UNITED STATES
GOVERNMENT
AND POLITICS

Chandler Publications in Political Science

Victor Jones, Editor

UNITED STATES GOVERNMENT AND POLITICS

SECOND EDITION

Jon Anthony Yinger
California State University, Fullerton

George K. Zaharopoulos
San Bernardino Valley College

Chandler
HARPER & ROW, PUBLISHERS
New York   Hagerstown   San Francisco   London

UNITED STATES GOVERNMENT AND POLITICS, Second Edition

Library of Congress Cataloging in Publication Data

Yinger, Jon Anthony, 1940-
   United States Government and politics.

   (Chandler publications in political science)
   Includes bibliographies.
   1. United States—Politics and government.
I. Zaharopoulos, George K., 1933-   joint author.
II. Title.
JK271.Y5 1974   320.4′73   73-20136
ISBN 0-352-18399-5

UNITED STATES GOVERNMENT AND POLITICS

SECOND EDITION

Jon Anthony Yinger
California State University, Fullerton

George K. Zaharopoulos
San Bernardino Valley College

Chandler
HARPER & ROW, PUBLISHERS
New York Hagerstown San Francisco London

103022

UNITED STATES GOVERNMENT AND POLITICS, Second Edition

Copyright © 1974 by Intext ., Inc.
Copyright © 1969 by Chandler Publishing Company

Library of Congress Cataloging in Publication Data

Yinger, Jon Anthony, 1940-
    United States Government and politics.

    (Chandler publications in political science)
    Includes bibliographies.
    1. United States—Politics and government.
I. Zaharopoulos, George K., 1933-   joint author.
II. Title.
JK271.Y5 1974   320.4'73   73-20136
ISBN 0-352-18399-5

Contents

103022

Preface

The reception of our 1969 edition has encouraged us to update the text—in part to avoid anachronisms that might distract the reader and, more important, to take into account the confrontations that began with the Watergate disclosures. In this regard we are particularly pleased to be able to reprint Richard Neustadt's engrossing and authoritative account of White House conduct a generation ago and now, "The Constraining of the President" from the New York Times Magazine, October 14, 1973. This discussion of the presidency, the Congress, the Parties and the cabinet points up the range and variety of those issues of political structure and process that confront us now and will continue to do so for a considerable period.

It seemed important to us, too, to give more attention in this edition to who we are as a people. We have therefore added a chapter developing a demographic profile of the American people and comparing some salient socioeconomic characteristics of the United States with those of other countries.

Our assumption in this book continues to be that the political process in the United States—in Washington and the states, in the large cities and the small localities—complex and diverse as it is, can be grasped and mastered by any citizen and specifically by the general student as well as one who majors in political science. We have tried to avoid an overemphasis on institutions and formalities and to focus as much as possible on facts and issues likely to have enduring relevance for our readers. We believe this can be achieved only by relating descriptions and explanations of political processes to the most urgent contemporary problems. Hence the institutional aspects of this book are kept to a minimum.

In our writing, we tried to act as mediators, relating the findings of the discipline to interesting and significant characteristics of our political life. Recognizing the schism, or at least difference in emphasis between the "traditionalists" and the "behavioralists" within political science, we have tried to draw on the best from both approaches. To make the American political system intelligible, we must discuss the Founding Fathers, the Constitution, and the problems that confront the American polity today—typical concerns of the traditionalists. And it is also important to point up the relationship between structure and function and the importance of social processes—particular emphases of the behavioralists.

For their help of many kinds in our preparation of the first edition of this text, we wish to thank again William J. Moore, Aram M. Sogomonian, Walter C. Schuiling, Gordon D. Munro, Austin Van Hove, Loren Smith, Larry Brewster, and Thelma Knea. We owe a debt of gratitude to a number of colleagues and associates who have offered us their interest, constructive criticism, and encouragement while we prepared this second edition. In particular we would like to thank Professors Henry J. Abraham of the University of Virginia, Victor Jones of the University of California, Berkeley, Brian Nelson of Florida International University, James F. Rowe of Valencia Community College in Orlando, Florida, Joseph R. Scheer of Gettysburg College, and the Department of Government staff of Tarrant County Junior College, Northwest Campus, in Hurst, Texas. We thank Ron Noggle for his help in gathering data for this edition, and our colleagues at both our institutions for their support and advice.

UNITED STATES GOVERNMENT AND POLITICS

Prologue

For the student of United States government and politics to understand
and appreciate the American system, he must be able to relate the critical
issues of his time to the evolution of the institutions and processes that
make up the system. The organization of this book aims to help the student see those relationships.

Chapter 1 presents a basic vocabulary of politics. Chapter 2 describes the environment in which the United States political system functions, including races and occupations, attitudes and beliefs, incomes and
life styles—all important parts of the nation's political culture. To get to
know what the political system is all about, it is essential to know something about the people who make up American society. This necessity
becomes apparent in Chapter 8, where we discuss the social bases of
American politics, and in Chapter 11, where we examine the problems of
law and order and the political challenges presented to the system by disadvantaged persons in America.

It is equally important for an understanding of American politics to
know something about the country's early political history. Many of the
issues confronting the American people in the formative years of the Republic have not yet been fully resolved. The question of separation of
powers arose in the Watergate investigation and became very much

alive in dramatic confrontations on television between the Senate Select Committee and President Nixon's advisers and between the president and Special Prosecutor Cox. Federalism—the division of power between the central government and the states—for example, is still an important issue. Chapter 7, on intergovernmental relations, discusses the operations of federalism in some detail in connection with the Nixon Administration's revenue sharing program. Designed to reverse the flow of power to Washington, that program is still controversial. Does the average citizen realize the extent to which this program affects his personal life and his pocketbook? Consider a specific dimension of revenue sharing as an illustration: If a man is a homeowner with an average income, he could expect some property tax relief from this program. The money that funds revenue sharing programs is drawn from the income sources of the federal government, primarily income tax receipts. Income taxes are far more progressive (the rich pay more, the poor less, proportionately) than local property taxes. On the other hand, the services supported by property taxes may be reduced because those who administer the local agencies may no longer feel obliged to maintain high levels of service as they did when they were locally accountable for the moneys raised.

The cornerstone of the democratic ideal is the concept of political equality. One of the issues confronting the American body politic today is whether this ideal of equality can ever become reality. Is it possible, for instance, for people to have widely different levels of income and still function as political equals? One of the points raised in Chapter 4 and again in Chapter 11 is precisely this. In Chapter 4 we ask, "How representative is the House of Representatives?" One of the ways in which it appears to be unrepresentative of the general population is that the income of House members begins with a base salary of $42,500 per year, about four times the average of family income in the United States. We are prompted to ask whether Congressmen can truly represent the interests of their average constituents rather than the special interests of the more affluent.

A critical issue of our day discussed in Chapter 11 is poverty. Federal government statistics indicate that the gap in income between the wealthy and the poor is wider today than it was in 1950. The question is whether United States institutions as presently constituted are capable of adopting the policies and implementing the programs that would begin to close the gap—and whether our government would be more "democratic" if they did so.

Public opinion polls indicate that cynicism about politics, politicians, and governmental institutions today has reached a new high. At the same time public apathy in these matters is also disturbingly high. Much of this cynicism and apathy is linked to presidential behavior over the past decade. The Vietnam experience, for example, disillusioned an entire generation of Americans. And if that were not enough to test people's confidence in the institution of the presidency, it was followed by a domestic scandal of unprecedented import, popularly known as the Watergate break-in and cover-up and the unprecedented resignation of the vice president. The political system has been seriously challenged. Can the presidency, the office that tops the system, regain the prestige and respect of the American people who are, after all, its main sources of power? In Chapter 10 the lessons of Vietnam are discussed in some detail. And in Chapter 5, dealing with the presidency, the Watergate scandal and its larger implications are analyzed.

Traditionally the most respected institution in the United States political system has been the Supreme Court. That public respect was undermined in the 1960s by a concerted attack on the Court by conservative elements who criticized Court decisions dealing with controversial social issues such as school desegregation, the rights of the accused, the right to privacy, and the school prayer issue. In Chapter 6 we examine the role of the judiciary as innovator. The impact of court decisions on social policy, especially of decisions of the Supreme Court, continues today even when a majority of the nine justices is clearly conservative. A major concern of the courts in this century has been civil rights and liberties. For instance, how should the demand for national security properly limit dissent? And how can a balance be maintained between the rights of an individual to express freely his political beliefs, even if they include a commitment to the idea of revolution, and the rights of society to enjoy security and order?

An informed citizen must himself confront challenging questions such as these. In each case there is a relationship between what political institutions do and the general direction that the society takes. As you examine in more detail the material presented in this book, keep in mind the necessary relationship among institutions, processes, and issues. No one of those three elements of a political system can be fully understood in isolation from the others.

Nor can the basic issues facing America during the 1970s be fully grasped in isolation from the distinctive manner in which Americans identify issues and the processes through which the issues are weighted and decisions about how to deal with them are made. As we elaborate in Chapter 11, issues are relevant because their resolution is desired in a particular way by articulate groups and in other ways by equally articulate opposing groups. Differences in objectives and in the means of achieving objectives are the substance of politics. The mode of politics is the established and institutionalized way in which a society identifies such issues and prescribes the constitutional manner of resolving relevant issues or controversies.

Our discussion of the Congress, the presidency, the judiciary, and the bureaucracy as well as parties and pressure groups shows that their effectiveness, responsiveness, efficiency, and representativeness are as important as the substantive problems and policies with which they must deal. The student and the practitioner, as well as the ordinary citizen, must constantly attempt to balance the values of our political system over against the values of immediate problem solving. We urge you, therefore, to be as alert to whether Congress can play its alloted role vis-a-vis the president, and vice-versa, as you are to the more dramatic social need to alleviate the miseries of poor people.

PART ONE
BACKGROUNDS AND PERSPECTIVES

The three chapters of Part One attempt to provide in brief form a conceptual and to some extent historical context for the remainder of the book: the six chapters of Part Two, The Political System of the United States; and the two chapters of Part Three, Foreign Policy and Domestic Problems.

Chapter 1, Government: Definitions and Forms, discusses the nature of government with particular reference to such concepts as the state, power, authority, and politics. This chapter also describes the various forms of democratic and authoritarian governments. The democratic forms include the federal, confederal, and unitary systems; while the discussion of authoritarian forms focuses on totalitarian governments. In addition, such concepts as liberalism, conservatism, radicalism, capitalism, and socialism are briefly described.

In Chapter 3, Framing the Constitution, the basis for government in the United States is described. The origins, underlying values, and some of the controversy surrounding ratification—much of which has continued to this day—are discussed. The complete text of the Constitution is provided as Appendix B.

Chapter 1
Government:
Definitions and Forms

The most basic thing to know about government is that it meets the twofold purpose of controlling people's actions and serving their needs—restricting and limiting behavior, promoting and guiding certain activities. The wide range of governmental functions is illustrated by the headlines of any newspaper, which reveal in dramatic form the many daily actions of government—local, state, and national—that have such far-reaching consequences for all our lives.

DEFINITIONS OF FUNDAMENTAL CONCEPTS

In order to understand the political system of the United States—or any other political system, for that matter—some basic concepts must be clearly comprehended. This section will define certain fundamental concepts inherent in modern government.

Government

Government, like death and taxes, is inevitable and essential for the life of man. This is so simply because man is a social creature. Man has certain needs which can be best satisfied if he is a member of a society. A society may be defined very simply as a mutual-benefit association. The smallest social unit is the family; the largest, the nation. (Some would say that the largest social unit is "the community of nations" or the international community.)

There are many definitions of *government*. For the purposes of this book, government may be defined as "the largest organization for ordering or controlling people's actions in a given society." If all men were unselfish and peaceable, there would be no need for government as we know it. As James Madison put it in *The Federalist*, No. 51, "If men were angels, no government would be necessary." A considerably more recent writer says: "Government is the organization of men under authority."[1] Men have found it advantageous to have government. Anthropologists tell us that even primitive tribes have hierarchical organizations performing functions similar to our governmental institutions.

Man has found it necessary to create government because he can best fulfill his own potential under its aegis and authority. Even though he must give up some of his individual freedom of action in order to live under government, he has discovered that the alternative to government —*anarchy* or the complete absence of government—is similar to conditions that exist in the jungle where the principle of "the survival of the fittest" prevails. Government, therefore, is for most men less objectionable than its counterpart, anarchy. As Thomas Hobbes wrote in the seventeenth century, life without government would be "nasty, brutish, and short."

Why is government essential for the orderly existence of man? The rationale for government derives from two functions which all governments perform, irrespective of political and ideological considerations. These two functions are *service* and *protection*. All governments provide certain services and protection for the governed—services and protection which individuals are either unable or unwilling to provide for themselves.

Among the myriad services provided by government in most civilized societies are unemployment compensation for persons out of work, social-security benefits for those too old to work, and programs and facilities for the education of the young, to mention but a few.

Although governmental services are of increasing significance, the fundamental reason for the existence of government is that it fulfills

---

[1] Robert M. MacIver, *The Web of Government* (New York: The Free Press, 1965), p. 6.

the basic human requirement for protection. The government provides protection from enemies, both external and domestic. This need for protection has existed since ancient times when our primitive ancestors discovered that by banding together they could defend themselves and protect their interests against more aggressive neighbors. Modern governments devote much energy and substantial wealth to the purposes of protection.

Most governments, including that of the United States, continually strive to reach a happy medium by attempting to devote effort and wealth for both services and protection. It can be said that a good government is one which is able to provide both necessary services and adequate protection. Beyond the concern that government perform these minimal functions, however, government should be judged by the quality of performance as well.

The State

The word *state* conveys different meanings to different people. To citizens of the United States, for example, it describes one of the fifty units that together constitute the federal union. To a follower of Karl Marx, the concept of the state implies power, force, coercion. Therefore, the state is something to be feared, distrusted, and eradicated at the earliest opportunity. To a Greek of the fourth century B.C., on the other hand, the term state defined one of the several independent and self-sufficient Greek city-states such as Sparta, Athens, Thebes. To some, the state is synonymous with the government. It is no wonder, then, there is so much ambiguity and confusion associated with the concept of state.

Most concretely, the term state is used to identify a people organized under a common government and occupying a piece of territory with well-defined boundaries or territorial limits. Thus the fifty "states" of the American federal union constitute *a state*. So do the "republics" of the Soviet Union, the "provinces" of Canada, the "départements" of France, and so on. (The differences between a federal system of government such as that of the United States and its counterpart, the unitary system, such as Great Britain's, will be discussed later in the chapter.)

What is the distinction between government and state? The state is different from the government in two important respects. First, the state includes the governed as well as those who govern. The government is the organ for the expression of the state's will and authority; it is more specific and obvious, and therefore closer to our experience.

Citizens come into daily contact with such governmental agents as police-men, lawmakers, bureaucrats. Second, governments come and go—in some societies they change fast and violently—but the state continues to exist; the state thus provides the necessary continuity of authority.

The distinction between *head of government* and *head of state* may help clarify further the difference between government and state. In most governmental systems, other than the presidential, the head of state is a different person from the head of government. For example, in Great Britain the Queen is head of state, while the prime minister is head of government. In West Germany the president is head of state, and the chancellor is head of government. In both systems the role of head of state is primarily symbolic and ceremonial, while the role of chancellor or prime minister is functional since he is concerned with the day-to-day problems of the government. In the United States the two offices have been combined in the American presidency.

Power

Closely related to both government and state are the concepts of power, authority, and sovereignty. Without these qualities the terms state and government would be meaningless.

The daily press reports on how the government uses its power to settle a strike or to persuade businessmen to rescind a price increase, how the government used its power to enforce the integration of schools and public facilities in the South. The government, it is reported, makes use of its power to contain the expansion of Communism in Europe or Asia or Latin America. A news story tells about someone who failed to pay his income taxes and the government using its power to make him pay, or to send him to jail for failing to do so.

Conservatives in the United States today argue that the power of the government is growing too rapidly and that it affects the rights and liber-ties of individuals adversely. Marxists argue that governmental power in capitalist societies is in the hands of small minorities or elites, who use it to exploit the workers and peasants. Yet others argue that the growth of governmental power has generally been beneficial to the individual.

It is readily seen, then, that the concept of *power* is central to the study of government and politics. There are some who would argue, as did Machiavelli in the 16th century, that government is nothing more than the technique for the manipulation of power.

Simply defined, power is the ability or the capacity to elicit com-pliance. In MacIver's words, it is "the capacity to control the behavior of others either directly by fiat or indirectly by the manipulation of available means."[2] In modern societies the state possesses a monopoly of coercive power.

This does not mean that everyone in a particular society respects the power of the state. In fact some do not obey the laws and commands of the state and thus may find themselves confronting its power; the tax evader is a good example. A person does not have to obey the laws and commands of the state if he is willing to pay the consequences of disobeying them. But the state's ability to elicit compliance includes its ability to impose penalties.

Authority

Power and authority are closely related. Authority implies a certain rightness or legitimacy which may or may not accompany the exercise of political power in a specific situation. When authority accompanies the exercise of power, it is said that it is legitimate power. When coercive power is used without authority or a general sense of its rightness, it is considered illegitimate. The exercise of power in dictatorial political systems usually seems to democrats to be of the latter type.

In the United States it is widely agreed that the decisions of the Supreme Court interpreting federal laws and the Constitution have a certain "rightness," which is called *authority*. This implies that people *ought* to obey these decisions although the Supreme Court has itself no coercive power to enforce them. And who endows the Supreme Court with such authority? The United States Constitution does, although it is not very explicit in this regard.

Perhaps an analogy between the baseball umpire and government will clarify the point. The baseball umpire has authority to call players "safe" or "out," to declare a pitch a "ball" or a "strike." Many different people in our society have some kind of authority—policemen, teachers, army officers, and others. All of them *derive* their authority and can exercise it within a very limited area of social activity. The baseball umpire cannot hand out traffic citations. Once he is out of the ballpark, his authority is finished. The baseball umpire *derives* his authority from the rules of baseball which give him the authority to call a player "safe" or "out." If the player does not agree with the umpire's decision, the rules empower the umpire to put him out of the game. The baseball umpire enforces the rules of the game of baseball; and government, through agents such as policemen, enforces the rules of society, some of which rules are the game of politics. Authority is an essential quality

---

[2] MacIver, *The Web of Government*, p. 66.

of government. If government is to maintain the orderly processes of society, it must endow its agents with authority.

> By authority we mean the established *right*, within any social order, to determine policies, to pronounce judgements on relevant issues, and to settle controversies, or, more broadly, to act as leader or guide to other men. When we speak of *an* authority we mean a person or body of persons possessed of this right. The accent is primarily on right, not power. Power alone has no legitimacy, no mandate, no office. Even the most ruthless tyrant gets nowhere unless he can clothe himself with authority.
>
> Robrt M. MacIver, *The Web of Government* (New York: The Free Press, 1965), p. 63.*

Sovereignty

On the occasion of state holidays and from the floor of national political conventions, politicians are fond of referring to their home states as "the great and sovereign" state of California or Alabama. This certainly makes for impressive oratory, but the phrase has little or no meaning.

Sovereignty—supreme legal authority—is characteristic of national states. The individual states of the United States are not truly sovereign because in our system of government, sovereignty is vested in the national government—in the federal union and not in its member states. True, the states are able to exercise a certain degree of independent political power, but they do not have any sovereign powers. Whenever there has been any question about the superiority of the national government, it has been quickly determined where sovereign authority is vested. A few examples will clarify this matter of sovereignty.

In 1957, Governor Orval Faubus of the State of Arkansas refused to abide by the Supreme Court's decision of 1954 calling for the racial integration of public schools throughout the United States. He felt that he had the authority, as his state's chief executive, to refuse to comply with the federal Court's decision. He soon came face to face with the sovereignty of the United States in the form of army paratroopers flown to Little Rock to enforce the laws of the United States—which, according to the Constitution, are superior to the laws of any state. If there remained any ambiguity about state sovereignty, it was settled by 1964 when federal marshalls prevented Governor Wallace of Alabama and

---

* Quotations like the one above appear throughout the text, adding a dimension to the discussion without being tied directly to the text. The authors and publishers express no position for or against the views stated in the quotations.

Governor Barnett of Mississippi from personally standing at the school-house door to block the admission of blacks to their states' institutions of higher learning.

There are three traditional tests for sovereignty: (1) whether the state sends and receives ambassadors, (2) whether the state is able to develop and execute its own foreign policy without outside interference, and (3) whether the state is able to protect its own borders and keep people in or out of its territory if it wants to do so. None of the fifty states of the American federal union meets these tests of sovereignty.

Politics

Aristotle, the Greek philosopher and political theorist, wrote that man is by nature a *political* animal. What he meant is that man appears destined to live in a *polis,* which to a Greek of the day could have been any one of the several city-states in existence. The ancient Greeks felt, and most civilized people feel today, that it is within an orderly social system that man can find happiness and fulfillment. Without government, it is doubtful that man would be able to survive, let alone progress. By the same token, government cannot exist without politics.

Politics, like most concepts involving human interaction, is difficult to define precisely. All sorts of meanings and connotations can be ascribed to the word *politics.* Three in particular stand out: politics as contest, as influence, and as process. It could be said, for example, that politics is the *contest* for power. Or it could be said that "Politics is the study of *influence* and the influential."[3] Certainly politics involves both the contest for power and the exercise of influence. Yet it involves much more.

Perhaps politics could best be described as a *process* by which men attempt to control or influence the behavior or attitudes of others. The most significant channel through which this process can take place is government. Political activity can take many forms. People may try to influence the politics of their government by demonstrations or mass meetings; they might utilize the press and other media of communication to alter or influence the course of government; or if everything else proves futile, they might resort to violence and revolution.

In most democratic societies, there are built-in methods for the expression of popular feeling on issues confronting the body politic. Such avenues as a free and competitive press, the free expression of

[3] Harold D. Lasswell, *Politics: Who Gets What, When, and How* (Gloucester, Mass.: Peter Smith).

public opinion, writing letters to legislators and editors of newspapers and magazines, and, most importantly, voting are the democratic methods for influencing public or governmental policy.

Democratic politics is above all a process of accommodation and compromise. A viable political system cannot really exist without these two qualities. A democratic society is normally a pluralistic society; it is made up of a great variety and diversity of groups, interests, and points of view. Unless these diverse interests are willing to accommodate one another and to arrive at compromises on many issues, the entire political system is likely to suffer. Consequently, politics is an activity of continuous compromises.

Politics may lead to public policies or may succeed in preventing the formulation of public policy. As one political scientist points out:

> . . . public policies are the outcome of the interplay among (1) broad general values, (2) the specific values of interest groups with different resources and opposing objectives, (3) a legal-institutional framework for making authoritative decisions, and (4) public officials who with their resources must ultimately make and administer the policies.[4]

Consensus and Consent of the Governed

Every stable political system must be supported by a basic *consensus* concerning the nature of the system itself. Consensus then can be defined as a broad agreement among the vast majority of the members of the body politic about the fundamentals of the political system. The vast majority of the people in the United States—Democrats and Republicans, Protestants and Catholics, workers and managers—are in general agreement in supporting the basic institutions and processes of the American political system; thus, a consensus does exist in this country. A preponderant majority accept the Constitution as the basis of the governmental system, a presidential as opposed to a parliamentary form of government, and a republican as opposed to a monarchical form of government—to name but three fundamental concepts about which there is consensus. Americans are not always in agreement on particular issues and policies confronting the government; but such issues of the moment are not among those fundamental values and institutions that make up the American consensus.

It follows that anyone who rejects these fundamental values is outside of this consensus. Those who demonstrate by their actions that

---

[4] T. Bentley Edwards and Frederick M. Wirt, *School Desegregation in the North* (New York and London: Chandler Publishing Company, 1968), pp. 7–8.

Politics is a term for describing the varied methods by which individuals and groups try to move government to stop conduct that is disturbing public order, to compele the settlement of some conflict that is threatening public order, to enforce some social change they want, or to refrain from enforcing some social change they dislike.

J. A. Corry and Henry J. Abraham, *Elements of Democratic Government* (New York: Oxford University Press, 1964), p. 7.

they are unwilling to work within the existing political framework to achieve their own ends, if they are numerous or powerful enough, undermine the stability of the political system itself. Extremists of the left and of the right, for example, might undermine the American system if there were so many of them actively plotting the overthrow of the government that they could not be dealt with successfully by existing law-enforcement agencies. Fortunately this remains merely a potential problem in the United States; such groups have never had enough appeal to undermine seriously the consensus upon which the system rests.

There is, however, a significant distinction between consensus and *consent of the governed*. Most Americans, as noted above, are in agreement about the broad outlines of the political system. They can differ, often substantially, about specific policies followed by the government of the day. But in a democratic system such dissent is not considered to be treason. This is because in a democratic system the vast majority of the citizens agree to accept the policies and acts of the government of the day even though for many persons such policies are not the ones they would have preferred. The principle at work here is known as the consent of the governed; that is, the citizens in a democratic society consent to be bound by the policies of the government of the day as long as that government enjoys majority support. Consensus—general agreement among the people about the fundamental values of the state—is the foundation upon which any stable system of government rests; while consent of the governed is an ingredient of a specifically democratic system.

The vitality of a democratic system depends upon keen competition for the consent of the governed. Those who happen to be in the minority at a given moment, the dissenters, remain committed to the fundamentals of the system because of the possibility that through the processes of that system they may become the majority. It is, after all, specific issues that divide us into competing political parties and groups. Those who are not members of the majority on a particular issue merely question the wisdom of this specific policy and are dissenters on this one issue. Dissenters in this sense are within the consensus; they accept the fundamentals of the political system, the institutions, processes, and procedures by which they may succeed in changing the policies and personnel who constitute the government of the day. Political stability in any system, then, depends on widespread consensus as to the fundamentals of that system, while in a democratic system the additional feature of consent of the governed suggests that for a particular government to be regarded as legitimate its policies must be endorsed by a majority of people comprising that system.

Citizenship

Persons who are full members of the American political community are called *citizens.* Other persons within the jurisdiction of a government are subject to its laws and they may, as in the United States, possess certain rights. Under the Fifth and Fourteenth Amendments to the Constitution all persons—citizens and aliens alike—are entitled to due process and equal protection of the laws. Only citizens, however, can vote or be elected to public office. Congress can forbid the employment of aliens in the public service or in industries related to defense. Aliens must register annually and notify the government when they change residence, and aliens are subject to deportation.

Citizenship in the United States can be obtained by birth on its soil, or in territories and other places under its jurisdiction as designated by Congress. Under prescribed conditions, children born abroad to a citizen of the United States are or can become native-born citizens. Aliens can become citizens by naturalization; that is, they are invested with citizenship by legal action under conditions laid down by Congress.

Citizens, whether native-born or naturalized, can lose citizenship by certain actions that constitute or imply its forfeiture: for example, by voting in the elections of a foreign state or by swearing allegiance to a foreign state. In the past naturalized citizens have been treated as second-class citizens in many ways and have been subjected to the possibility of revocation of their citizenship for acts which native-born citizens could commit with impunity. In 1964, however, in *Schneider* v. *Rusk,** the United States Supreme Court held invalid an act of Congress revoking the citizenship of former aliens who maintain "a continuous residence for three years in the territory of a foreign state of which he was formerly a national or in which the place of his birth is situated." Justice Douglas,

* All Supreme Court decisions mentioned in the text are cited in full in Appendix A.

speaking for the Court, said:

> We start from the premise that the rights of citizenship of the native born and of the naturalized person are of the same dignity and are coextensive. The only difference drawn by the Constitution is that only the "natural born" citizen is eligible to be President.

Any citizen of the United States, however, can voluntarily give up his citizenship, usually for the purpose of attaining citizenship in another country. This is a right established by Congress which is not recognized by many other countries.

FORMS OF GOVERNMENT

In his long struggle to improve his condition, man has experimented with many forms of goverment. History tells us, for example, that a certain historical era was characterized by autocracy or absolutism, or that one of the by-products of the French Revolution of 1789 was the introduction of democratic ideals throughout Europe. It should be noted at the outset that man is still experimenting with ways to govern himself. And experimentation is likely to continue because, it seems, man is never satisfied with what exists. This section cannot undertake a discussion of all the numerous forms of government known in the history of man. Rather it will deal with the general types: *democracy; authoritarianism;* and *totalitarianism,* the twentieth-century manifestation of authoritarianism. The section will also discuss the subtypes of governmental forms: *federalism, confederalism,* and *unitary government.*

Democracy

As a form of government, democracy is widely admired. Admiration, however, does not mean that it is universally, or even widely, accepted. Virtually everyone pays lip service to democratic ideals, while in truth most of the civilized world is governed undemocratically. This is paradoxical but not at all unusual. Even dictators, of both the Communist and Fascist variety, use the word "democracy" for rhetorical purposes.

President Ayub Khan of Pakistan referred to his regime as a "guided democracy"; so did President Nkrumah of Ghana. Actually, there is not very much democracy in either Pakistan or Ghana. More perplexing, and even contradictory in terms, are the East European Communist countries which call themselves "peoples' democracies"— as if there could be another kind. Such confusion and misunderstanding of the term *democracy* have roots in the following factors. First, it is an ideal form of government to which most people aspire. Second, democracy in the modern world is vastly different from what it was in Athens four centuries before the birth of Christ. Finally, the term is misused by Communists, who reject it as a political concept and instead emphasize economic considerations.

But what is democracy? Every schoolchild knows that it is "government by the people." Oddly enough, this simple definition is correct. The word *democracy* comes from two Greek words: the words *demos,* meaning people or multitude, and *kratos,* which means government or authority. Put together these two words spell *demokratia,* from which is derived *democracy.*

The definition alone does not tell what democracy is. "Government by the people" is not sufficient; it requires elaboration. Democracy has also been defined as government of laws and not of men. This definition is also correct but inadequate. Rather than another, perhaps more detailed, and more comprehensive definition of democracy, the list below offers a set of requirements which democratic government must meet. These criteria can be used to determine whether a government is democratically based or not. As a rule, if a government does not meet all or most of these criteria, it is not democratic.

1. A constitution. Democratic government derives its authority from a constitutional framework which is based on the principle of majority rule. A constitution is a document or a series of documents and principles which serve as the basis for the relationship between government and governed. A constitution is designed to perform two distinct functions: to *define* the authority and to *limit* the power of the government. It provides the framework for government by laws not by the fiat of individuals who occupy positions of political power. Thus in most dictatorships there is a conspicuous absence of a constitution because it may inhibit the whim of the dictator.

In order to be effective, that is, to define the authority and limit the power of the government effectively, a constitution must be meaningful. It must have some significance to both the governing group and the governed. It goes without saying that this is not true in much of the world today. In many countries, constitutions serve as a facade for the rule by a small group or elite who do not hesitate to disregard the constitution whenever necessary. A good case in point is the Soviet Union, which has had a written constitution since 1936. On paper the Soviet constitution appears democratic, but in practice it is not since it makes the Communist party the only legal political party in the Soviet Union.

This has led close observers of the Soviet political system to declare that Soviet constitutional principles differ substantially from Soviet political realities.

2. A free press. A press which is not controlled by some agency of the government is vital to the existence of democracy. It performs an educational role—a role that is essential to the democratic body politic. A free press is the unofficial watchdog of democracy, exposing scandals, inefficiency, and corrupt practices in government. A free press can serve as a link between government and people; it can let policy makers know what the public thinks and vice versa. Dictatorships are afraid of a free press. Normally one of the first acts of a dictator is to suppress or rigidly control all newspapers and magazines which do not equivocally support his regime. This fact alone indicates how significant the role of the press is to democratic government and politics.

While freedom entails responsibility, a free press is not always responsible. In fact, democracies frequently experience irresponsible behavior on the part of the press. But that is the price democratic man must pay for maintaining freedom of the press. The assumption is that most men are reasonable and will choose the sedate and responsible over the sensational and irresponsible newspaper or magazine.

3. Political Parties. Democratic government cannot function well without competitive political parties. If a system is to be called democratic, it must have at least two political parties that compete for the voters' favor.[5] Political parties have been described as the backbone of democracy—an essential structure of the democratic political organism. Political parties perform several functions necessary for the smooth operation of democratic government. They develop ideas and programs for the body politic. They provide personnel for the running of the government. They offer to the public alternative courses of action and a sense of participation in the policy-making process.

Competitive political parties are anathema to dictators. We cannot think of even one dictatorship which allowed more than one political party to exist. In fact, dictators make certain that political opposition is eliminated and kept from organizing. One of Lenin's earliest

[5] It is often pointed out that both India and Mexico are "one-party systems"; yet both are considered democracies. Strictly speaking, they are not one-party states since there are parties other than the official party which are free to criticize the government. To the extent that these minor parties are not competitive, such systems fall short of the democratic ideal.

moves after the Bolshevik Revolution of 1917 was to suppress the several opposition groups. This process has been followed by Mussolini, Hitler, Franco, and all other tyrants since.

4. Elections.   There can be no democracy without periodic elections. To democratic government, elections are as essential as oxygen is to animal and plant life. As plants and animals cannot survive without oxygen, so the democratic organism cannot survive without elections. Elections serve two purposes: they afford the public an opportunity to participate in the making of policy; and they provide the public with a group of individuals to run the government for a certain period of time.

Elections must be held periodically and with appropriate notice to the electorate. Whether it is every two, three, four, or seven years makes no difference, but they must be held. The party in power cannot decide to put off elections indefinitely because it wants to stay in power. If elections are to be of any value, the electorate must have a genuine choice between parties and candidates who offer alternative programs and ideas. In other words, elections must be something more than a ritual designed to impress outsiders, which is the case in most dictatorships.

5. Majority rule and minority rights.   Democratic government is based on the principle of majority rule. When the ballots are counted after an election, the political party or the individual who received a sufficiently greater number of votes (usually a plurality or a majority) than any other party or individual is entitled to assume office. The person or party that won the election is allowed to take over the government even though those in power may not like the election results.

The principle of majority rule goes hand in hand with the corollary of minority rights. The logic is that once the majority assumes power, it should not turn on the minority and try to suppress it. Today's minority in democratic societies should have the opportunity to become tomorrow's majority. And if the majority would like to be treated with respect and kindness when it becomes the minority (something common in democracies), it should behave appropriately toward the opposition.

Republicanism

Modern democracy can best be defined as *limited and representative government*. This section will discuss the differences, if any, between the concepts of democracy and republic.

A few years ago, the ultraconservative John Birch Society created the slogan OURS IS A REPUBLIC NOT A DEMOCRACY—LET'S KEEP IT THAT WAY to refer to the American system of government. The implication is that there is a great difference between democracy and republic and that the latter is better than the former.

To be sure, there is a difference between democracy and republic. Political scientists and constitutional lawyers may argue about the merits and shortcomings of each, but why would the John Birch Society show an interest in such an obscure and academic issue? A possible explanation is that, as originally conceived by the Founding Fathers, the term *republic* implied "limited democracy." That is, the republic was conceived as a compromise between monarchy (rule by one), against which the colonists had fought a revolutionary war, and democracy, which some of the framers of the Constitution considered rule by the mob and therefore undesirable. Nevertheless, confusion about the two exists, and the student of government should be able to tell the difference.

The term *republic* comes from two Latin words: *res,* meaning affair, and *publica,* which means public or people. United, these two words form the Latin *respublica* from which is derived *republic.* The most commonly used definition of *republic* is "representative democracy." But one might ask: What other kind of democracy is there? The answer is "direct or pure democracy."

As practiced in ancient Greece, democratic government demanded the direct participation of the small number of citizens in the making of decisions which affected the community. This was possible in the Greek city-states where the number of actual citizens was very small. But that was the first time—and in a very real sense the last time—*direct* democracy was practiced. The term *republic* did not come to denote representative government until the time of the American and French Revolutions.

Is the United States a republic or a democracy? It is both. The United States is an indirect democracy. Representatives are elected by the people to go to an appointed place, whether to Washington, D.C., or the state capital, and make decisions. In a vast and variegated country such as the United States, there can be no alternative to indirect democracy. The people hold the men and women they elect responsible for making good decisions for the entire society; and if they do not like the way their elected representatives are doing things, they have the power to vote them out of office and give someone else the opportunity to represent them.

The difference, then, between pure democracy and republic on the one hand and indirect democracy on the other, is one of representation. It revolves around the question "Who governs?"

The Elitist Thesis

The question "Who governs?" is of special concern to scholars who attempt to understand and explain modern government. It is natural that in a democracy the people—the masses—do influence government policies and actions, at least most of the time. Democracy, like any other value system (such as pragmatism in philosophy or Christianity in religion), has its defenders and critics, its supporters and detractors. The elitist critique of the condition of democracy in the United States is of particular interest, for it has attracted the attention of an entire generation of social science students. The elitist critique offers what seems to be convincing evidence that the American political system is something different from what conventional textbooks and high school civics courses claim.

The elitist thesis goes something like this: American politics is not really as it appears on the surface; the masses do not actually shape government policies but are instead led by a small group of individuals, the "power elite," who make decisions about social policies without much concern for public attitudes. This thesis was first formulated by the sociologist C. Wright Mills in 1956 in *The Power Elite*, a book that enjoyed wide popularity, stimulating a debate that is still continuing. Other scholars have elaborated on Mills' thesis. Most notable is the work of social psychologist G. William Domhoff, whose book *Who Rules America?*, published in 1967, contends that the upper class in American society is indeed the ruling class. And in a 1972 volume, *Fat Cats and Democrats*, Domhoff argues that while the Democratic party is regarded as the party of the common man in American politics, in fact its main contributors and financial supporters are extremely wealthy persons, that is, "fat cats," who have controlling influence on party policies and the selection of candidates. These people are motivated by class interests rather than by a benign concern for democracy or the two-party system.

The elitist thesis is further elaborated in a popular American government textbook. Written by political scientists Thomas R. Dye and L. Harmon Zeigler, *The Irony of Democracy: An Uncommon Introduction to American Politics*, is all that the subtitle implies. For example, Dye and Zeigler begin the second edition of their text with the poignant statement that "Elites, not masses, govern America" (p. 3). A few pages later the meaning of elitism is cogently explained in propositions like this: "Society is divided into the few who have power and the many who do not. Only a small number of persons allocate values for society; the masses do not decide public policy" (p. 7).

One can readily see why the elitist thesis has struck a responsive chord in the contemporary student generation. It seems to provide the most plausible explanation for some recent policy blunders, notably the war in Indochina. But elitist theory—like any other all-inclusive explanation of social phenomena—does not provide all the answers. The statement that "Elites, not masses, govern America," for instance, though undeniably true, explains little. For no one who has any awareness of modern democratic theory and practice would make the claim that the masses "govern" America or any other society for that matter. Since the experiment with direct democracy was briefly tried and quickly abandoned in ancient Greece, democratic theorists have said only that the masses should influence and indirectly affect government policy in democracies—not that they should directly "govern" or rule.

Authoritarianism

If democracy is limited and representative government, *authoritarianism,* which is unlimited or absolute and unrepresentative government, is the opposite of democracy. It is a form of government that does not rely on the consent of the governed and does not derive its authority from the body politic.

Authoritarianism is not new. In fact, it is much older than democracy. Authoritarian government prevailed in China, Egypt, Persia, and Greece before the Greek discovery and acceptance of democracy. Authoritarian rule is still prevalent in most of the world today. Modern authoritarianism (or absolutism) has had various forms. These range from the tyranny of Stalin and Hitler to the less oppressive but still dictatorial rule of men like Franco in Spain, Salazar in Portugal, and Castro in Cuba to the authoritarian style of political leaders like Nasser of Egypt and Ayub Khan of Pakistan.

By its very nature, dictatorship is antidemocratic. Dictators of all ideological orientations reject the most basic assumption of democracy —that individuals have rights against the state—and try to prove that democracy as a form of government is corrupt and inadequate. They do not hesitate to emphasize the shortcomings and weaknesses of democracy, which are real and obvious; and they never cease mocking democracy and some of its basic institutions such as parliaments and political parties, which are portrayed as collections of spineless and unprincipled individuals.

"Hi there, folks! I'm your new strong man."

Drawing by Handelsman; © 1967 The New Yorker Magazine, Inc.

As with democracy, certain institutions, processes, and ideas are characteristic of dictatorship and can be found in all dictatorial regimes.

1. Reliance on the leader.   Historically, all dictatorships have shown dependence on particular leaders. The leader's role in a dictatorship is of the utmost importance. It is the leader who is expected to personify the nation and to solve its problems. And while the leader cannot solve every problem singlehandedly, he takes all the credit for what is done by his subordinates and assistants. In some dictatorships the leader takes an interest even in the most minute matters. Ngo Dinh Diem of South Vietnam, for example, had to approve every divorce granted in his country and every passport issued by his government.

Many dictators possess what the German sociologist Max Weber called *charisma,* a special gift of leadership qualities. The charismatic leader is endowed with certain powers that cause people to follow him and obey his orders or wishes. How else can one explain the intensity of the German people's devotion to Hitler? That Lenin was able to take over and almost alone lead the Bolshevik Revolution of 1917 can be partly explained by the fact that he was a charismatic figure—a personality that radiated confidence and demanded support.

Many democratic political leaders likewise possess charisma. In fact, many analysts feel that in modern democracies charisma is essential for electoral success. The worth of charisma depends, then, on whether this very important political asset is used for good or for evil, whether it is utilized for demagoguery or for constructive political ends such as the mobilization of public opinion in support of a policy beneficial to the body politic.

2. Reliance on ideology.   Another element which is often part of dictatorship is *ideology.* So necessary is ideology to the viability of totalitarian dictatorship especially (discussed below) that any dictator who hopes to stay in power for long will *develop* an ideology if he has not come to power with ideological support in the first place.

Ideology has been given a variety of definitions. For present purposes, however, the following definition seems appropriate:

> Ideology is a comprehensive, consistent, closed system of knowledge, to which its adherents turn to get answers to all their questions, solutions to all their problems.[6]

In other words, ideology is something to which the dictator can turn to explain or justify virtually every one of his policies or moves.

In modern times the two predominant ideological orientations have been Marxism-Leninism and Fascism. Both fit the above definition of ideology in that each of them offers a simple approach to the complex problems facing modern society. Both Soviet Marxism and Fascism claim to have discovered easy solutions to man's perplexing difficulties and needs. The hardships and deprivations that man goes through in his effort to reach the desired goals can be very simply explained by referring to a set of readily available ideological clichés. For example, Marxists explain historical phenomena and the human condition as depending primarily on economic factors. In addition to glorifying the state, as Mussolini did and Franco does, historically Fascists of whatever variety have worshipped the state as a living organism having a will and a pur-

---

[6] Herbert J. Spiro, *Government by Constitution* (New York: Random House, 1959), p. 180.

pose of its own. Fascists of the Nazi variety explain everything—social, political, historical, and economic phenomena—from the standpoint of superior and inferior peoples and races.

3. Reliance on propaganda and slogans. Dictators rely very heavily on propaganda and slogans to perpetuate their rule. While democracies also use propaganda in order to mobilize public opinion, dictatorships constantly utilize the delicate art of propaganda to saturate the mind of the public with preferred opinions and partial truths. Propaganda can be defined as a systematic, continuous, and deliberate effort to indoctrinate people into a system of beliefs or ideas (which may or may not be based on reality). The dictator often uses propaganda to appeal to the most irrational and emotional part of human nature; thus he hopes to affect the actions of the individual through an appeal to his emotions.

In advanced democracies, more than in other systems, politicians make an effort to appeal to human reason rather than to human emotion —to the mind rather than to the heart. They assume that democratic man is sufficiently intelligent to reject the most outlandish lies and hard-to-fulfill promises. And while democratic politicians often do not hesitate to stretch the truth, they cannot hope to become and remain successful in politics unless they are able to convince their constituents that they can produce more than empty promises and impressive oratory. One of the traditions of modern democracy is that propaganda be kept at a minimum, while actual performance is emphasized. The point here is that in a democracy a variety of conflicting views, even if they are confusing, allows the public a choice among alternatives; more importantly, it offers a greater possibility for truth to emerge.

Authoritarian government, on the other hand, in order to maintain its hold over the public mind, must substitute propaganda for law. Propaganda, under these circumstances, becomes a normal activity of the government. Very often a ministry or separate department of propaganda is established (almost always euphemistically called the Ministry of Information) to coordinate the government's propaganda activities. And with the development of modern communications media, the dictator's ability to propagandize is immense. Perhaps the most notorious, and by far the most imaginative, minister of propaganda in the twentieth century was Joseph Goebbels, who served Hitler faithfully until the demise of the Third Reich.

To keep the public constantly susceptible to its propaganda, the authoritarian government uses slogans extensively. These slogans normally call for very simple solutions to some of the long-standing problems facing the society. Some of these problems may be wholly imaginary, and the solutions proposed highly unrealistic. Thus, ALL LAND TO THE PEASANTS, a slogan used during the Bolshevik Revolution, and DEATH TO THE JEWS, constantly heard in Nazi Germany, have much in common. They offered simple definitions of a "problem" and proposed even simpler solutions. The slogan, then, is employed to elicit and bring to the surface deep-rooted hatreds and long-standing biases and prejudices held by one social class or group against another.

What has been said thus far about propaganda and slogans is illustrated by the following quotation on their use in modern Egypt. The statement emphasizes the reliance of modern authoritarianism on propaganda for various purposes. Characteristically, the Egyptian ministry of propaganda is called the Ministry of National Guidance.

> Mass propaganda is an essential feature of Nasser's regime. The radio, the press and the pulpit are carefully controlled by the State. No dissentient voice is tolerated. The political slogans of the regime, the values, ideas and goals of modern Egypt, are manufactured at the top, are passed down through the machinery of the Ministry of National Guidance and through the Arab Socialist Union—the state political party—and are then spoon-fed to the people. Nasser's speeches form an essential part of school and university curricula.[7]

4. Reliance on police and terror.   Another distinguishing characteristic between a democracy and a dictatorship is the latter's reliance on the police as an instrument of terror. The midnight "knock on the door"—whether by Stalin's N.K.V.D., Hitler's Gestapo, or Franco's Guardia Civil—has become a common occurrence in modern dictatorships. Whereas in democracies the police are accountable to elected public officials, in dictatorships they are accountable only to the "leader." As such they are merely instruments of the leader's will, often acting in such a manner as to force the public into abject submission and docile obedience. While not all doors are knocked upon at midnight and not all homes are summarily searched, even in the most oppressive dictatorships, the possibility of such acts is sufficient to instill into the people a fear, which makes arbitrary search and seizure a very subtle form of terror.

Totalitarianism

In the world of today, which is characterized by a number of political, social, and economic isms, *totalitarianism* represents the most cen-

---

[7] Patrick Seale and Irene Beeson, "Egypt Confronts Its Population Explosion," *New Republic* (May 7, 1966), p. 11.

tralized form of political organization. This phenomenon is so much a part of the twentieth century that it may safely be said to be "a child of our time." An eminent American diplomat-historian has written that totalitarianism "has demeaned humanity in its own sight, attacked man's confidence in himself, made him realize that he can be his own terrible enemy, more bestial than the beasts, more cruel than nature."[8]

One might begin to define *totalitarianism* by stating that it is a condition in which massive power—not only political power but also social, economic, and military power—is concentrated in the hands of one or a few. Thus, the leadership or the government can exercise absolute control over the individual under its authority. The way a man lives, works, learns, behaves, and even the way he thinks, are to a great degree determined by the government, which has a totality of power at its disposal.

Totalitarianism is dictatorship in the extreme. It reached its peak of effectiveness in the Soviet Union under Stalin, in Germany under Hitler, and in Communist China under Mao Tse-tung. In these societies, the whim of the leader or dictator was the law of the land, and extreme measures were utilized to see that his will was strictly obeyed.

Federalism

Whether a system of government is set up on the *federal, confederal,* or *unitary* model has little to do with whether it is democratic or authoritarian, just or oppressive. Thus it is that the United States and the Soviet Union are federally structured countries and that Great Britain and Mussolini's Italy were organized on the unitary model.

In a federal system of government, political power is divided between two levels of government. Some power is given to the central or national authority, and some is given to the regional parts or units. The United States, for example, has a government which, because of the conditions that existed before and during the Constitutional Convention of 1787, was set up on the federal model. The Constitution makes definite provisions for the *division of power.* It states very plainly that certain powers are to be given to the central government while others are left to the states or to the people. As a consequence, the individual citizen of the United States comes in contact with these two levels of government: (1) that of the state in which he resides, and (2) that of

---

[8] George F. Kennan, "Totalitarianism in the Modern World," in Carl J. Friedrich, ed., *Totalitarianism* (New York: Grosset, 1964), p. 17.

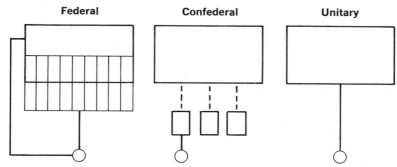

Figure 1-1. Federal, confederal, and unitary forms of government.

the entire union, the central government. For example, each of the fifty states in the federation has its own system of courts and its own laws covering criminal offenses not explicitly dealt with in federal statutes.

A federal system of government such as exists in the United States requires a written constitution to spell out how power is to be divided— which powers are to be given to the central or national authority and which powers to each of the several regional units. A constitution, therefore, serves as the source from which governmental authority springs. And in order to see that a federal constitution is rightly interpreted, the system provides a referee (in the United States, it is the Supreme Court) with ultimate authority to determine what the constitution means.

As indicated above, the United States is only one among many nations and political systems which are federally structured. Our neighbors to the north, Canada, and to the south, Mexico, have federal systems of government. So do the Australians, the Brazilians, the West Germans, the Swiss, and many others. While there are differences from one federal system to another, these differences usually involve the distribution of power: how much is to be located in which level of the system.

Some have described federalism as a marriage of convenience—an agreement between partners to form a close relationship for mutually beneficial purposes. These purposes might involve trade, defense, or communications. The analogy is not too far-fetched. Historically, the main reason for the creation of federations has been to accomplish ends which the individual state, province, or republic could not accomplish without the assistance of others. And it is normally this mutuality of interests that keeps federations together.

Confederalism

A confederation is a weak form of federalism. When a number of independent states come together, usually for reasons of defense, they form a coalition which is called an *alliance*. After the purposes of the alliance have been fulfilled—either the enemy has been defeated or the danger has subsided—the alliance breaks apart. A *confederation* is a step beyond an alliance in that a permanent authority or body is established to oversee the affairs of the alliance and to open up some new avenues for cooperation.

Early in the Revolutionary War, in 1777, the Second Continental Congress proposed what they called "a firm league of friendship" based on the Articles of Confederation. The new government, requiring unanimous adherence of the thirteen colonies, was not formally organized until 1781, when Maryland finally approved the Articles. By its very nature a confederation is incapable of acting as a cohesive unit; it is an imperfect union. The problems afflicting the American colonies after 1777 led some concerned citizens to call together at Philadelphia a constitutional convention in 1787 in order, as the Preamble to the Constitution states, "to form a more perfect Union." The assumption certainly was that the confederation was weak and unable to solve some of the acute problems facing the new and inexperienced nation.

Unitary Government

Federal political systems are relatively new in human experience, and they are still greatly outnumbered by unitary governments. In a federal system, power is divided; in a unitary system, power is united or fused. In the unitary form of government, power is concentrated in the central government which, in turn, may disperse some of that power to local units. The prime examples of unitary states are Great Britain and France. The crucial point is that in the British system it is London that determines how much power, if any, Scotland shall have. Similarly, in the French system it is Paris that decides whether the chief administrative officer of the province of Normandy shall be replaced or have his powers increased or reduced.

In a unitary political system, a written constitution is not necessary, because there is no question as to where power is located—everyone knows that it is located in the central government. Still, a constitution does *define* and *limit* the power of the government—any government. Therefore, virtually every government today, regardless of form, has a constitution.

APPROACHES TO DEMOCRATIC GOVERNMENT

Democracies insist on maintaining what in contemporary terms is called "diversity," a condition in which more than one approach may be employed by the government to reach desired social goals. Above all, democratic man does not depend on absolutes—on rigid, unalterable positions or values. Rather, he is characterized by flexibility, a willingness to compromise and to make concessions in order to maintain the orderly processes of society.

This section will examine two approaches to democratic government: *conservatism* and *liberalism.* These two approaches have alternated in influence over the years, and on close examination it becomes possible to discover elements of both in all governmental systems. In light of the current controversy in United States politics about whether one or the other approach is the better, an analysis seems to be in order.

Conservatism

As a political attitude, conservatism implies the desire to conserve or to maintain the existing order, the status quo. Conservatives are generally opposed to radical political, social, and economic reforms. The word *radical* is important in the preceding sentence because the impression should not be given that conservatives by definition oppose any kind of change merely for the sake of opposition. The true conservative values the experience of the past, which he views as the accumulation of wisdom, moral principles, and tradition. By the same token, he opposes any kind of change which is based solely on theory—in other words, something that has not proved its worth in actual practice. In the American tradition, the genuine conservative could be called a *pragmatist*—one who, after he has made certain that something works well, accepts it, oftentimes grudgingly to be sure.

Modern political conservatism has its roots in the eighteenth century when it emerged in reaction to the political and social upheaval of the French Revolution. (Modern economic conservatism emerged as a result of the Industrial Revolution in the middle of the nineteenth century.) The leading figure in the development of modern political conservatism, the one to whom conservatives turn for inspiration and ideas, was the British political leader and philosopher Edmund Burke. His speeches in Parliament together with his writings serve as the fountainhead of conservatism's political principles. Apprehensive about the influence of the French Revolution on tradition-bound English society, Burke used all his oratorical skills to oppose it. Burke and his followers argued that England's traditional institutions such as the monarchy, the aristocracy, and the church were a bulwark against the revolutionary influences from across the Channel. Therefore, the power of these institutions should be maintained for the good of the realm.

In the United States there have been no established institutions such as a state church, a monarchy, or a rigid aristocracy to defend. Thus American conservatism, following the attitudes of men like Alexander Hamilton, turned its attention to the fundamental question "Who governs?" or more precisely "Who should govern?" Were the people, the average men, capable of governing themselves, or should an elite group, by reason of their education, background, and financial success, govern? The basic question was whether majority rule was possible. Hamilton and his supporters argued against majority rule, while Jefferson and his followers insisted on the full implementation of the principles enunciated in the Declaration of Independence, declaring that all men are free and equal and that they have certain rights that cannot be taken away, including the right of self-government.

Conservatism has changed significantly in the past fifty years. At least in the United States, conservatives are no longer concerned with

---

. . . both the conservative and the liberal tradition in America have common roots in a highly individualistic conception of the nature of society. They have differed largely over the means by which the individual is to be served. Conservatives have resisted egalitarian liberal measures on the grounds that they are really leveling devices designed to obliterate any real distinction by reducing all to a least common denominator and that they often represent an assault on the rights of private property, which conservatives feel to be the foundation of real freedom. As a result, much of the political conflict of American history—particularly since the Civil War—has centered around the proper role of the government in relation to the economy. On the whole, the proponents of laissez-faire have succeeded in resisting governmental expansion—except in those limited areas in which they themselves desired interventions—until quite recent times. Thus it can be argued that, in terms of policy output, the American political tradition can best be labeled conservative. On the other hand, at the level of formal political thought, American thinkers have generally been part of the liberal-reform tradition. At best, *this* group wins only occasional victories. In the sense that the term is used here, the American liberal has *normally* been in the minority. The fact that he is no longer in the minority has significant consequences. . . .

James P. Young, *The Politics of Affluence* (New York and London: Chandler Publishing Company, 1968), p. 7.

the philosophical question "Who governs?" (although the query "How much government?" is raised). Today's conservatives are primarily concerned with economic questions and the role of the individual in a mechanized, highly complex society. Present-day conservatives oppose expansion of the "welfare state," but they have shown some willingness to accept moderate changes and reforms.

There are certain groups in contemporary American politics that claim to belong to the conservative position. On closer examination, however, these groups are anything but conservative because the programs they advocate and the principles they espouse are designed not to preserve and improve what has been established and accepted but to change conditions radically to suit their desires and political preferences. Perhaps the best term to describe these groups is not "conservative" but "reactionary." So-called conservative groups in post World War II American politics generally have two things in common: rigid anti-Communism and implacable opposition to programs of social welfare. The challenges posed to American democracy by such extremist groups as the John Birch Society, the Minutemen, and the American Nazi party will be discussed in the final chapter of this book.

Liberalism

While conservatism desires the preservation of the status quo, which is viewed as almost sacred because it involves the accumulation of experience, liberalism accepts little as sacred merely because it is old and established. As a political philosophy, liberalism stresses a belief in inevitable progress and improvement while maintaining faith in the basic goodness and perfectibility of man. Unlike radicalism, which demands sweeping changes, liberalism depends on steady, methodical, rational change.

Like conservatism, liberalism has its roots in the past. It developed in Europe in the latter part of the eighteenth and early part of the nineteenth century as an expression of dissatisfaction with the existing order. It gained momentum as a result of the American and French Revolutions and, because it reflected the interests of a growing middle class of merchants, artisans, and professional men, it soon became a formidable political force. The liberalism of this period, often termed classic liberalism, called for such things as noninterference of government in business, the extension of suffrage (the vote), and other political liberties such as freedom of the press and the separation of church and state. Later on during the nineteenth century, liberals took on such unpopular causes as the issues of slavery and imperialism, both of which were viewed as infringing upon the rights and liberties of individuals.

From Europe and Great Britain, liberalism was transplanted to the United States, where its most faithful and articulate exponent was Thomas Jefferson. His influence on the American political system cannot be overemphasized, with its strong attachment to the rights and liberties of the individual and the firm belief in the goodness of man. The Jeffersonian ideal has been so firmly implanted in the American political tradition that, in this regard, all Americans can be considered Jeffersonian to a great extent.

Modern liberals no longer insist that the state should not interfere in economic affairs and that the individual alone should determine his future and destiny. This change in attitude occurred following the Industrial Revolution and rise of Marxism. Marx argued that classic liberalism was conservatism of another color; in fact, it was even worse because it allowed for the exploitation of one class by another. Marx called for revolutionary changes in the economic structure which would affect the social and political structures as well. Thus liberal attitudes were reevaluated in light of the threat from revolutionary Marxism. Liberals after Marx came to think it appropriate for the government to guarantee the welfare of all individuals and to prevent any group in society from gaining undue influence over any other group. Such policies would make the Marxian prediction of class struggle unlikely to come true.

By the beginning of the twentieth century, this new liberal attitude reached the United States and found expression in the Populist movement and later in Theodore Roosevelt's Progressive party and in Woodrow Wilson's administration. It was further extended during Franklin D. Roosevelt's New Deal. Such measures as a federally regulated minimum wage, improved working conditions, progressive taxation, as well as other welfare measures such as social security, unemployment insurance, and medical care for the aged are examples of the influence of liberalism on the American political and economic system.

Liberalism stresses political, civil, and religious liberties. Liberals, therefore, have been unequivocally opposed to both Communism and Fascism, although there are some persons who mistakenly believe that liberalism is one step removed from Communism. There are, nevertheless, radical liberals who, like conservative extremists, use the name of liberalism to attain their purposes, which are usually not at all related to genuine liberalism. Thus radicals—whether of the right or of the left —reject existing institutions and demand sweeping political and economic change.

CAPITALISM AND SOCIALISM

The terms *capitalism* and *socialism* are used with increasing frequency in contemporary America. These terms have been assigned a variety of connotations by people who use them as daggers, so to speak, to defend or to attack what they consider "the American way of life" or certain trends and tendencies in modern American politics. Groups on the far right, for example, use the term "creeping socialism" to refer to the present condition of the American economy, while extreme leftists argue against what they call "monopoly capitalism." These terms, which were originally intended to define simply and precisely the nature of an economic system, are now being assigned all sorts of social and political, along with economic, connotations.

Actually, *capitalism* and *socialism* are economic terms, not political concepts. Either can work in conjunction with democracy or dictatorship. For instance, the capitalism of the United States differs substantially from the capitalism of Hitler's Germany or of Mussolini's Italy. The socialism of the Soviet Union is vastly different from Sweden's. The economic system of socialism can function within a democratic framework as well as within a totalitarian political system; so can capitalism. Thus the socialism of Sweden and of Great Britain is called "Democratic Socialism," while a book published in the United States a few years ago carries the title *The Case for Democratic Capitalism*,[9] implying, of course, that there can be undemocratic capitalism as well.

What, then, characterizes the economic system of capitalism in its classic form? Four features are vital:

1. Private ownership of property.
2. Private operation of the means of production and distribution.
3. The profit motive.
4. Competition.

On the other hand, socialism emphasizes:

1. Community ownership of the means of production and distribution.
2. State ownership of property.
3. The welfare state.
4. Economic planning.

Neither capitalism nor socialism exists in its pure form anywhere in the

[9] Harold Chase and Paul Dolan, *The Case for Democratic Capitalism* (New York: T. Y. Crowell, 1964).

world. Most modern countries, including the United States, which is by far the most successful capitalistic country in the world, are quite eclectic about their economic regulations. They do not hesitate to use whatever controls work best, or to avoid controls, to provide prosperity and well-being. Thus the American economic system includes elements of socialism such as unemployment insurance, old-age benefits, and some degree of planning. In recent years the Soviet economic system too has become somewhat more pragmatic. Soviet industrial managers have discovered that the profit motive is a powerful incentive and may help increase production and at the same time improve the quality of goods produced.

GLOSSARY

Authority The established right within any social order, to determine policies, pronounce judgments, or settle controversies.

Authoritarianism Unlimited or absolute and unrepresentative government.

Capitalism An economic system that includes private ownership of property, private operation of the means of production and distribution, the profit motive, and competition.

Charisma A special gift of leadership qualities.

Citizen A full member of the political community.

Confederalism A weak form of federalism; a coalition or alliance of independent states with a permanent authority or body which is established to oversee the affairs of the alliance.

Conservatism A political philosophy characterized by a desire to conserve or maintain the existing order, assigning great value to the experience of the past.

Consensus A broad agreement among the vast majority of the members of a body politic about the fundamental values of the political system.

Democracy Government by the people, whether direct or indirect and representative.

Elitism The belief that some individuals, groups, or classes are especially suited to make decisions for society as a whole.

Federalism A system of government in which political power is divided between two levels, in the United States between the Federal government and the several states.

Government The largest organization for ordering or controlling the actions of persons in a society.

Ideology A comprehensive, consistent, closed system of knowledge.

Liberalism A political outlook supporting governmental change and based on a belief in inevitable human progress and improvement and faith in the basic goodness and perfectibility of man.

Politics   A process by which men attempt to control or influence the behavior or attitudes of others.

Power   The ability or the capacity to elicit compliance, whether by persuasion or by force.

Propaganda   Systematic, continuous and deliberate efforts to indoctrinate persons into a system of beliefs and ideas, which may or may not be based on reality.

Republic   A form of government wherein the leaders are in some fashion representative of and responsible to the people.

Socialism   An economic system that emphasizes community ownership of the means of production and distribution, state ownership of property, the welfare state, and economic planning.

Sovereignty   The distinctive characteristic of the supreme lawful authority of a state that sends ambassadors, secures its own borders, and has the ability to make foreign policy without foreign interference.

State   A people organized under a common government and occupying a piece of territory with well-defined boundaries or territorial limits.

Totalitarianism   Massive and unresponsible political, social, economic and military power concentrated in the hands of a few.

Unitary (form of government)   A central government in which power is concentrated and which arbitrarily delegates authority to any political subdivisions such as states, counties, or cities.

SUGGESTIONS FOR FURTHER READING

ARENDT, HANNAH. *The Origins of Totalitarianism.* 2nd ed.; New York: Meridian, 1958

ARISTOTLE. *Politics.* Many editions.

BARBER, JAMES DAVID. *Citizen Politics.* Chicago: Markham, 1969.

CAREW-HUNT, R. M. *The Theory and Practice of Communism.* Baltimore: Penguin, 1963.

CORRY, J. A., and HENRY J. ABRAHAM. *Elements of Democratic Government.* New York: Oxford University Press, 1964.

CRICK, BERNARD. *In Defense of Politics.* Baltimore: Penguin, 1964.

DAHL, ROBERT A. *Preface to Democratic Theory.* Chicago: University of Chicago Press, 1956.

DJILAS, MILOVAN. *The New Class.* New York: Praeger, 1957.

EBENSTEIN, WILLIAM. *Today's Isms.* Englewood Cliffs, N.J.: Prentice-Hall, 1973.

FRIEDRICH, CARL J. *Constitutional Government and Democracy.* 3d ed.; Boston: Ginn, 1964.

FRIEDRICH, CARL J., and Z. B. BRZEZINSKI. *Totalitarian Dictatorship and Autocracy.* 2d ed.; New York: Praeger, 1966.

FROMM, ERICH. *Escape from Freedom.* New York: Holt, Rinehart & Winston, 1941.

HOFFER, ERIC. *The True Believer.* New York: Harper & Row, 1951.

INGERSOLL, DAVID E. *Communism, Fascism, and Democracy.* Columbus, O.: Charles E. Merrill, 1971.

LERNER, MAX. *America as a Civilization.* New York: Simon & Schuster, 1957.

MAC IVER, ROBERT M. *The Web of Government.* New York: The Free Press, 1965.

MAYO, HENRY B. *An Introduction to Democratic Theory.* New York: Oxford University Press, 1960.

PLATO. *The Republic.* Many editions.

ROSENAU, JAMES N. *The Dramas of Politics.* Boston: Little, Brown & Co., 1973.

SKINNER, B. F. *Beyond Freedom and Dignity.* New York: Knopf, 1971.

VAN DYKE, VERNON. *Political Science: A Philosophical Analysis.* Palo Alto: Stanford University Press, 1960.

WELDON, T. D. *The Vocabulary of Politics.* Baltimore: Penguin, 1960.

Chapter 2
The People of the United States

Whether government be "of the people, for the people, and by the people," as we hope it is in the United States, or whether the mass of people have little or nothing to do with governing themselves, the number, character and distribution of the inhabitants of a nation are important factors in the operation of any political system. In the prologue we mentioned some of the major issues facing the people of the United States in the 1970s. This chapter will present a general profile of the peoples of America which, when considered together with historical and constitutional factors, can help us to understand the special ingredients that affect the political culture of the United States. The chapter should also demonstrate the diversity and large scale of the problems that our political system must cope with.

THE LAND

In land area, the United States is one of the largest countries in the world—less than half the size of the Soviet Union but almost as large as Canada or China. One characteristic of the United States is the vastness and variety of its landscape. Climatic conditions range from the frozen, virtually uninhabitable parts of Alaska to the tropical and semitropical climates of Hawaii, California, and Florida. There are the fertile plains of the middle part of the United States and the immense deserts of the Southwest; majestic mountains like the Rockies, and great, legendary rivers such as the Mississippi.

This diversity in landscape contributed to the creation of distinctive life styles, and hence of political patterns, in different sections of the country. This sectionalism is now diminishing, in large part because of innovations in communications, especially television, and transportation, especially the jet airplane.

Population Growth

In population, the United States is the fourth largest country in the world, after China, India, and the Soviet Union. In 1970 over 203 million persons were living in the United States, up from 179 million in 1960, an increase of almost 25 million persons in 10 years. Between 1950 and 1960 the national population expanded by 28.4 million persons, making a total increase of about 50 million during the lifetime of most readers of this book.

In 1940, before the outbreak of World War II, our population was only 132.2 million. The baby boom following the war plus a significantly high birthrate even after the boom subsided has added 71 million persons since 1940. (The population of the world, moreover, has doubled in the past 35 years.)

Even though the birthrate began to drop in the 1960s and is now below the levels of the 1930s, it has been estimated that with no foreign immigration and with a birthrate at replacement levels, it would be 70 years (2040) before our population stopped growing. For at least several generations, then, and perhaps for longer depending upon our reproductive habits, our population will be growing.

What difference does changing population size make? Opinions differ on the consequences of a large and growing population. Right now, however, there is an increasingly vocal concern for a degenerating environment and lower quality of life that, it is feared, will be the results of a larger population. Many cities and counties are now taking steps to limit or control the rate of their growth in order to hold on to suburban or rural communities and to avoid the costs of providing facilities and services to accommodate additional people.

The Commission on Population Growth and the American Future in 1972 reported that:

> There is hardly any social problem confronting this nation whose solution would be easier if our population were larger. Even now, the

dreams of too many Americans are not being realized; others are being fulfilled at too great a cost. Accordingly, this Commission has concluded that our country can no longer afford the uncritical acceptance of the population growth ethic that "more is better."

The questions of what is an optimum population and how to achieve it easily become political questions. Experts answer differently, and some insist that the questions themselves should not be asked. The conflict and the temporary resolution of the conflict by changes in public opinion, and the action of organized citizen groups and of government agencies illustrate the political process that are discussed in this book. The size, distribution, and character of our population shape the dimensions, nature, and possible solutions of the issues facing America in the 1970s.

The postwar babies, now the young adults of the United States, are a good example. As soon as they reached school age, shortages of classrooms and teachers developed in the elementary schools and these shortages each year moved up a grade into the high schools, colleges, and universities. By the time the flood began to reach the upper levels, an oversupply of teachers and facilities began to develop in the lower grades, and this condition is moving up the ladder annually.

An important factor in explaining the heavy school enrollment is the trend throughout the twentieth century for a steadily increasing proportion of children and youths to be enrolled in school. Table 2-1 shows that the percent of those between 5 and 24 years old enrolled in school has increased from 58.2 in 1930 to 73.8 in 1970. Changes within

Table 2-1. Percentage of age groups, 25–34 years old, enrolled in school: 1910–1970.

	Total 5–34 years	Total 5–24 years	5–24 years old						
			5–6	7–13	14–15	16–17	18–19	20–24	25–34
1970	57.2	73.8	72.4	97.3	95.9	89.3	56.6	21.3	6.1
1960	53.1	71.7	63.8	97.5	94.1	80.9	42.1	14.6	4.6
1950	(NA)	62.5	55.8	95.7	93.1	74.5	32.3	12.9	(NA)
1940	(NA)	57.7	43.0	95.0	90.0	68.7	28.9	6.6	(NA)
1930	(NA)	58.2	43.2	95.3	88.8	57.3	25.4	7.4	(NA)
1920	(NA)	(NA)	41.0	90.6	79.9	42.9	17.8	(NA)	(NA)
1910	(NA)	(NA)	34.6	86.1	75.0	43.1	18.7	(NA)	(NA)

(NA) = not available

Source: U.S. Bureau of the Census, *Census of Population, 1970; General Social and Economic Characteristics: U.S. Summary,* Table 73.

the three upper age groups, 16–17, 18–19, and 20–24, have been particularly striking.

Other phenomena are associated with the rapid increase in the number of teenagers and young adults. Automobile accidents have increased at the same rate as has the teenage component of the population, the component which has higher rates of accidents per person. The crime rate is higher among persons under 25 years of age than among older groups, which fact helps to explain statistically the increase in criminal acts.

> About 28 percent of the reported increase between 1960 and 1970 in the number of arrests for serious crimes can be attributed to an increase in the percentage of population under 25. Another 22 percent of the increase can be explained by the growing size of the population and other demographic factors. Thus, population change alone accounted for about half of the reported increase in the number of arrests for serious crimes over the last decade.[1]

Housing and jobs are coming to be major problems for people born during the baby boom. They are, of course, matters which must be handled through the political and economic systems. Increasingly the public sector is becoming more important in regulating and subsidizing activities in the private sector to provide both housing and jobs. The Census of 1970 again helps us to identify some of the characteristics of demand and supply.

As people grow into young adulthood they form households. The number of households in the United States will increase by one third by 1980, a much higher rate of increase than that of the total population. This means about a million and a half new households each year. If, as most Americans seem to wish, each household should have its own housing unit, this calls for an enormous increase in housing construction.

Government is deeply involved in housing, which involves it in almost all aspects of the structure of cities, physical planning and land use controls, subdivision controls, provision or regulation of utilities, regulation or subsidy of institutions that finance home building, provision of streets, highways and other transportation facilities. In fact the whole system of private property, including private housing, is based upon laws that have been developed over centuries. A critical public question today is whether the new householders, most of them young, will be able to purchase a home. Again government will be faced with

---

[1] Commission on Population Growth and the American Future, *Population and the American Future* (Washington, D.C.: 1972), p. 22.

acting to reduce the cost of home construction or to subsidize the purchase or rental of homes or both.

POPULATION DISTRIBUTION

The absolute number of people is important; equally significant is the way in which they are distributed around the country. Population density is closely associated with a way of life. This is most easily seen when we recall that for most of our history we have been predominantly a rural people. Even though cities have grown in population more rapidly than the countryside throughout our history, it was not until this century that the United States became predominantly urban. So fast was the pace of change that we hardly had become an urban nation before we found ourselves metropolitan.

> Americans are a metropolitan people. Most families live in metropolitan areas; most births, deaths and migration take place in them. But the traditions and nostalgia are farm and small town.[2]

Almost all of the population growth of the 1960s occurred in metropolitan areas. Today 69 percent of Americans are crowded into the 10 percent of the land area of the United States that constitute the 243 Standard Metropolitan Statistical Areas (as defined by the Bureau of the Census). The nonmetropolitan population, 31 percent of the total, is spread out over 90 percent of the land.

Many people are concerned with the deterioration of the environment that accompanies the continued concentration of Americans in metropolitan areas. Everyone is aware of the many campaigns of the Sierra Club, the Audubon Society, the Wilderness Society, and numerous state and local groups to improve the quality of air and water, to preserve open space from further urban encroachments, and to reduce travel by automobile.

We too often associate a quality environment with sparsely settled land. However, since most Americans live in metropolitan areas, pollution is essentially a metropolitan problem. Even within metropolitan areas there are disparities in environmental quality as there are in many other social and economic characteristics. The poor are concentrated in the inner core of our metropolitan areas. As the United States Council on Environmental Quality said in its 1971 report:

> Air pollution, a problem for nearly all of the Nation, lays its pall most heavily over the inner city in many metropolitan areas. Open space,

[2] *Population and the American Future*, p. 25.

parks and recreational opportunity are high priorities for a better environment. Yet in the inner city they are lacking to a higher degree than in other parts of the urban complex. Problems of noise, sanitation, and congestion affect nearly all sectors of the larger cities. But overcrowding, rats, flaked lead paint, deteriorating housing, and ever-present litter and garbage are afflictions more typical of the inner city.

Not only is there an uneven distribution of population in the nation, but there is a selective distribution of population within metropolitan areas as well. Some wealthy and middle-income whites live in central cities, but most of them live in the suburbs even though many continue to work downtown. The central cities, in turn, are the concentrations of the poor and racial minorities. Many of these people are unskilled and find that those jobs they can fill are moving out to the suburbs.

In 1969, for instance, 11 percent of the families in central cities had incomes below the poverty level as compared with 5.6 percent in suburban parts of the metropolitan area. Of the total number of families, 7.2 percent in central cities were receiving public assistance and only 3.5 in the suburbs. Of the families with incomes below the poverty level, 28.8 percent in central cities were receiving public assistance and 17.4 in the suburbs.

For 50 years population has been growing more rapidly in the suburbs than in the central cities and in 1970 the suburbs had become more populous than the central cities of two thirds of the metropolitan areas of 250,000 or more. There is no reason to expect any change in this long-time trend. On a one-man, one-vote basis, central cities can be outvoted in regional, state, and national elections.

POLITICAL GROUPS

A number of other political implications can be drawn from this brief statistical and demographic portrait of the United States. For one thing, the political system will continue to be pressured to satisfy the needs and aspirations of some social groups. Blacks, for example, will persist in their struggle for a share of the political power, and for equal treatment in jobs, housing, and education. The proportion of the total population they comprise is likely to increase rather than decrease in the foreseeable future. Also, younger people—those under 25 who make up half the population—have special needs and political attitudes that have to be taken into account. As do senior citizens (about forty million persons in the United States are over 55). Political parties and politicians that fail to respond to the special desires of any of these groups could find that they do so at their political peril.

Potentially, the most powerful group in American politics is women. Women have been labeled a minority group; but they are anything but a minority since they outnumber men by about four million. The nation was given a taste of women's determination to become more actively involved in politics and in the problems of American society during the political conventions and campaigns of 1972. In fact, a woman (Jean Westwood) for a short time headed the Democratic National Committee, a position of significant political power and influence.

The suggestion has been made that the best way to understand the political system of one's own country is to look at it from the outside, say Japan or Great Britain—to become thoroughly acquainted with the "political culture" and institutions of another society, say Japan or Great Britain, and compare them to those of one's own country. Understandably, most of us cannot move abroad in order to do that. It is possible, however, by reading about different countries, especially their political and constitutional histories, to compare and contrast them at least generally to the United States.

COMPARATIVE PERSPECTIVE

In Table 2-2, we have gathered statistical information to provide a comparative perspective. The United States is compared to eight other countries: The Soviet Union is included because it has long contested with the United States for power and influence and is one of the two most important industrial and military powers in the world. Four other European nations—Great Britain, France, and West Germany because they belong to that relatively small number of nations that are called "developed," and Sweden, a small nation of about eight million persons with a highly developed economy and affluent society—are included. Japan is an Asian nation that experienced a phenomenal rate of economic growth in the 1950s and '60s and is the third most important industrial power in the world today—after the United States and the Soviet Union. Another Asian nation, India, is not as fortunate as Japan in economic development. Her limited resources and rapid population growth inhibit the possibilities of accelerated economic development. Somewhere between India and Japan, on most scales, is the world's most populous country, China. For China, however, reliable statistics are unavailable

Table 2-2. Comparative national demographic and economic indicators: The United States and selected countries.

	U.S.A.	U.S.S.R.	Great Britain	France	West Germany	Sweden	Japan	India	Brazil
1. Per capita income in dollars	3814	1678	1513	2106	1910	2905	1288	73	263
2. No. of persons per physician	650	433	860	770	580	800	910	4830	1670
3. No. of persons per hospital bed	120	107	90	80	90	70	80	2410	290
4. Infant mortality per 1000 births	19.8	24.4	17.9	15.1	23.5	13.1	15.3	139	112
5. Life expectancy in years	71	70	71	71	71	77	71	50	55
6. Passenger cars per 1000 inhabitants	450	7	200	220	200	250	80	1	20
7. Telephones per 1000 inhabitants	510	20	220	200	200	500	200	5	15
8. TV receivers per 1000 inhabitants	399	127	284	210	262	401	214	(NA)	72

Sources: *United Nations Demographic Yearbook, 1970 United Nations Statistical Yearbook, 1970; New York Times Almanac, 1971.*

Note: Per capita income data for USSR, Sweden, India, and Brazil are for 1968. Data for all other countries are for 1969. Numbers 6 and 7 are estimated by the authors based on *Yearbook* data.

in many of the categories listed. Brazil belongs to that category of nations social scientists refer to as "developing." When the demographic and economic statistics of India and Brazil are compared to those of the more developed nations of Europe and the United States, one can readily grasp the immensity of the problems faced by countries like India and Brazil. It is also possible to understand why many of the underdeveloped or developing countries of the world have experienced political instability and authoritarian rule in recent years, for there seems to be a strong correlation between economic backwardness and political turmoil.

As indicated in Table 2-2, we have selected eight measures for comparison, ranging from per capita income (the total personal income generated in one year divided by population) and rate of infant mortality (the number of children per thousand who die before their first birthday), to number of telephones and television receivers per 1000 population. It ought to be emphasized that these figures are not the sole basis for comparing and evaluating other cultures. They merely provide a statistical basis for comparison and contrast, employing well understood indicators. And since gathering the type of data necessary to produce statistical yearbooks is a tedious and time-consuming business, it is not possible to have completely up-to-date information on many countries.

Wealth

On the basis of the data collected in Table 2-2, a number of conclusions about the United States are possible. The United States is by far the richest nation in the world today. Compare, for instance, per capita income of the United States with that of the other countries listed. The difference between the per capita income of the United States and that of even the developed countries of Europe is striking; only Sweden comes close to the United States in this category, and even there the difference is $1,000. But the comparison becomes stark indeed when per capita income—and every other indicator—is compared between the United States, India, and Brazil.

Now compare the numbers of persons per physician and per hospital bed. In the first category, the Soviet Union tops the list (only 433 persons per physician) with West Germany and the United States second and third respectively. But then compare the same statistics for India and Brazil. The indicator for number of persons per hospital bed probably tells us a great deal about the statistics on infant mortality and life expectancy. Sweden, for example, has the lowest ratio of persons per hospital bed (70:1) and the lowest rate of infant mortality (13.1 per 1000) while life expectancy is 77 years. India, on the other hand, has the highest ratio of persons per hospital bed (2,410:1) and also the highest rate of infant mortality on the list; life expectancy in India is 50 years.

Statistics on number of passenger cars, telephones, and television receivers per 1000 population suggest that the United States, Japan, and the countries of western Europe (with the exception of the Soviet Union, whose economic system has not been geared to meeting the needs of the

"What campaign? What election?"

Editorial cartoon by Frank Interlandi, © 1972 The Los Angeles Times, reprinted with permission.

consumer) are consumer societies; in those countries the economy grows and profits by satisfying the material needs of the population. In this regard, the United States is the consumer society par excellence, with Sweden following close behind.

Up to this point we have presented a statistical summary of the United States; several other nations were brought into the picture to provide a comparative perspective. In 1963, Gabriel A. Almond and Sidney Verba published a book which examined the attitudes of people in five democratic countries with widely different political experiences toward their government and political system. The results were published under the title *The Civic Culture.*

National Pride

Table 2-3 contains a summary of attitudes about government in the United States, Great Britain, West Germany, Italy, and Mexico. A selected number of citizens in these five countries were asked to list the things about their country that made them most proud. It is significant that 85 percent of the American respondents expressed pride in the governmental and political institutions of the country, as compared with 46 percent for the British, 7 percent for the West Germans, only 3 percent of the Italians, and 30 percent for the Mexicans.

Remember that this study was conducted in the late 1950s. One must assume that if the same questions were asked today in the United

Table 2-3.   Aspects of their nation in which respondents took pride

Percentage of those who say they are proud of	U.S.	U.K.	Germany	Italy	Mexico
Governmental, political institutions	85	46	7	3	30
Social legislation	13	18	6	1	2
Position in international affairs	5	11	5	2	3
Economic system	23	10	33	3	24
Characteristics of people	7	18	36	11	15
Spiritual virtues and religion	3	1	3	6	8
Contributions to the arts	1	6	11	16	9
Contributions to science	3	7	12	3	1
Physical attributes of country	5	10	17	25	22
Nothing or don't know	4	10	15	27	16
Other	9	11	3	21	14
Total number of cases	970	963	955	995	1,007

Soure: *The Civic Culture* (Boston: Little, Brown, 1965), p. 64.

States, the number of those who express pride in governmental and political institutions would not be as high as 85 percent. This can be attributed to the Vietnam experience which, for a variety of reasons, disheartened many citizens. Also the pressures of modern life, and the development of a counterculture among young people, including changing attitudes toward the family, the church, and authority in general tend to erode positive attitudes toward government. In December, 1971, the Gallup organization surveyed public opinion with the question: "On the whole would you say you are satisfied or dissatisfied with the way the nation is being governed?," nationally only 37 percent expressed satisfaction while 54 percent expressed dissatisfaction (9 percent had no opinion).[1] And in a related study, Professor Arthur Miller found that between 1964 and 1970 the American people's trust in their government declined almost 20 percent. At the same time public cynicism about politics and politicians increased dramatically. To some extent this cynicism and lack of interest was reflected in the 1972 elections; only 56 percent of those eligible to vote actually went to the polls, the lowest percentage since 1948 when 52 percent voted.

GLOSSARY

Consumer society A country whose economy is primarily geared toward producing goods and services for use (consumption) by its citizens.

Demographic Information concerning the vital statistics of a nation: total population, age, racial composition, income, and the like.

Developed nations Those nations with a high degree of industrialization and a high GNP (over $1000 per capita annually).

Developing countries Those countries which are now beginning to industrialize their economies and modernize their societies (and their political systems).

Gross national product The total value of all the goods and services produced by a country, usually measured for a single year.

Per capita income Income per person; found by dividing the total personal income of a country (for a given year) by its population.

Political culture The political values, attitudes, and beliefs that are characteristic of a nation.

Senior citizens Persons over 55 years of age.

SUGGESTIONS FOR FURTHER READING

ALMOND, GABRIEL A., and SIDNEY VERBA. *The Civic Culture*. Princeton: Princeton University Press, 1963.

---

[1] *The Gallup Opinion Index*, Report No. 81, March 1972.

BANKS, ARTHUR S., and ROBERT B. TEXTOR. *A Cross-Polity Survey.* Cambridge: MIT Press, 1963.

CARTER, GWENDOLEN M., and JOHN H. HERTZ. *Government and Politics in the Twentieth Century.* New York: Praeger, 1973.

HODGE, PATRICIA L., and PHILIP M. HOUSER. *The Challenge of America's Metropolitan Population Outlook—1960 to 1985.* National Commission on Urban Problems, Research Report #3. Washington, D.C., 1968.

KEY, V. O. JR. *Public Opinion and American Democracy.* New York: Knopf, 1965.

LANE, ROBERT E. *Political Life.* New York: The Free Press, 1969.

LIPSET, SEYMOUR MARTIN. *Political Man.* Garden City, N.Y.: Doubleday, 1963.

LUBELL, SAMUEL, *The Hidden Crisis in American Politics.* New York: Norton, 1971.

MC GIFFERT, MICHAEL. *The Character of Americans.* Homewood, Ill.: Dorsey, 1970.

U.S. Commission on Population Growth and the American Future. Research Reports:
1. *Demographic and Social Aspects of Population Growth*
2. *Economic Aspects of Population Change*
3. *Population, Resources and the Environment*
4. *Government and Population: The Governmental Implications of Population Change*
5. *Population Distribution and Policy*
6. *Aspects of Population Growth Policy*
7. *Statements of Public Hearings of the Commission*

U.S. Commission on Population Growth and the American Future. *Report: Population and the American Future* (Washington, D.C., 1972).

WALTTENBERG, BEN J., and RICHARD M. SCAMMON. *This USA—An Unexpected Family Portrait of 194,067,296 Americans Drawn from the Census* (New York: Doubleday & Co., 1972).

WILLIAMS, ROBIN M. JR. *American Society: A Sociological Interpretation.* New York: Knopf, 1970.

Chapter 3
Framing the Constitution

To some people the Constitution connotes something which is dead, useless, and irrelevant. To many others it is a mystical object which inspires a sort of religious awe. Both of these attitudes ignore the real importance of the Constitution as a vital part of the contemporary legal and political system. In the 1780s when it was written, a number of highly emotional and politically divisive issues confronted its authors. The Constitution, whatever else it may be, is a repository of the efforts of those men in Philadelphia to come to grips with very real human problems. Many of those issues remain with us today. In this chapter we will look at seven of them.

Seven of the issues that had to be resolved by the framers of the Constitution were: (1) the legitimacy of the Constitution replacing the Articles of Confederation; (2) Madisonianism (checks and balances) versus Jeffersonianism (popular consensus); (3) a presidential versus a parliamentary form of government; (4) bicameralism versus unicameralism; (5) slavery in regard to representation, taxation, and regulation of the slave trade; (6) the separation of powers; and (7) the territorial division of powers (federalism).

Each of these issues has its counterpart in political problems that have confronted the United States in recent history. This is not to say, however, that the Founding Fathers anticipated all the problems which this country would face in the years ahead. To mention one glaring oversight, the men at Philadelphia neither expected nor provided for the nationwide, popularly supported political parties that have proved to be so important a part of America's political history. Despite the fact that by the time of the American Revolution two relatively strong political parties had developed in England (Whigs and Tories) and that opinion in the United States before the adoption of the new constitution was rather sharply divided between advocates of a stronger central government (Federalists) and opponents of "consolidated" federal power (anti-Federalists), the framers of the Constitution made no provisions whatsoever for the functioning or regulation of political parties.

THE LEGITIMACY OF THE CONSTITUTION

The first question facing leaders of the thirteen states a decade after the Declaration of Independence was whether the original constitution, the Articles of Confederation, should be improved or replaced. Although the inability of the confederated states to cope with vital problems—notably, protection against outside enemies and the regulation of internal and external trade—had caused grave concern, especially among more affluent individuals, the amending process prescribed by the Articles stymied reform. For the Articles required that amendments be approved by the Congress and by the legislatures of all thirteen states.

To meet the challenge, representatives of Virginia and Maryland, having agreed about regulating commerce on the Potomac, called a general convention at Annapolis in 1786. Only five states sent delegates, but these proposed a second convention to be held at Philadelphia the following year "to devise such further provisions as shall appear to them necessary to render the constitution of the federal government adequate to the exigencies of the Union." Congress reluctantly approved, and twelve states sent delegates, only Rhode Island refusing.

As sweeping as the changes suggested in 1787 were, there is no inherent reason why they could not have been grafted onto the existing Articles. Indeed, many sections of the Constitution are identical with parts of the Articles, and other sections are quite similar both in form and in content. What, then, was the reason for drafting a new document rather than amending the Articles? Amendment of the Articles seemed out of the question because of the unlikelihood of convincing each of the thirteen states to give its approval. Reluctant states would have been in a very powerful position; almost inevitably one state or a group of states would withhold approval unless the other states granted a desired concession. This sort of difficulty had been encountered in earlier attempts to change the Articles.

During the Philadelphia convention the majority agreed that the business at hand should be to write a new constitution and to design machinery for ratifying it which would not require the unanimous consent of all thirteen states. This decision is embodied in Article VII of the Constitution. According to this article, ratification depended not on the acceptance of all thirteen states—which adherence to the provisions of the existing Articles of Confederation would have required—but rather the approval of only nine of the thirteen. In this sense the Constitution could be considered illegitimate or even illegal.

Congress had authorized the calling of a convention in Philadelphia for the sole purpose of revising the Articles of Confederation. Echoing the authorization from Congress, some state legislatures specifically instructed their delegates to consider only amendments to the Articles and not a substitute document. In addition, Congress directed that no changes could take effect unless approved by Congress and accepted by all the state legislatures. As things turned out, however, the new constitution was ratified neither by the old Congress nor by the state legislatures. Instead it was ratified by *conventions* in each of the states, to which Congress was directed to submit the document by its thirty-nine bold signers.

It should be emphasized, however, that disagreements were sharp and discussion vigorous, both at the convention and in the subsequent months of debate over ratification. We are all familiar with the principal arguments of the so-called Federalists, or supporters of the proposed constitution. They are laid out and developed classically in *The Federalist,* originally written as "letters to the editor" by John Jay, Alexander Hamilton, and James Madison.

Many of their arguments in favor of ratification seem to have been devised in order to knock down straw men—so obvious is its defense more than 150 years after its adoption. With the republication of popular editions of the essays and pamphlets of the anti-Federalists it has become clear that the supporters of the proposed constitution were fighting a real battle with skillful adversaries.

While ratification of the Constitution violated the existing Articles of Confederation, and while the convention which wrote it was not authorized to do so by Congress, succeeding generations have come to regard the Constitution with the reverence and awe usually reserved for sacred objects. In their blind worship of the Constitution, many people believe that the problems the United States faces today are the result of having "strayed away" from the bedrock principles of the Constitution. Thus the Constitution is seen as a necessary and sufficient description of how citizens and government should act if the system is to operate harmoniously. How ideal it would be if the Constitution had been perfect when written and were able to solve all problems the nation faces today. Unfortunately, neither is the case.

While the Constitution was not expected either to be a perfect document or to meet every problem imaginable, it has served the country well over almost two centuries. This remarkable record is due at least as much to the men who have interpreted and applied the Constitution as to those who wrote it. There is nothing magical about the

---

To the People of the State of New York:

There is an idea, which is not without its advocates, that a vigorous Executive is inconsistent with the genius of republican government. The enlightened well-wishers to this species of government must at least hope that the supposition is destitute of foundation; since they can never admit its truth, without at the same time admitting the condemnation of their own principles. Energy in the Executive is a leading character in the definition of good government. It is essential to the protection of the community against foreign attacks; it is not less essential to the steady administration of the laws; to the protection of property against those irregular and high-handed combinations which sometimes interrupt the ordinary course of justice; to the security of liberty against the enterprises and assaults of ambition, of faction, and of anarchy. . . .

. . . A feeble Executive implies a feeble execution of the government. A feeble execution is but another phrase for a bad execution; and a government ill executed, whatever it may be in theory, must be, in practice, a bad government.

Alexander Hamilton, "Advantages of a Single Executive," *The Federalist*, No. 70.

Constitution as written; what is impressive is the fact that the Constitution has proved flexible enough to allow novel solutions to new problems and yet durable enough that the basic outlines of American government have not changed significantly since 1789. Instead of worshipping the document itself, modern Americans might be better advised to be thankful for the accidents of history which have caused the United States system of government to be what it is today. Its survival and its strength were not always as certain as they now appear to be—and are due as much to the nation's many great leaders, the serious challenges they have confronted, and their responses to these challenges as to the Constitution itself.

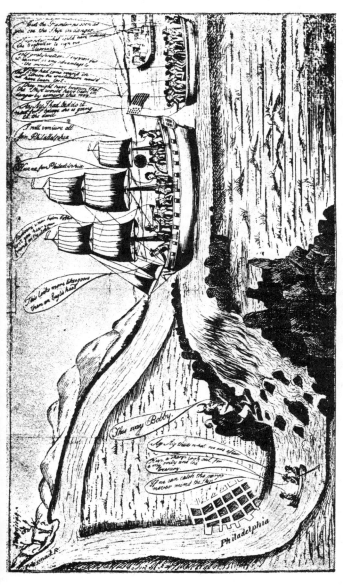

"Congress Embark'd on board the Ship Constitution of America bound to Conogocheque by way of Philadelphia," by an anonymous artist (1798). Hard feelings engendered during the ratification debate were carried over into the developing party divisions of the first decade under the Constitution. This cartoon attacks the role of former United States Senator Robert Morris (a Hamiltonian Federalist with extensive properties in Philadelphia) in removing the capital from New York to Philadelphia. (From the Historical Society of Pennsylvania collection.)

CHECKS AND BALANCES VERSUS POPULAR CONSENSUS

The first chapter examined the differences between the abstract concepts of conservatism and liberalism, noting attractive features in both approaches. If the philosophies of a large number of national leaders, past or present, were analyzed, it would not be surprising to learn that most of them incorporate elements of both approaches in their own conceptions of government. At the time the Constitution was written, conservatives like James Madison were concerned with placing enough power in the hands of the new federal government to avoid the problems encountered under the weak government of the Articles of Confederation. Liberals like Thomas Jefferson, on the other hand, were concerned with limiting the powers of the central government and protecting individual liberties. While the philosophies of both men incorporate elements of conservatism *and* liberalism, it may prove useful to consider that their divergent approaches as representative of the type of debate that was going on at the convention.

To begin with, it should be noted that the Founding Fathers, as colonists, had been familiar with two-house legislatures. They were also familiar, to some extent, with the operations of representative government, including separately elected executives and legislatures, and with an independent judiciary. Even so, these as well as other features of the new constitutional system were extensively debated at the convention.

Madison is usually credited with having devised the system of checks and balances, which has become an integral part of the American form of government. He felt that any government must face the threat that some interest group, or faction, might take over the government and use governmental power for its own purposes. Convinced that factions were more likely to dominate small political systems than large ones, Madison favored a large republic which would include people with different geographic, occupational, and ethnic backgrounds. Since the danger of factions would be greater within each state than within the republic as a whole, Madison preferred that the central government be stronger than the state governments. He did not want to abolish the state governments, but definitely thought they should be subordinate to the federal government.

Even in a large republic, with the diversity of factions and interest groups that would be represented, Madison felt there was a danger that some group might dominate the machinery of government. This danger could be reduced, not by eliminating factions (which he felt would be impossible without destroying liberty), but by separating the formidable

"That's the way our system works -- each branch of government watches the other two, and the people watch dumbfounded!"

Editorial cartoon by Frank Interlandi; © 1973 The Los Angeles Times, reprinted with permission.

powers of the federal government into three distinct branches: *executive, judicial,* and *legislative.* Even though a faction might be able to control one branch, the chance that all three branches of the government could be controlled by a single group, Madison thought, would be very small indeed. Among the three branches, Madison believed that the one most susceptible to majority tyranny was the legislative. At the constitutional convention this danger was anticipated by dividing the legislative branch into two parts: a Senate and a House of Representatives, with the members of each to be elected for terms of differing lengths and by different methods. In this way, ambitious politicians in each branch—and in the two houses of the legislative branch—would check one another. As Madison suggested in *The Federalist,* No. 51, ambition would check ambition in a harmonious system of mutual frustration.[1]

If Madison had to choose between political harmony and political frustration, he would be inclined toward frustration. To him, harmony was but a step away from tyranny, and majorities could be every bit as tyrannical as minorities. Frustration, on the other hand, meant inaction, indecision, and equilibrium. And it was better that the government not act at all than act tyrannically. He also was concerned with the possibility that a power-seeking group might even constitute the majority, in which case the system would succumb to "tyranny of the majority," as he called it.

Jefferson, unlike Madison, was not primarily concerned with checking and balancing the powers of the federal government. While Jefferson did believe in the concept of limited government, he felt that in a democracy the people themselves would provide the best restraint and the only reliable protection against the arbitrary use of government power. He felt that no artificial system of checks and balances could prevent the usurpation of power by a demagogue or tyrant if the people were willing to submit to his rule. Whereas Madison tended to be somewhat wary of the common man, and thus felt it necessary in some ways to "insulate" some governmental institutions from the whims of popular control, Jefferson trusted the common people more than the leaders. "Sometimes it is said that man cannot be trusted with the government of himself. Can he, then," asked Jefferson, "be trusted with the government of others?"

Jefferson was not concerned with limiting the power of the federal government, which he did not see as a major problem in a democracy, but with insuring that all branches would work in harmony and cooperation with one another. If the powers of government had to be separated into several branches, then each branch should be made as democratic as possible; that is, each branch should be directly answerable to the people for its actions and its policies. Jefferson was heartily in favor of the consensus approach to government (discussed in the opening chapter of this

---

[1] James MacGregor Burns has written a fascinating and very readable account of the Madisonian and Jeffersonian positions at the constitutional convention: *The Deadlock of Democracy: Four-Party Politics in America* (Englewood Cliffs, N.J.: Prentice-Hall, 1963). Especially interesting are Chapters 1 and 2.

book). He emphasized positive governmental action on any issues about which the general public was in wide agreement. Above all, Jefferson did not want a government that was indecisive or incapable of acting.

Jefferson's faith in the good sense of the common man suggests some rather idealistic assumptions about human nature. He believed, above all, in the perfectibility of man. Thus any man could be expected to make a "right" decision on a given issue if he were only well enough educated and sufficiently well informed on the facts surrounding the issue. While Madison emphasized man's shortcomings and the need for government to make provisions for dealing with them, Jefferson dwelt on man's positive attributes and the desirability of government's letting him alone whenever possible. Whereas Madison was quick to point out

". . And once again Watergate proves that our three branches of government provide the finest system of checks, balances and mutual insult!"

"Grin and Bear It" by George Lichty; © Field Enterprises, Inc. 1973, courtesy of Publishers-Hall Syndicate.

the unchanging elements of human nature and thus the likelihood that difficulties facing government and society would increase in the future, Jefferson believed implicitly in the idea of progress and expected that the problems of his day would be greater than those of succeeding generations. Finally, Jefferson made the idealistic assumption that the common man was as capable of understanding complex problems as were government specialists. He felt, therefore, that the people as a whole should make the important decisions—even on highly technical matters —which faced the country.

How have these two approaches to the American system of government worked in practice? It is one of the ironies of history that as president, Madison was unable to operate effectively the system of checks and balances which he was so brilliantly instrumental in designing. In a sense it could be said that he was caught in his own trap, for Madison's term as president was one of constant bickering and rivalry among the three branches of government. Although it is not possible here to examine in detail the problems which Madison faced as president, it is worth noting that during Jefferson's tenure in the presidency these difficulties were largely absent. Madison's administration was a not-so-harmonious system of mutual frustration, while Jefferson's was one of cooperation and consensus.

In general, United States political history has exhibited a cycle of sorts—with bickering, inaction, and indecision at the low points in the cycle and harmony, cooperation, and consensus at its high points. Usually, the high points seem to occur when the nation faces a grave threat of some kind and when a dynamic leader manages to obtain a widespread consensus for his particular programs intended to meet this challenge. While consensus is never complete, a high degree of it was achieved by such presidents as Washington, Jefferson, Jackson, Lincoln, Theodore Roosevelt, Woodrow Wilson, and Franklin Roosevelt. By contrast, the low points in the cycle occur when there is no perceived crisis and when there is no widespread agreement on how best to approach the nation's problems. It would not be accurate to place *all* other presidents in this category; but it is true that "consensus" presidents occupy the White House less frequently than do "mutual-frustration" presidents.

PRESIDENTIAL VERSUS PARLIAMENTARY GOVERNMENT

As mentioned earlier, Madison opposed vesting a monopoly of political power in one institution, whether it be the legislature or the executive.

Some political theorists, like Jefferson, who did not oppose a powerful legislature, looked to the parliamentary system of eighteenth-century England as an example. Others, like Hamilton, favored a powerful executive. They chose as their model a state government like New York's where a great deal of power resided in the governor. The arguments of the advocates of a parliamentary system centered on the principle of majority rule and the responsiveness of the legislature to the "general will." Legislatures, they felt, were much less likely to act capriciously or arbitrarily than executives.

Hamilton and those who agreed with him were not so concerned with majoritarianism and the general will as they were with the need for leadership and efficiency in government. They felt that the poor record of the government of the Articles of Confederation was adequate demonstration of the need for a political system capable of responding to challenges and crises quickly and effectively. A parliamentary government, or a government with legislative supremacy, could not achieve these objectives. They observed that when the English government acted, it was due to the initiative of a strong and perhaps tyrannical monarch like George III, or a powerful prime minister. In any case, action seldom originated in the legislature itself. In the Hamiltonian view, when the English Parliament did assert its supremacy, inefficiency and bungling were the result. The same could be said for political affairs in those American states which did not have a strong executive, and even more particularly under the Articles of Confederation with its powerless and impotent office of president.

In a *parliamentary* system, in theory at least, the prime minister is a creature of the legislators; he acts for them. Thus when he ceases to enjoy their support and confidence, he must resign. Theoretically, then, there is no separation of power. In practice, of course, the prime minister and his cabinet *function* separately from the legislature, and to some extent independently of it. Under a *presidential* system, the president and the legislature are constitutionally separated. They were elected separately, they are housed separately, and they operate separately —in theory at least. But in practice, most presidential systems have seen the necessity of executive-legislative cooperation. Thus, when it comes to the infighting of practical politics, the president and the legislature are often doing precisely the same kinds of things: he is trying to get certain legislation passed, and the legislators are trying to influence or even control the operation of the various departments of the executive branch. These relationships are shown in Figure 3-1.

At the constitutional convention, Hamilton and those who favored a strong president were adamant in defending their position. The forces

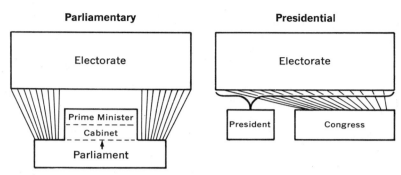

Figure 3-1. Parliamentary versus presidential system of government.

favoring legislative supremacy were hurt by Jefferson's absence (he was in Europe at the time of the convention) and Patrick Henry's departure in protest after the convention had gotten under way. The "presidential" forces had another advantage, in that Madison, although not in complete or even substantial agreement with Hamilton, nevertheless favored an independent president strong enough to check the powers given to the new federal Congress. The resulting compromise, which Madison was instrumental in engineering, represented a defeat for those who favored a parliamentary form of government or a weak executive.

As will become apparent in the discussion of Chapter 4, the office of president has steadily increased in power both absolutely and relatively. Today the president of the United States is unquestionably the most powerful political figure in the country. Moreover, the presidency is probably the most powerful democratic executive institution throughout the world. As his power has grown, many students of American government have become concerned at the relative loss of power by Congress. Indeed, some reformers have called for the scrapping of the presidential system entirely, and changing over to an English-style parliamentary government. Under such a system, they argue, the chief executive, or prime minister, would at least be responsible to his fellow members of parliament between elections. At it is, Congress seems to be a less and less effective check on presidential power. For a number of reasons, however, the likelihood of a fundamental change in the American system of government seems very small at present.

BICAMERALISM VERSUS UNICAMERALISM

The adjective *cameral* comes from the Latin word for "chamber"; thus a *bicameral* legislature is one with two chambers or houses. The Articles of Confederation provided for a unicameral legislature, the Congress. As legislatures go, the unicameral is a more democratic form than the bicameral because it is more directly responsive to the general will, or public opinion. At the beginning of the Philadelphia convention, it was assumed that the new government, like the old, would be unicameral. But delegates from the small states, like New Jersey and Rhode Island, were thinking in terms of a legislative body in which each state would be represented equally so that New Jersey's vote would count the same as New York's or Virginia's. This was how the Articles of Confederation had worked, and it was not very surprising that the small states were anxious to continue this type of arrangement. But equal representation of states was anathema to the delegates from the large states. On this point they were adamantly majoritarian; that is, they favored representation strictly on the basis of population. Thus if Virginia had ten times the population of New Jersey, it should have ten representatives for every one of New Jersey's. This approach, in turn, was unacceptable to the small states. Why should they give up a system where they were the equals of the large states for one in which their voice would be insignificantly small?

The solution to this dilemma was not entirely satisfactory to either side. The Connecticut Compromise, as it was called, not only balanced the interests of the small states against those of the large, but also represented a compromise between two different theories of representation. One, the elitist theory, was embodied in the Senate, members of which would not be popularly elected but instead would be chosen by state legislatures.[2] The other approach to representation, the principle of "one man, one vote," was followed in choosing members of the House of Representatives. Radical democrats and delegates from large states rightly pointed out that this compromise would allow fourteen Senators (out of a total of twenty-six) representing the least-populous states to block legislation favored by the vast majority of American citizens.

This objection is still relevant today, when more than half of the population of the United States is concentrated in nine states (California, New York, Pennsylvania, Illinois, Ohio, Texas, Michigan, New Jersey, Massachusetts), which have only eighteen out of one hundred senators. Thus the states with 51.4 percent of the population have only 18 percent of the seats in the Senate. On the other hand, the delegates from the small states were being quite realistic in trying to maintain

---

[2] This system was changed by the Seventeenth Amendment, ratified in 1913, which provides for the direct election of Senators.

their importance in national politics. If this compromise had not been struck, it is quite likely that a number of the smaller states simply would not have ratified the Constitution.

It is interesting that some of the same arguments heard in 1787 regarding the two approaches to national representation are being heard today with regard to representation in *state* legislatures. The case of *Baker* v. *Carr* (1962) and subsequent decisions of the United States Supreme Court have applied the "one man, one vote" principle to state legislatures as well as to districts for the United States House of Representatives. Some have asked why representation in *both* houses of state legislatures now must be based on population, while in the United States Senate it continues to be based on geography. The answer to this question is that the states within the federal system are more than mere geographic or administrative subdivisions of the central government. But the same cannot be said of the counties and other units of local government *within* states. Each of the first thirteen states had a history and a political system unique to itself. Union would have been impossible *except* for a federal arrangement guaranteeing the continued separate existence of each of the (now fifty) states. Counties, which have been the basis for some state-senatorial districts, as in California, have no special status and may be abolished by the state at any time. This is simply another way of saying that the United States government has a *federal* form whereas the states have a unitary form. For this reason special representation makes sense for states within the federal system, but does not for counties within each state.

SLAVERY

Another of the difficult circumstances faced by the men who met at Philadelphia in 1787 was slavery. More precisely, there were three issues which had to do with the larger question of slavery: (1) Which people would be counted for purposes of apportioning seats in the House of Representatives? (2) Which would be counted for purposes of taxation? (3) What provisions would be made regarding the flourishing trade in African slaves? None of these questions was solved to the complete satisfaction of anyone. Each of them was resolved by a compromise which had serious implications for later political and social developments. These compromises, though, were the least successful of any incorporated into the Constitution of 1787.

On each of these matters the battlelines were drawn on almost strictly regional lines. With regard to apportionment, for example, the

South was made up primarily of large plantations and medium-sized farms whose Caucasian owners wanted their slaves to be counted in the allocation of seats in the House of Representatives. They did not want blacks to have any voice in politics, of course, but they wanted to benefit themselves from the relatively heavy population in the region of which about one-third were blacks. Northerners generally opposed counting blacks on two grounds. First, it was simply viewed as a gimmick to give the South a greater voice in the House, and, second, many people were beginning to feel that it was wrong for whites to pretend to speak for blacks when they were denied any effective political voice. While there were some Southerners who shared these views, just as there were some slaveholders in the North, for the most part the issue was one of the North versus the South.

On the question of counting citizens for purposes of taxation, the tables were exactly reversed. Southern whites felt that blacks should not be counted since they were neither citizens nor property owners. It is possible that some Southerners took this argument seriously, although it appeared to Northerners as a thinly veiled attempt by Southerners to avoid paying their fair share of the national financial burden. Some Southerners raised anew the cry of "taxation without representation," since many Northerners were willing to see blacks counted for apportioning taxes but not for apportioning representatives. The solution to this dilemma was the Three-Fifths Compromise: five slaves would have the same weight as three whites both for purposes of taxation and representation. Thus the South was overrepresented in terms of actual participating citizens, but in a sense it had to pay for this representation when taxes were apportioned among the states. In fact, the South gained more than it lost, since forms of taxation other than direct levies against the states were the primary sources of revenue between 1789 and 1861.

The final problem involving slavery faced by those at the constitutional convention had to do with the slave trade itself. Revulsion against the barbarous treatment of blacks forcibly removed from their homes in western Africa prompted many humanitarians, social reformers, and political liberals to advocate a provision in the new Constitution outlawing slavery. In addition to the expected opposition from slaveholders, the proposal met opposition from another important group as well: the New England shipping industry. Some merchants were still making fortunes in the slave trade even as late as 1800. In addition, many plantation owners were afraid that the whole economy of the South would stagnate without a constant influx of new slaves to work the virgin lands to the west. The debate regarding the prohibition of the slave trade was long and bitter. Again a compromise was the only feasible solution if the convention were not to collapse. This time the agreement was simply to postpone the issue (Article I, Section 9, Clause 1): "The Migration or Importation of such Persons [slaves] . . . shall not be prohibited by the Congress prior to the Year [1808]." This provision was a bitter defeat for those who wanted to abolish slavery, but as with other less-than-perfect compromises, it was essential to securing the adoption of the new document.

As with other issues which resulted in compromises at the constitutional convention, the slavery issue would return in another form to haunt the body politic in subsequent years. Indeed, when Chief Justice Taney wrote the majority opinion in *Dred Scott* v. *Sandford* (1857), he referred to the Three-Fifths Compromise (which made a distinction between whites, "free persons," blacks, and "all other persons"), the slave-trade compromise, and distinctions between "citizens" and "persons"[3] as proof that the Founding Fathers believed that blacks did not enjoy the rights of citizens, that they were inferior to whites, and that they should be treated as chattel, or property. The ultimate upshot of this decision was the Civil War. In fact, it took the Thirteenth, Fourteenth, and Fifteenth Amendments to repudiate the views of Chief Justice Taney and those who shared his interpretation of the Constitution. The profound impact of these civil-rights amendments will be seen in Chapters 8 and 10 in the discussion of civil rights today.

THE SEPARATION OF POWERS

The Constitution is much more closely in accord with Madison's ideas than with Jefferson's. Formally, at least, the powers of the three branches of government are made to appear quite distinct: legislative, executive, and judiciary. As mentioned above, Madison was wary of concentrating most of the powers of government in one branch—or, more accurately, he did not want too much power in the hands of one group. Borrowing from the French political philosopher Montesquieu, Madison believed that the three branches of government could be made separate from each other, and approximately equal in power, by giving each branch effective weapons to assure its independence of the other two branches. These weapons are commonly referred to as *checks and balances*. In

---

[3] For example in Article IV, Section 2: "The *Citizens* of each State shall be entitled to all Privileges and Immunities . . ."; but "A *Person* charged in any State with Treason, Felony, or other Crime. . . ." (Emphasis added.)

essence, they consist of powers to be used in opposing ill-considered actions of one of the other two branches (these are the *checks*), and powers to be exercised independently of the other two branches (these are referred to as *balances*).

In the Constitution the Congress has the longest and most impressive list of powers of the three branches. In fact, it might appear on the surface that Madison's fear of majority tyranny would be well justified if some powerful group should dominate the Congress. The first and most obvious check against such a development is structural: Congress is divided into two houses. Thus the bicameral organization of Congress not only assures two different kinds of representation (this could have been achieved by having both Senators and Representatives in one house), but also provides a check against hasty and ill-considered action which might emanate from either chamber (Madison was particularly worried about this danger in the House). Another self-contained check, which applies to the House of Representatives, is the requirement that *all* congressmen must run for reelection every two years. This reduces the chance that any cohesive majority might maintain itself in power for an extended period of time.

There are two sources of external checks on Congress, as provided in the Constitution. The first of these is the president. He has an arsenal of weapons which are designed to block congressional action which he deems undesirable or to spur action which he thinks necessary. Although these powers are discussed more fully in the chapter on the presidency, it might be useful to simply list the more important ones here: the veto; the opportunity to call Congress into special session; the "State of the Union" message; and the special-message power. The second major external check on Congress is the power of the courts, especially the Supreme Court, to declare acts of Congress unconstitutional. This power of *judicial review* will be discussed in some detail in Chapter 5. Although judicial review has proved to be a very important source of limitations on congressional power, it is not spelled out in the Constitution itself. There are indications, however, that many of the men at Philadelphia anticipated that the Court would exercise this power. Madison, in particular, felt that it was essential to an effective system of checks and balances.

Checks on presidential power come from Congress and the courts. Congress can override a presidential veto with a two-thirds majority vote. The Senate must approve all presidential appointments and ratify all treaties. In addition, funds for all executive programs and activities must be provided by Congress. This "power of the purse" has been one of the most effective weapons available to Congress in dealing with the president. Finally, Congress has at its fingertips the threat of impeaching the president.

The courts, in turn, must interpret laws passed by Congress which empower the president to act. In some instances a restrictive interpretation of a statute may have the effect of checking executive action. And just as the Supreme Court can declare acts of Congress unconstitutional, it can, and occasionally does, declare actions of the president unconstitutional. An example of such a decision came in 1952, in *Youngstown Sheet and Tube Co.* v. *Sawyer,* when the Supreme Court declared unconstitutional President Truman's seizure of the steel industry in response to a nationwide steel strike which had had crippling effects on the Korean War effort.

The power of the courts, which is less obvious than that of Congress or the president, is checked in more subtle ways. First, the president appoints judges to all federal courts. But if a court has been handing down decisions with which the president does not agree, it may be a number of years before he has the opportunity to appoint enough new members to make much of a change in the composition of the court since judges are appointed for life. The courts, however, have no power to enforce their decisions; they must depend on the cooperation of the Justice Department of the executive branch. Congress, in turn, can create or abolish federal courts at all levels except the highest—the Supreme Court is the only federal court created by the Constitution. Congress also fixes the appellate jurisdiction of the Supreme Court. Thus Congress can place a whole category of cases beyond the reach of the Supreme Court. Finally, Congress fixes salaries of all federal judges, although they cannot be lowered for a given judge during his lifetime. Moreover, the number of justices of the Supreme Court is determined by Congress and has ranged from five to ten, though it has remained fixed at nine for the past century. There is nothing but tradition prohibiting Congress from changing the size of the Court.

A less subtle attempt by some key members of Congress to limit the power of the Court came in the summer of 1968—although there have been similar attempts in the past. The 1968 episode involved proposed restrictions on the Court's appellate jurisdiction in certain types of criminal cases involving the rights of the accused. Many people feel that recent Supreme Court decisions involving these rights will impede law-enforcement efforts. This effort to undermine the authority of the Supreme Court came very near to succeeding.

The "checks," then, are limitations on power. The "balances" half of the formula consists of grants of power to each branch to equal the powers of the other branches. Thus Congress has the power to pass laws affecting a vast array of national issues. The president has the power of appointment and direction of the administrative branch, which enforces the laws and implements national programs. The Supreme Court interprets laws and other actions of Congress and the president. An important aspect—perhaps the crucial element—in balancing the three branches of government consists of insuring their independence of each other. Thus, the members of the Senate, as originally constituted, were to be elected by state legislatures, and answerable neither to the House nor to the president. Members of the House of Representatives are elected by single-member districts and are answerable neither to the president nor to the nation as a whole. The president is chosen by the nation at large and is independent of both the Congress and the courts. Judges, although chosen by the president, hold their posts for life, thus insuring their independence. The balance half of the equation, then, consists of positive grants of power to be exercised independently of the other branches.

The theory seems neat and simple: legislative, executive, and judicial power, separated into three branches, each checked and balanced by the others. This is the theory, and this is the system described in the Constitution. But in practice it is impossible to imagine a system in which these powers could or should be exercised entirely independently. Actually, as will be seen, one of the president's important roles is that of chief legislator—initiator and sponsor of the vast bulk of legislation which Congress must consider and act upon. Also, in fulfilling administrative responsibilities, the executive branch has developed a number of independent regulatory commissions and agencies which, in many cases, hear disputes within their jurisdiction and operate as courts of law in deciding these disputes; again, clear separation is clouded. Congress, in impeaching federal officials and in judging its own members, functions as a court. Moreover, Congress, in managing its own affairs, executes and administrates. The courts, in turn, are often found to be making "political decisions"—a power supposedly reserved to Congress. Finally, the Supreme Court oversees much of the management of the lower federal courts, thus performing a function which is more typical of the executive branch.

If the aim of the Founding Fathers was merely to apportion the power of the federal government among three different branches, then they succeeded. But if their aim was to establish three branches whose functions would be totally distinct, then they failed. The lasting contribution of Madison and those who shared his views was to distribute power so that no man, group of men, or branch of government would ever be able to exercise total power. More important than separation, then, is the checking and balancing of power. The fact that each branch of the government to some extent exercises powers which are more characteristic of one of the other branches does not detract from the worth of what Madison called the "separation of powers."

THE TERRITORIAL DIVISION OF POWERS—FEDERALISM

The decision to divide power between the federal government and the states was viewed by the framers of the Constitution as the most effective means to balance and check federal power. But in view of the immediate past history of the thirteen states as of 1787, some sort of *territorial division of powers,* or federal scheme, was necessary. The issue facing the constitutional convention was not whether the nation would have a unitary or a federal system, but rather how best to allocate powers that surely would have to remain divided on some sort of territorial basis. The chief difficulty with the Articles of Confederation was that the provisions left the bulk of power to the individual states and gave very little to the central government. This arrangement exactly fitted the description of a confederation as described in Chapter 1. Many of the men at the constitutional convention opposed abandoning the confederal arrangement. They felt that their duty was to improve the existing system, not to abolish it. But the majority believed, rightly or wrongly, that the failure of the Articles was in large part due to the *form* of government. In fact, economic and social difficulties in the thirteen states were at least as much to blame for the breakdown of the national government as was its form, but it was true that the confederal form had grave deficiencies.

In developing a workable division of powers between the national government and the states, the Founding Fathers had to decide whether to emphasize the powers of the former or the latter. Most of the men at Philadelphia agreed that the central government would have to have some new powers not enjoyed under the Articles. These would include, at a minimum, the power to (1) regulate commerce among the states and with foreign nations, (2) raise and maintain an army and a navy, (3) levy taxes directly on the states, and (4) establish a uniform national currency. But beyond these provisions the Federalists thought that in other matters the central government should be dominant as well. The anti-Federalists felt that the powers of the central government should be strictly limited and that in all matters not specifically mentioned in the Constitution the states, and not the federal government, should reign supreme. Those who hold this position today are known as "states-rightists."

The views of the Federalists on the division of power are found in the Constitution in the final clause of Article I, Section 8:

> The Congress shall have Power
> To make all Laws which shall be necessary and proper for carrying into Execution the foregoing Powers . . .

and in Article VI, Clause 2:

> This Constitution, and the Laws of the United States which shall be made in Pursuance thereof; and all Treaties made, or which shall be made . . . shall be the supreme Law of the Land; and the Judges in every State shall be bound thereby, any Thing in the Constitution or Laws of any State to the Contrary notwithstanding.

The Federalists naturally emphasized the supremacy of the "Constitution, and the Laws" and the anti-Federalists the phrase "in Pursuance thereof." But over the years the Supreme Court has found that most laws enacted by Congress have been passed "in Pursuance" of the Constitution; in other words, it has not found the words "in Pursuance thereof" to be a very substantial limitation on federal power. In the words of Chief Justice John Marshall, in *McCulloch* v. *Maryland* (1819), at page 421: "Let the end be legitimate, let it be within the scope of the constitution, and all means which are appropriate, which are plainly adapted to that end . . . are constitutional."

A more persuasive case for the anti-Federalists and the contemporary states-rightists can be based on the Tenth Amendment to the Constitution: "The powers not delegated to the United States by the Constitution, nor prohibited by it to the States, are reserved to the States respectively, or to the people." From this passage, which is in direct contradiction of Article VI, derive the concepts of "delegated powers" and "reserved powers." Traditionally, those who are opposed to the idea of a strong central government like to think that the federal system was created by the states, and thus derives all of its powers from them. And what the states give, the states can also take away, so their thinking goes. They fail to notice that the Tenth Amendment refers to powers delegated to the federal government by the *Constitution,* not by the states. The Civil War settled once and for all the question of whether states can withdraw their consent to be part of the federal system. They cannot.

The concept of "reserved powers," also embedded in the Tenth Amendment, has maintained greater currency. The idea expressed here is that there is an irreducible core, a certain minimum number of functions, which are exclusively the prerogative of the state governments. Traditionally these include the police power and education, the two most frequently cited. The failure of the Constitution to spell out exactly which powers are reserved to the states, however, has left a very ambiguous situation indeed. Even in law enforcement and education, the federal government today is having a tremendous impact. With increasingly precise federal standards of police conduct, local law-enforcement officers are often, in effect, enforcing federal rules rather than strictly state regulations. And in education, federal grants are beginning to set some minimum standards by which states will have to abide. There is still a long way to go, however, before law enforcement and education are the sole or even primary responsibility of the federal government. The point here is that when the federal government decides to act, there is very little in the Constitution—even in the Tenth Amendment—to prevent its doing so.

It is an undeniable fact that federal power has grown more rapidly than state power. The legal bases for this expansion are usually given as the Commerce Clause of Article I and the Fourteenth Amendment. The political causes can be seen in two factors: the complex problems of modern life, and the unwillingness or inability of the states to deal with these matters. There are many problems which, by their very nature, seem to require federal controls and federal standards. These include conservation, air and water pollution, automation, persistent unemployment, and transportation. There are other matters which could conceivably be handled at the state level, such as crime prevention, education, and social welfare. But because of the inability of many states—especially the poorer southern states—to fulfill the minimum aspirations of their people, the federal government has had to act in these areas as well.

CONCLUDING NOTE

Each of the issues discussed in this chapter was hotly debated at the constitutional convention, and the result was embodied in the document itself. Because these issues were so controversial, much in the document is ambiguously written. And so the problems are by no means solved, and many of the same debates crop up again and again—often in new guise, many times in their original form. An understanding of these issues is as crucial to a knowledge of contemporary political problems as it is to a basic comprehension of the Constitution. The next six chapters (Part II) will discuss how the United States constitutional system works in practice—that is, the specific institutions which comprise this political system. The last two chapters of the book (Part III) with present the leading challenges, foreign and domestic, which confront the system today.

GLOSSARY

Bicameral   Two-chamber, usually with reference to legislative bodies.

Checks and balances   Powers of each branch of government used to oppose ill-considered actions of one of the other branches (*checks*), and powers exercised independently of the other two (*balances*).

The Federalist   A series of articles written in the late eighteenth century favoring ratification of the Constitution.

Legitimacy   Sanction by law or custom.

Parliamentary system   A system of government wherein the executive and legislative body are one and power to rule is theoretically unseparated.

Presidential system   A system of government wherein the executive and legislative bodies are distinct and power to govern is divided.

Ratification   The formal act of approving or sanctioning.

Separation of powers   A phrase referring to the division of powers of the federal government among the executive, legislative, and judicial branches.

Unicameral   One-chamber, usually with reference to legislative bodies.

SUGGESTIONS FOR FURTHER READING

BEARD, CHARLES A. *An Economic Interpretation of the Constitution of the United States.* New York: Macmillan, 1913.

BAILYN, BERNARD. *The Ideological Origins of the American Revolution.* Cambridge: Harvard University Press, 1967.

BROWN, ROBERT E. *Charles Beard and the Constitution of the United States.* Princeton, N.J.: Princeton University Press, 1956.

CORWIN, EDWARD S. *American Constitutional History.* Edited by Alpheus T. Mason and Gerald Garvey. New York: Harper and Row, 1964.

FARRAND, MAX. *The Framing of the Constitution of the United States.* New Haven, Conn.: Yale University Press, 1913.

The Federalist Papers. Various editions.

HOLCOMBE, ARTHUR N. *The Constitutional System.* Chicago: Scott, Foresman, 1964.

HOLCOMBE, ARTHUR N. *Our More Perfect Union: From Eighteenth Century Principles to Twentieth Century Practice.* Cambridge: Harvard University Press, 1959.

KELLY, ALFRED H. and WINFRED A. HARBISON, *The American Constitution: Its Origins and Development.* New York: Norton, 1955.

LEWIS, JOHN D., ed. *Anti-Federalists versus Federalists: Selected Documents.* New York and London: Chandler Publishing Company, 1967.

MC ILWAIN, CHARLES T. *The American Revolution: A Constitutional Interpretation.* Ithaca, N.Y.: Cornell University Press, 1958.

PRITCHETT, C. HERMAN. *The American Constitution.* 2d ed.; New York: McGraw-Hill, 1968.

ROSSITER, CLINTON. *1787: The Grand Convention.* New York: Macmillan, 1966.

PART TWO
THE POLITICAL SYSTEM OF THE UNITED STATES

Americans tend to take for granted the division of government into three branches: legislative, executive, and judicial. But this kind of arrangement is by no means the only possible one. To mention only one alternative that is quite different from the American system, the British Parliament for all practical purposes encompasses the executive (the leaders of the majority party), and the highest court (a special committee of the House of Lords) in addition to the legislature itself. Another possible arrangement would be the division of one type of power, for example, the executive power, between two distinct offices, say, a prime minister and a president. This is the case in the French system and the German system, to name only two.

It is also important to note that, although Congress makes laws, the president enforces laws, and the courts settle disputes arising under laws, there is also some overlap of the functions of the three branches. Congress occasionally takes a small hand in enforcing laws and in settling disputes. Likewise, the president and the courts make policy, which has the same effect as writing laws, a job supposedly left to Congress. In fact, there is much more to the operations of the three branches of government than might appear by merely reading the Constitution or by referring to oversimplified charts on government organization and procedure. Although a knowledge of the Constitution is important, as is a basic understanding of the bill-passing process and the organization of the executive branch, the actual work of each of these institutions consists of much more than merely reading the Constitution, passing bills, or sending interoffice memos. It is the total operation of each of these branches, then, with which the chapters that follow are concerned.

In Part Two there are also chapters on relations between federal, state, and local governments in the context of federalism in the United States; parties and pressure groups; and civil rights and liberties.

Chapter 4
The Congress

Article I, Section 1, of the Constitution states that: "All legislative Powers herein granted shall be vested in a Congress of the United States, which shall consist of a Senate and House of Representatives." Chapter 3 described how, as a result of the Connecticut Compromise, the Founding Fathers decided to establish a bicameral or two-house legislature rather than a unicameral one such as the Congress of the Articles of Confederation. The opening sentence of the Constitution also tells us that legislative power is to be shared by the two houses, meaning that neither can pass a law without the concurrence of the other. And, finally, this sentence shows the desire to separate clearly the powers of government, allocating the legislative power exclusively to Congress. But to the extent that the president or the courts make policies which have about the same effect as Congress' passing laws, the American system is not functioning the way the Founding Fathers thought it would.

POWERS AND FUNCTIONS

The powers of Congress appear to be spelled out unmistakably in Section 8 of Article I of the Constitution. There 25 specific powers are listed, with a final clause giving Congress the power "To make all Laws which shall be necessary and proper for carrying into Execution the foregoing Powers." But it is this very Necessary and Proper Clause (or Implied-Powers Clause) that has been the center of a major controversy over the proper scope of congressional power. The Supreme Court has handed down a number of decisions on this point. Essentially the Court has held two things in this regard. The first is that the Implied-Powers Clause does not give to Congress any powers which are not among the 25 enumerated and, second, that laws involving the federal government in new spheres of activity, such as banking or minimum-wage regulation, are constitutional if they are necessary in order to carry out one of the enumerated powers. In practice Congress has most often justified its entry into new fields of legislation, such as social security, airplane fares, and civil rights, on the basis of the Commerce Clause (in Article I of the Constitution) which gives to Congress the power to regulate interstate commerce. Thus, when Congress enters some new field or finds it necessary to enact some new regulation, it very often justifies this new activity on the grounds that *not* to act would have an adverse effect on interstate commerce. Since a great many matters can be shown to have a direct or at least an indirect effect on the commerce of the nation, it is not surprising that this clause has opened the way for a great variety of kinds of legislation.

A two hour debate session provides a good opportunity for individual members to talk to their colleagues. Right now, for example, there are about six members I want to see, either to find out about legislation or to discuss legislation in which I'm particularly interested or which directly affects my district. While you are on the floor, you have an ideal opportunity to chat with colleagues and get business done which it proves impossible to accomplish in any other way. An opportunity is afforded to participate in a clearing house sort of operation in which valuable information can be forthcoming. It is similar to the way London coffee houses used to be.

Statement by a Congressman appearing in Charles L. Clapp, *The Congressman: His Work as He Sees It* (Washington, D.C.: The Brookings Institution, 1963), p. 137.

The most important function of Congress, as might be expected, is to make laws. In the technical language of social science, Congress is referred to as a rule-making body, the executive branch as the rule-enforcing body, and the courts as performing the function of settling disputes. To say that Congress is a rule-making body is to emphasize its constitutional role of passing laws and thus of making national policy. Most of the men at Philadelphia in 1787 clearly intended that Congress should make basic policy decisions rather than the president or the courts. As the following sections indicate, however, both the president and the courts do have a hand in policy making. So policy making and law passing are not always identical; only Congress can actually make laws. The president may veto them and the Supreme Court may declare them unconstitutional, but only Congress can pass them in the first place.

Most of the other powers of Congress are simply derivatives of the law-passing or policy-making power. Most laws enacted by Congress either explicitly or implicitly raise the question of how the policy is to be paid for. The power of the purse is one of Congress' most potent weapons. Regardless of what policies the president may desire, or even succeed in getting Congress to enact as laws, they will come to nothing unless paid for with money appropriated by Congress. This is true of domestic programs, such as the war on poverty, medical care for the aged, federal aid to schools, or the federal highway program. And it is true for foreign-policy measures, such as support for the United Nations, paying the costs of the United States Army, or giving economic aid to an ally. Likewise, Congress must provide funds to support the day-to-day operations of the government—salaries for the law clerks who assist the justices of the Supreme Court; funds to remodel the buildings on Capitol Hill; or money for paper clips, staples, and erasers for the civil servants who work in the executive branch. By threatening to tighten the purse strings, Congressmen can frighten thousands of bureaucrats in Washington, cause local officials dependent on federal funds to listen to congressional advice, and even show the Supreme Court that they disapprove of something it has done. When it is said that Congress has tightened the purse strings—or loosened them—specifically what is meant is that Congress has passed an appropriations bill which either cuts back or increases the amount of money it will authorize to support the vast number of activities which are within the federal government's sphere of authority.

Another tool Congress may use, in addition to passing laws and authorizing government expenditures, is to conduct investigations, not only of the operations of the executive branch, but also of social and economic situations. The only significant limitation on the investigatory power of Congress is that it can only be used if it will lead, or could reasonably be expected to lead, to the enactment of a specific law; that is, congressmen cannot conduct investigations just because they enjoy conducting them. Such inquiries must have something to do with Congress' law-making function. The Supreme Court has held that investigations enable Congress to inform itself about important issues and for this reason are a reasonable use of congressional power. The Court also has required that witnesses called before congressional committees be granted some of the constitutional rights of witnesses or defendants in a courtroom. The investigative function of Congress has been abused on some occasions by ambitious senators or congressmen who have used it as a means of seeking personal publicity or of smearing the reputation of private individuals for no legitimate reason. The former House Un-American Activities Committee and the Senate Internal Security Subcommittee have been especially criticized for violations of civil liberties as will be noted in Chapter 9. Other committees, however, such as a recent Senate committee to investigate the Watergate scandal, have used the process of investigation to bring shocking facts to public attention and as the basis for legislation to curb various campaign abuses.

Congress also informs the public through its publications, its debates, and its committee hearings. Most libraries subscribe to the *Congressional Record,* a daily account of the proceedings of both houses. Although the *Record* contains a great deal of useless and inaccurate material, it is extensively quoted by newspapers, and any citizen who is interested can subscribe for $100 a year. Each committee of Congress publishes all of its public hearings as well as numerous other documents, all of which are available to the public for the asking. The debates of Congress are informative at times, but unbearably dull at other times. Usually the testimony given at committee hearings is more informative than are the actual debates on the floor of the House or Senate. Often, segments of committee hearings which are particularly newsworthy are carried over television and are reported in daily newspapers. Although Congress may seem to have more weighty concerns than to keep the public informed on what the federal government is doing, the importance of this free flow of information to the survival of democracy itself can hardly be overemphasized. No matter what the intentions of the leaders might be, if they operated without the healthy light of publicity, they might well adopt authoritarian policies before any effective public protest or resistance could be organized.

In addition to passing laws and informing the public, Congress does a number of other things with less regularity. It proposes constitutional amendments, it meets in joint session every four years to count the votes of the electoral college which elects a new president, and, if no candidate receives a majority, the House of Representatives elects the president from among the top three candidates. The House also has the power to impeach federal officials—from the president on down—and if an official is formally charged with wrongdoing (that is, impeached), the Senate must try him. The most notorious case of impeachment was of President Andrew Johnson in 1868. Although Johnson was impeached (formally charged) by the House of Representatives, the Senate fell one vote short of the two-thirds majority necessary to find him guilty. Another power of Congress is that of admitting new states to the Union. There was a great deal of debate and a number of votes taken before the most recent states, Hawaii and Alaska, were admitted to the Union by Congress. Finally, the Senate has the right to approve (by a two-thirds vote) or reject federal treaties, and to approve or disapprove presidential nominations to high posts in the administration and in the military.

Each house of the Congress handles its own internal affairs, rules, elections, and admission of members. Ordinarily, the rules under which each house operates are not very controversial and are enacted every January at the beginning of a new session (a "Congress" consists of two sessions each lasting one year). Even though the very same rules may have been in force in the House during the previous session, no agreed-upon rules of procedure exist until they are either reenacted or revised. In the Senate the same rules carry over from one session to the next unless specific changes are made at the beginning of the session. Occasionally, a particular rule will be the subject of intense debate. An example is the conflict that periodically arises over Senate Rule 22, which allows the filibuster.

A mere description of the Congress by the Constitution would miss a number of characteristics which are every bit as real as the formal, constitutional attributes. One of the primary features of the United States Congress which is not spelled out in the Constitution is that it acts as a *brake on majority action*—that is, on the making of public policy to reflect the expressed desires of more than half of the electorate. This may sound shocking to the reader who had imagined Congress as the embodiment of action and, above all, as a representative assembly for the whole American people. But Congress is designed more for inaction than for action, and its behavior does not always accurately reflect the will of the American people. As a review of Chapter 3 makes clear, this characteristic of Congress is what Madison and many of the other Founding Fathers intended. If the reader keeps in mind Madison's idea that the American political system should be a harmonious system of mutual frustration, the description of congressional behavior in this chapter will make sense. Some of the factors which impede majority action in Congress are the multiple constituencies of Congress, the committee system (and its corollary, the principle of seniority), certain rules of debate in the Senate, the method of representation in the House, and the role of the House Rules Committee. Although there are other obstacles to majority action in Congress, these are the key factors and the ones to be examined here.

MULTIPLE CONSTITUENCIES

It is commonly supposed that the Congress of the United States represents the entire American people. But no one in the Congress actually represents the American people as a whole; that is, congressmen and senators are not drawn from one constituency (the nation) but from multiple constituencies (their local districts and states). There are, in fact, 535 constituencies represented in Congress—representatives of 435 districts make up the House of Representatives, and 100 senators representing as many different constituencies make up the Senate. It is true that each state has two senators, so that in a sense there are only 50 distinct constituencies represented in that chamber. But the two senators from a given state are elected in different years, on the basis of different issues, and by different electorates (some of the people who vote in 1974 may not vote in 1976, and by 1976 citizens will be voting who were not qualified to vote in 1974). Thus, 100 different voting publics or constituencies were responsible for choosing the men who now make up the senate, and each Congress is itself made up of 535 different constituencies.

This factor of the multiple constituencies of Congress is important to an understanding of Congress' role as a brake on majority action. With no one person in Congress representing the nation as a whole, it should be obvious that most of its members are most concerned with doing those things which are demanded by the people who elected them and who will, they hope, reelect them. But what about issues on which a majority in the nation as a whole is demanding action? One such issue is federal aid to education.

A majority of the people in the United States have favored direct federal aid to education for some time—not everyone, and not on precisely the same terms, but a majority has favored some sort of aid nonetheless. This issue can be traced back at least to the early 1950s. But action was not finally taken until the 89th Congress passed the Federal Aid to Education Bill in 1965. Why did it take so long? There are many reasons for this example of congressional inaction. The 1960 aid to education bill, for example, was defeated by a coalition of southern Democrats and conservative Republicans because it contained provisions prohibiting aid to segregated schools. The 1961 bill was

"It warms my heart to know that, when I'm elected, each and every one of you wonderful people will be a constituent of mine."

Drawing by B. Tobey; © 1966 The New Yorker Magazine, Inc.

defeated by a coalition of Catholics, who insisted on government aid to parochial schools, and the traditional conservative opposition. (The role of pressure groups in policy making is more fully discussed in Chapter 8.) This opposition to federal aid to education illustrates the factor of multiple constituencies. Very few congressmen or senators would be defeated specifically because they did not act on federal aid to education. But they might very well be defeated if they did not get some particular program approved which would directly aid their own area, such as a federal highway or dam project. They might also be defeated if they did not take care to speak out for the economic interests of their region (for example, favoring high tariffs on imported cotton and cotton goods if they come from a cotton-growing region). This emphasis on local problems and local issues goes a long way toward explaining why it is that programs such as federal aid to education, which affect the whole country but which are not supported in certain key constituencies, are not high on the list of priorities for House or Senate action. So even though sentiment in the nation as a whole favors such a program, until enough members of Congress specifically feel pressure from their districts for passage, or until the one truly national elected official—the president—takes it upon himself to work very hard for passage, such programs are likely to die in Congress, despite majority support for them.

The fact that the 89th Congress did act on a number of measures which were favored by the majority of American people is the exception which proves the rule. This same majority had favored most of these measures for more than a decade and a half—federal aid to educaton, medical care for the aged, a comprehensive civil-rights bill, and federal action to curtail air and water pollution, to mention but a few. Congress had acted as a brake on majority action on all of these proposals since the early 1950s, and it had done so largely because of the multiple constituencies. And in each case, until enough pressure built up in enough separate districts, and until the president himself would take strong and decisive action, little was likely to be done—in spite of the fact that a majority of the American public might favor action. The members of Congress are locally elected and locally responsible, and it is much less likely that any of them would be defeated at the polls because of their failure to act individually on issues favored overwhelmingly by the people in their own individual constituencies.

THE COMMITTEE SYSTEM

Another feature of Congress which is partly responsible for its role as a brake on majority action is the committee system, particularly the principle of seniority, which is an integral part of that system. Most of the real work, the substantive work of Congress, is done by committees, not by either house as a whole. There is so much work to be done that there must be a division of labor. And so it is that work is divided up among committees—standing committees, subcommittees, select committees, joint committees, and conference committees, to name the more important types.

The real workhorses of Congress are the standing committees, 21 in the House and 17 in the Senate. A *standing committee* is supposed to be a microcosm of the house, with about the same ratio of Republicans and Democrats, liberals and conservatives, Westerners, Midwesterners, Southerners, and New Englanders, as in the whole house. As we will see, however, some key committees fall short of meeting this ideal balance. The standing committees each take up proposed legislation covering a designated subject area, and although there is occasionally some overlap, the system functions well in terms of dividing up labor in order to get through the mountain of bills introduced during each session of Congress (sometimes as many as 6000). In the Senate the membership of the standing committees ranges from 7 (District of Columbia) to 24 (Appropriations). In the House of Representatives their size ranges from 9 (Internal Security) to 55 (Appropriations). These figures suggest two things: First, committees are slightly larger in the House than in the Senate and, second, committees which handle more important subject matter are larger than other committees (the Appropriations committees in both houses are the largest, followed by the Armed Services Committee and the Foreign Affairs Committee in the House and the Committee on Foreign Relations in the Senate). The standing committees in both houses are listed below, showing the parallel committees where they exist.

Senate	*House*
Aeronautical and Space Sciences	Sciences and Aeronautics
Agriculture and Forestry	Agriculture
Appropriations	Appropriations
Armed Services	Armed Services
Banking, Housing and Urban Affairs	Banking and Currency
Commerce	Interstate and Foreign Commerce
District of Columbia	District of Columbia
Finance	Ways and Means
Foreign Relations	Foreign Affairs
Government Operations	Government Operations
Interior and Insular Affairs	Interior and Insular Affairs
Judiciary	Judiciary
Labor and Public Welfare	Education and Labor
Post Office and Civil Service	Post Office and Civil Service
Public Works	Public Works
Rules and Administration	Rules
Veterans' Affairs	Veterans' Affairs
	House Administration
	Internal Security
	Merchant Marine and Fisheries
	Standards of Official Conduct

Just as there is a division of labor within each house as a whole, so there is a division of labor within each standing committee. Some standing committees may have as many as four or five permanent *subcommittees* which do much of the work of the parent committee. For example, both the Senate Foreign Relations Committee and the House Committee on Foreign Affairs have a subcommittee for Latin American affairs. The subcommittee is typically a microcosm of the parent committee, just as the latter is usually a microcosm of the whole house. There are also *select committees,* or special committees, which are not permanent, but are set up for some specific purpose, for example, to investigate a series of air disasters. (The Watergate matter was investigated by a select committee.) A *joint committee,* that is, a committee whose membership includes both senators and representatives, may be either permanent or temporary. There are twelve permanent joint committees, such as the joint committees on atomic energy, on the economic report, and on defense production.

A *conference committee* is a special variety of nonpermanent joint committee. A conference committee is set up when the House and the Senate pass the same bill in different form. Consisting of three congressmen and three senators, the conference committee is supposed to iron out the differences and report back to both parent bodies. If a compromise cannot be worked out after three attempts, usually the bill is dropped altogether. It should be apparent, then, that if the members of the conference committee do not share the views of most of their colleagues, it is very difficult for a compromise hammered out in the conference committee to be accepted by the parent bodies, the House and the Senate. And so it is very pertinent to ask: Who appoints the members of these conference committees? The answer is that they are appointed by the chairman of the appropriate standing committee in each house.

The power to appoint conferees is just one of a number of formidable powers possessed by committee chairmen. The committee chairmen also have the power to call the committee into session, fix its agenda, and guide the passage of legislation considered by the committee when it is reported on the floor. These powers add up to a tremendous potential for helping to pass or to block legislation favored by the majority. If the chairmen of the various committees were in general agreement with the majority of their colleagues, it would seem that needed legislation could be passed with relative ease. But if, as is often the case, the committee chairman opposes the views of most of his colleagues, then he is in an excellent position to exert a minority veto—to act as a brake on majority action. And this is a role that many committee chairmen relish. What is the reason for the lack of consistency between the views of the majority and the views of many of the committee chairmen? The answer is, in large part, the operation of the principle of *seniority*.

Before the seniority method was adopted for making committee assignments and selecting chairmen of committees, there was a great deal of bitterness and conflict over these questions at the beginning of each session of Congress. The traditional methods of making these decisions—wielding influence, twisting arms, and making deals—became so unseemly, so cumbersome, and so unworkable that both houses, independently of each other, adopted the seniority principle for making these appointments. Simply stated, seniority means that members who have been around the longest get the choicest committee assignments. The corollary (which is perhaps the most important aspect of seniority) is that *within* each committee, the member of the majority party with the longest continuous service will automatically be the chairman.

Committee chairmen in both houses of Congress have tremendous power to spur majority action or to impede it. As might be expected, chairmen who are generally sympathetic to the views of the majority frequently do make use of their special powers—calling meetings, fixing the agenda, presiding over meetings, appointing subcommittees, and representing the committee when reporting back to the whole house on a bill—to facilitate majority action. But committee chairmen are not always in sympathy with the views of most of their colleagues. In fact it is often the case that a committee chairman represents minority views. The explanation for this is the rule of seniority, described above. The member of the majority party who has had the longest continuous service on the committee is automatically its chairman. But which members are likely to have the longest service? Those who come from "safe" districts and are reelected term after term. And where are these "safe" districts? They are in one-party areas, for the most part, where the real contest for power is the primary election rather than the general election; the winner in the primary is usually as good as elected in the general election. Most of these one-party areas are in the South where, in the past, few Republicans were elected (this pattern is now slowly changing), and in the farm belt (Iowa, South Dakota, Nebraska, and Kansas), where few Democrats are elected. Thus when the Democrats have a majority in Congress, majority-party members with the longest service are southern Democrats. And when the Republicans have a majority in Congress, majority-party members with the longest service are farm-belt Republicans. Hence the seniority rule in practice means that, depending on which party has the majority, committee chairmanships have traditionally gone to a disproportionate number of southern

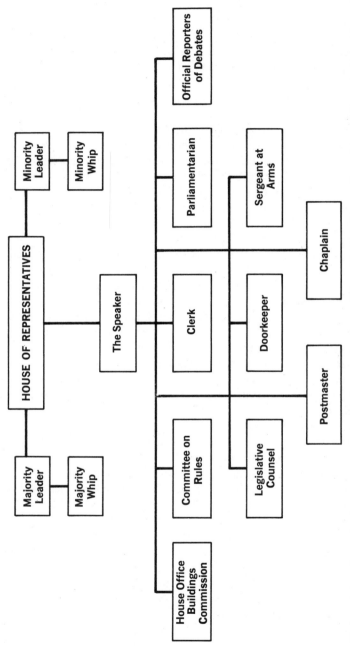

Figure 4-1. Organization of the House of Representatives. (From *United States Government Organization Manual,* 1966–67 p. 608).

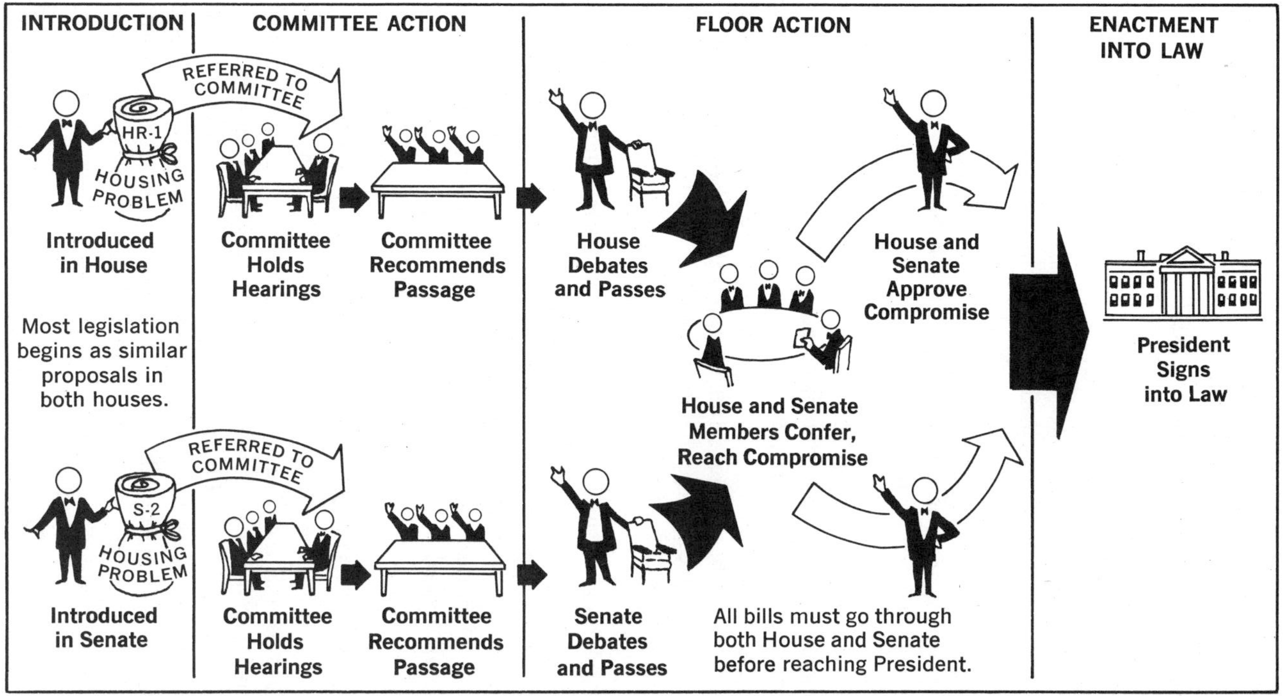
INTRODUCTION
COMMITTEE ACTION
FLOOR ACTION
ENACTMENT INTO LAW
REFERRED TO COMMITTEE
HR-1
HOUSING PROBLEM
Introduced in House
Committee Holds Hearings
Committee Recommends Passage
House Debates and Passes
House and Senate Approve Compromise
Most legislation begins as similar proposals in both houses.
House and Senate Members Confer, Reach Compromise
President Signs into Law
REFERRED TO COMMITTEE
S-2
HOUSING PROBLEM
Introduced in Senate
Committee Holds Hearings
Committee Recommends Passage
Senate Debates and Passes
All bills must go through both House and Senate before reaching President.

Figure 4-2. How a bill becomes law. This graphic shows the most typical way in which proposed legislation is enacted into law. There are more complicated, as well as simpler routes . . . and most bills fall by the wayside and never become law. (From *Congressional Quarterly*, 1965, p. 164a.)

Democrats or farm-belt Republicans.[1] But southern Democrats and farm-belt Republicans often hold political views quite out of keeping with those held by the majorities within their respective parties. So the seniority rule in practice means that committee chairmen, with their life or death power over legislation, are often opposed to majority views.

Highly significant also in the functioning of Congress is the choice of formal leaders in both houses. The organization of the House of Representatives is shown in Figure 4-1. In the House, as in the Senate, party caucuses elect the formal leaders—with the exception of the presiding officer of the Senate, who is the Vice President of the United States. The formal leadership, as might be expected, reflects the views (often, minority views) of legislators, and not necessarily the views of the majority of Americans.

In the 93rd Congress (1973–1974) the Democratic Caucus of the House of Representatives adopted new rules which took away the power of party leaders to appoint members to committees and gave to Democratic committee members the power to choose the ranking Democratic committeeman (who would be the chairman as long as the Democrats have a majority in the House). Interestingly, this new-found power in the hands of the rank-and-file members resulted in relatively few shifts from the assignments that would have been made under the seniority system.

Figure 4-2 shows, in simplified form, the formal steps usually followed in the enactment of legislation. As has been suggested throughout this chapter, the legislative process is in reality much more complex than could be shown in a schematic diagram. Nevertheless, the figure illustrates the positions of power in the legislative branch, where policy is most likely to be influenced.

IMPEDING MAJORITY ACTION—RULES OF THE SENATE

One of the most misunderstood characteristics of debate in the Senate, and an important factor in understanding how Congress acts as a brake on majority action, is the *filibuster*, a device that a minority may use to block majority action by the Senate. This may be done by talking and talking and talking interminably until the majority gives up and agrees to move on to other business. Filibusters may last days, weeks, months,

---

[1] In the 93rd Congress (1973–1974), 12 out of 21 committee chairmen in the House were from southern states; in the Senate 11 out of 17 committee chairmen were southern.

or even longer. Filibusters are possible in the United States Senate because of Rule 22. This rule, also known as *unanimous consent*, permits any senator to speak as long as he wants on a bill before action can be taken. He does not even have to be talking about the bill itself. There is no rule in the Senate that debate must be germane, that it be pertinent to the bill at hand. So a Senator may talk about his campaign plans for the coming election, or he may read articles from the *New York Times* or even from a book of Mother Goose. One senator, Wayne Morse of Oregon, was noted for reading passages from Shakespeare when engaged in a filibuster.

But Rule 22 now does attempt to provide a remedy for the filibuster. This remedy is known as *closure* or *cloture*. It was incorporated into the rule because of the overuse of the filibuster, which is in fact an abuse of the privilege. Often, after a particularly bitter debate when opponents of a bill had managed to defeat it by filibustering it to death, there would be a move to modify the unanimous-consent rule. It was after a particularly bitter encounter of this kind in 1917 that the rule was modified to allow for cloture, or stopping of debate, by a two-thirds vote of the total Senate membership. But this was a compromise measure, and it proved virtually impossible to get such a vote (the cloture rule was used only four times between 1917 and 1959). So there have been repeated attempts to go even further than the 1917 cloture rule.

The reaction against Rule 22 was particularly acute after a southern filibuster in 1958 which resulted in killing a civil rights bill. It was largely in reaction to the 1958 filibuster that Rule 22 was modified in 1959, at the beginning of the 86th Congress. The change was not very earth-shattering—changes in Senate rules seldom are. Over the bitter opposition of the southern bloc, it was agreed to require only two-thirds of those senators present and voting, instead of two-thirds of the Senate membership, to cut off a filibuster. Since 1959 if two-thirds of the senators on the floor are willing to vote for cloture, a filibuster can be stopped. But here is the catch: seldom is such a large majority willing to restrict the freedom of their colleagues to say whatever they want, for a cloture motion is always taken as a slap against those conducting the filibuster. Thus in the summer of 1966, when the southerners were filibustering against the 1966 civil rights bill, Mike Mansfield, the majority leader, garnered 55 votes to end the filibuster, but he could not get a two-thirds majority. (Since 1959 cloture has been successfully invoked only three times.) So the Senate never voted on the bill, and the entire piece of legislation, including sections that had very wide support, went down to defeat.

The filibuster is just one of a number of devices in the United

States Senate by which a minority can prevent majority action. It is also possible to use other delaying tactics which have the effect of preventing majority action, such as calling for the reading of the Journal. At the beginning of each day's session, the presiding officer of the Senate asks if there is any opposition to passing over the reading of the Journal. This is about the same procedure as that used by the chairman of a club when he asks for "any additions or corrections to the minutes." The difference is that the typical club minutes take only a short while to read, whereas the Journal of the Senate may take four or five hours. For this reason, it is standard procedure in the United States Senate for the presiding officer to ask and receive unanimous consent to dispense with the reading of the Journal. But if even one senator wants to hear the Journal read that day's session is, in effect, lost, and the Senate will operate on an every-other-day basis: one day for action and the following day to read back the Journal. The reason that the Senate Journal takes so long to read is that it includes virtually every action, every motion, the content of every bill proposed, and in detail every action taken on the floor of the Senate the previous day.

A third obstructionist tactic that can be used in the Senate is to request that no committees meet while the Senate is in session. As with the reading of the Journal, this provision seems innocent enough. But it must be remembered that most of the work of Congress is done, not on the floor of the House or the Senate, but in committee sessions. And because there is so much work that needs doing, committees are meeting constantly. In fact, it is often disappointing to visitors of the nation's capital to find that there is seldom anything very exciting happening on the floor of the Senate, and that typically there are only a handful of senators present at any one time on the floor because most of them are off in committee meetings doing the more important work. But all of this committee work stops if just *one* member of a committee requests that his committee not meet that day. By this tactic, it is possible to stop the work of a particular committee for a whole session, and thus to prevent committee action on an item of legislation that this minority of one might oppose.

None of the tactics discussed above is illegal or has fallen into disuse. Each of them—and other tactics like them—can be used and is used to prevent the Senate from acting, to frustrate the will of the majority. As Woodrow Wilson once said, "The Senate of the United States is the only deliberative body in the world which cannot act when a majority is ready to act." And the reason that a majority of the Senate often cannot act when it wants to is that these rules and others like them can be used for the purpose of preventing action.

The student might reasonably ask at this point why it is that something is not done to facilitate majority action in the Senate. The answer is twofold. First, the Senate prides itself on being the greatest deliberative body in the world. The upper chambers of most other legislatures have lost much of the real political power they used to have. The role of the British House of Lords, which is the closest parallel of the United States Senate in the English system of government, has declined to the point of being little more than ceremonial. The Senate, however, while retaining much of the relaxed atmosphere and informality of procedure which characterize an upper house, has also retained every bit of the power allocated to it by the Constitution. Senators are very proud of the fact that they can exercise this great power without the rigid rules and restrictions which make the procedure and debate in the House of Representatives more formal and less personal. The members of the Senate pride themselves on the clublike atmosphere which prevails there even today. Because this characteristic of the Senate makes that body unique in the world, suggestions to modify or eliminate it are not very welcome.

A second and related reason for opposition to changing the rules of the Senate is the firm belief of most senators that new rules are unnecessary. It is true that rules exist, although comparatively few in

"Thanks for the opportunity to address myself to that point, Bob. As you know, I've long advocated a full and frank disclosure of all income. Many colleagues, for what I'm sure are honorable reasons, hold the opposite view, and in this government, God bless it, the majority rules. . . ."

Drawing by Lorenz; © 1967 The New Yorker Magazine, Inc.

number, which are designed to anticipate most problems which come up. What does not exist, though, is a set of rules which is designed to prevent minorities from obstructing the work of the majority. To many senators this is not a matter for concern; the rules work well most of the time not only because they are good rules, but also because most senators are gentlemen most of the time and do not abuse the rules. Any substantial overhaul of the rules, then, would be a tacit admission that United States senators do not warrant the high respect generally accorded them. Because the Senate tends to regard itself as a sort of elite body, adopting elaborate and restrictive rules would be inconsistent with its self-image. The freshman Senators who call loudly for reform—and there are always a few—are thus likely to make themselves unpopular with their colleagues because they are saying, in effect, that those colleagues are incapable of governing themselves.

IMPEDING MAJORITY ACTION IN THE HOUSE

There are four ways, basically, that policies favored by a majority of Americans are frustrated in the House: (1) the size of the House, (2) the short terms of its members, (3) its rules, and (4) its composition.

Ironically, the Senate in recent years has proven itself more responsive to the pressures of public opinion than the House. This is certainly the reverse of what the Founding Fathers anticipated or planned. A major factor in the comparative unresponsiveness of the House is its size. It is one of the largest legislative bodies in the world. The Supreme Soviet (the USSR equivalent) is even larger, with 767 members (but it is not known for its responsiveness to the popular will either). In general, there seems to be an inverse relationship between the size of a legislative body and its ability to translate the wishes of its constituents into public policy.[2]

A second factor which impedes the policy-making function of the House is the two-year term of its members. The original idea behind the two-year term was to keep the representatives close to the people. With the demands of modern campaigning, however, the effect is to divert a large portion of a congressman's time and energy into campaigning for reelection every other year and to increase more and more the influence of powerful and wealthy interests who contribute to his campaign chest.

[2] An exception might be the British House of Commons which has 630 members. Even so, it is not the House of Commons, in reality, which writes legislation, but the Cabinet, which is chosen by Parliament.

The third ingredient in the House's impotence is its own rules. The rules which govern the activities of the House of Representatives are more numerous and far more stringent in terms of facilitating majority action. But in a discussion of the House, careful distinction needs to be made between the *formal* provisions which govern the consideration and passage of legislation and the *actual* process. Formally, a majority in the House can act whenever it wants and on whatever matters it chooses. However, despite the formal guarantees, a minority veto acts in the House just as it does in the Senate. The rules under which the House is governed are quite different from those of the Senate, but the effect is much the same: the majority is often prevented from acting. But, whereas any member of the Senate who wants to obstruct action can do so, in the House the power of legislative obstruction is exercised by a select few. Positions which lend themselves to the obstruction of majority action in the House are the committee chairmanships and the House Rules Committee. The rules which govern the operations of the House give exceptional power to committee chairmen and to the Rules Committee.

As was noted above, the committee system in Congress gives a great deal of power to chairmen, power which can be used to promote legislation favored by the majority or to block it. Also noted were: the existence of multiple constituencies, which means all members, including chairmen of committees, are locally chosen and locally responsible; the advantage of incumbency in campaigns, which insures that many members will be elected from safe rural constituencies; and the seniority principle (although somewhat modified in 1971), which elevates men from these very same safe districts—these three facts taken together add up to committee chairmen who are more likely to block majority action than to expedite it.

Another aspect of procedure that may block majority action in the House of Representatives concerns the House Rules Committee. In 1910 a revolt which had been brewing over the powers of the Speaker of the House was finally resolved by reducing the Speaker's powers and giving some of them to the House Rules Committee. The Speaker had had the power, for example, to refer bills to committees, to recognize members wishing to present bills before the whole House, and even to determine whether or not amendments to bills would be in order. Clearly, these were very substantial powers to reside in the hands of a single man. It was felt, therefore, that by the transfer of much of this power to the Rules Committee the process would be more fair and more responsive to the majority will. But that shift in power made membership on the Rules Committee a coveted position, and House members with the most seniority took advantage of it by choosing seats on that committee. Who, then, would get these favored positions of power? Farm-belt Republicans and southern Democrats.

Originally, the Rules Committee was set up to act as a sort of traffic cop. Few people in Congress or out of it would find any fault with the committee if it acted only as a traffic cop; but with so much power to determine the fate of legislation, and with this power in the hands of Congressmen who are not representative of the majority, it was perhaps inevitable that the Rules Committee would do more than merely regulate the flow of legislation. Since acquiring these added powers in 1910, the Rules Committee has become more like an undertaker than a traffic cop, although there have been some reforms aimed at lessening this aspect of the committee's role. Members of the committee have come to consider it their duty to exercise more than procedural control of legislation. They have busied themselves with additional hearings and investigations on the subject matter of legislation; they require additional testimony of witnesses; and they alter the content of legislation passed on to them by the standing committees, often killing entirely legislation that they do not favor.[3] It is this activity of the Rules Committee—what it does to legislation favored by the majority and passed on to it by the standing committees—that has been the source of the bitter criticisms that have been levied against the committee.

The fourth explanation for members of the House being out of step with their constituents has to do with who the members are, that is, the composition of the House. United States Congressmen are older, better educated, and wealthier than most of their constituents. Furthermore, most Congressmen are men (only 14 out 435 were women in 1973), white, and lawers or businessmen.[4] As pointed out in Chapter 3, the average age in the United States is 28. The median age of voters is 43. The average Congressman is 52—older than in any other major Western democracy. The typical United States adult has completed 11 years of education; the overwhelming majority of Congressmen, on the other hand, are college graduates, and a majority hold higher degrees, usually in law. The average United States family income in 1972 was $10,285 per year; Congressmen earn $42,500 plus various allowances and other outside income. Figure 4-3 illustrates these comparisons.

---

[3] Instances of such obstruction by the Rules Committee are cited by Joseph S. Clark, *Congress: The Sapless Branch* (rev. ed.; New York: Harper and Row, 1965), pp. 131–136.

[4] In 1973, 221 members of the House listed their profession as lawyer and 155 were in business or banking. *Congressional Quarterly Weekly* 31 (1) (January 16, 1973), p. 15.

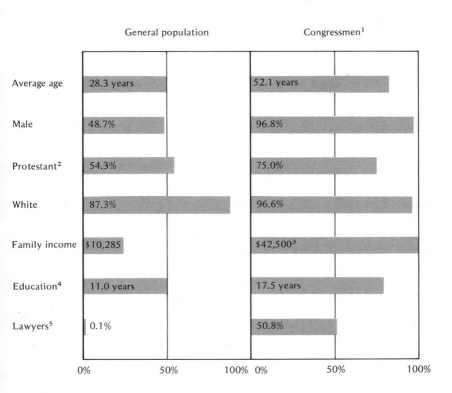

General population   Congressmen[1]

	General population	Congressmen[1]
Average age	28.3 years	52.1 years
Male	48.7%	96.8%
Protestant[2]	54.3%	75.0%
White	87.3%	96.6%
Family income	$10,285	$42,500[3]
Education[4]	11.0 years	17.5 years
Lawyers[5]	0.1%	50.8%

0%   50%   100%   0%   50%   100%

Sources: Figures adapted from *U.S. Statistical Abstract, 1972,* and from the *Congressional Directory, 93rd Congress, First Session (1973).*

[1] Members of the U.S. House of Representatives only.

[2] In the general population, the percentage who are Protestant is based on the number of total churchgoers.

[3] Base salary only; outside income, travel allowance, and other expenses not included.

[4] Average number of years of formal education completed by adults.

[5] Lawyers in general population based on ABA members (136,451) as of 1972 as a percentage of the total work force (87.7 million).

Figure 4-3. How representative is the House of Representatives?

Obviously a legislative body made up of members so untypical of the general population is not going to be responsive to many of the policy preferences of great numbers of citizens. We would expect, from this picture of the House, that its members would more faithfully represent business interests than consumer interests. In general that expectation is borne out.

The Senate, of course, is as unrepresentative as the House in many of the dimensions discussed above. At the time of this writing there was only one black senator (Edward Brooke, R—Mass.) and no woman member of the Senate. And while senators get the same basic salary as congressmen, their outside income is generally higher. Yet it was never intended that the Senate faithfully reflect the electorate it serves. For many of the Founding Fathers, and most citizens today, this is expected of the House. But the expectation is not realized.

The composition of the House has until recently been unrepresentative with respect to the rural–suburban–urban divisions in United States society. The actual mechanism creating this unrepresentativeness is known as the *rural gerrymander*. In the years between 1900 and 1920 a basic shift occurred in United States society that was not reflected in the House of Representatives. In 1900 a majority of the population lived in rural areas, but by 1920 a majority lived in cities. Congressional districts, however, remained predominantly rural. This was allowed to happen by not carving up the districts allotted to a state, in a way that fairly represented the more populous areas, the cities. The result was that congressmen from the rural districts remained almost as numerous as they were in 1900, faithfully reflecting the rural values and interests of an earlier age.

The rural gerrymander is now becoming a thing of the past because of three landmark decisions of the Supreme Court: *Baker* v. *Carr (1962), Wesberry* v. *Sanders (1964),* and *Reynolds* v. *Sims (1964).* In the Baker case the Court agreed that Baker, a citizen of Tennessee, was denied his constitutional rights because of the rural gerrymander. The Tennessee legislature had not redrawn its state legislative districts since 1901, and during the intervening sixty years the rural areas had declined in population while both Nashville and Memphis had grown to several times their 1901 population size. The result was that persons living in Nashville and Memphis had only a fraction of the voting power of those living in the rural areas of Tennessee—a pattern typical of a majority of the states in 1962.

In the Baker case the Court merely sent the case back to a lower federal court, stating that it was justiciable (that is, it could properly be decided by a federal court). In *Wesberry* v. *Sanders* the Supreme

Court for the first time gave guidelines: No congressional district should have a population more than 15 percent over or under population of the average district.

The real bombshell, as far as most states were concerned, was the case decided in June of 1964, *Reynolds* v. *Sims*. In that case the Supreme Court applied the nearly equal population guidelines ("one man, one vote") to both houses of state legislatures. The point here is that the rural gerrymander—and the rural-biased state legislatures which have permitted it—are a thing of the past as a result of these three landmark Supreme Court decisions. As long as the rural gerrymander was used in determining the makeup of the House of Representatives, faulty representation might permit a national minority to impose its will on the Congress. On February 21, 1973, however, the Supreme Court upheld in *Mahan* v. *Howell* a reapportionment in Virginia which relaxed considerably for state legislatures the nearly equal as possible rule applicable to the U.S. House of Representatives.

CONGRESSIONAL REFORM—INTERNAL CHANGES

For a time in the middle 1960s, it appeared that major changes were taking place in Congress which would make it more responsive to majority wishes. The most decisive change was the congressional election of 1964. In that year overwhelming majorities of pro-Administration Democrats were elected in both the Senate and the House of Representatives. This top-heavy majority of more than 2 to 1 in both houses meant that for the first time in decades "presidential" Democrats and "presidential" Republicans were the dominant faction, in James M. Burns's terminology in *The Deadlock of Democracy*. Indeed, the 89th Congress (1965–1966) enacted an amazing number of laws that no administration had been able to get through Congress for years. The point here is that it requires a lopsided and hard-to-obtain majority, predisposed to decisive action—plus dynamic presidential leadership— to overcome the antimajoritarian organization of Congress.

The change in the political complexion of the House in 1964, in particular, made possible a few internal reforms that many felt would have lasting significance. The most important of these was the enactment of the 21-day rule in January of 1965. The 21-day rule has to do with legislation deadlocked in the House Rules Committee. If that committee refuses to take action on a bill, under the new rule, the chairman of the committee originally sponsoring the bill may take it out of the hands of the Rules Committee after 21 days. A related development was the change in the composition of the Rules Committee so that the conservative coalition of anti-Administration Democrats and conservative Republicans no longer was in the majority. Howard Smith of Virginia, conservative chairman of the Rules Committee, was defeated in his primary battle for reelection in June of 1966. After serving for 18 consecutive terms in the House, 83-year-old Smith was involuntarily retired.

A third development that many thought would result in a more liberal Congress and thus improve the possibilities for reform was the enforcement of the Supreme Court's decisions on legislative reapportionment. Because of these rulings, it was felt that the House of Representatives in the 1970s would become more representative of urban interests and thus more liberal. Since state legislatures must be apportioned on the basis of population, they would draw congressional districts which would favor the urban majority. This new majority in the House, in turn, would be more reform-minded.

All three of these hopes were disappointed. First, the top-heavy Democratic majorities which characterized the 89th Congress appear to have been due to a very special combination of circumstances not likely to be repeated often, if at all. The congressional elections in the fall of 1966 returned the old conservative coalition to power. It should not be inferred that there is any conservative conspiracy to prevent progress, but the noteworthy achievements of the 89th Congress were due in large part to massive Democratic majorities in both houses that proved to be unstable. And when the political complexion of Congress is more evenly divided, as it was from 1960 to 1964, and has been since 1966, Congress tends to retard rather than advance progress and reform.

Second, the 21-day rule was not as effective as many had hoped it would be. That rule depended on the initiative of the committee chairmen to wrest legislation from the Rules Committee; but the majority of the committee chairmen are southern Democrats, when the Democrats are the majority party, who often oppose legislation favored by the majority. So they did not use this power often and many bills died in the Rules Committee just as before. The 21-day rule was abandoned in January 1967.[5]

Third, reapportionment has resulted in a shift in power away from the rural areas. But the shift has not been as expected, from the predominantly conservative rural areas to the liberal urban centers. Rather, conservative rural areas for the most part have relinquished control to

[5] What eventually did change the role of the Rules Committee was the retirement of William Colmer (D.—Miss.) (Howard Smith's replacement as Chairman) in 1972. In 1973 a more liberal Democrat, Ray J. Madden (D.—Ind.), became Rules Committee chairman.

conservative suburban areas, for there is where the bulk of the nation's population is found. On many issues, voters in the suburbs are every bit as conservative as those in rural areas. On social-welfare matters, for example, people living in the suburbs tend to oppose high government spending or deficit financing. Thus, reapportionment did not automatically make Congress or state legislatures more liberal.

The absence of an expected "liberalizing" of national and state politics following reapportionment of many state legislatures and congressional districts can be seen in part in the resurgence of Republican strength after the 1966 elections. This Republican domination of state politics continued in many states until the early 1970s. By 1973 the Democrats controlled a substantial majority of governorships and state legislatures, but this shift occurred five or six years after court-ordered reapportionment. Reapportionment, then, does not appear to have been a major advantage to Democrats in a strictly partisan sense.

Neither does reapportionment seem to have had a significant "liberalizing" effect on state politics as many experts predicted it would. It should be observed that when the terms *conservative* and *liberal* are used in reference to types of national and state legislative programs, there are several dimensions that should be taken into account. Residents of suburban areas often take a conservative position on social-welfare issues, but they may be relatively more liberal than people from the core city on questions that involve the acceptance of the principle of social equality or issues that involve political rights.

Several studies conclude that: working-class people dominate the politics of the central city; upper-class people dominate the politics of the suburbs; the largest number of Americans today live in suburbs, not central cities or rural areas; patterns of political preferences tend to show themselves more related to local population density rather than to regional location; on social welfare issues, suburbanites are more conservative than rural dwellers or city dwellers.[6] These studies and recent state and local election results make it reasonable to conclude that the impact of reapportionment has not been a triumph for liberals or for Democrats per se.

Nevertheless, reapportionment has had the effect of making Con-

---

[6] See Angus Campbell et al., *The American Voter* (New York: Wiley, 1960), pp. 100–108; Samuel A. Stouffer, *Communism, Conformity, and Civil Liberties* (New York: Doubleday, 1955), p. 139; Seymour M. Lipset, *Political Man* (New York: Doubleday, 1960), p. 104; V. O. Key, Jr., *Political Opinion and American Democracy* (New York: Knopf, 1961), pp. 99–120; and Norral D. Glenn and J. L. Simmons, "Are Regional Differences Diminishing?" *Public Opinion Quarterly*, 31 (Summer, 1967), pp. 176–193.

gress and state legislatures more representative than in the past. So, although newfound suburban legislative control is not necessarily liberal, at least it is in keeping with the principle of majority rule. In summary, then, the unusual constellation of circumstances which made the 89th Congress one of the most productive on record is not likely to be repeated. And other changes which might have appeared hopeful on the surface have not prevented a return of the traditional conservative-dominated elements in Congress.

OTHER SUGGESTIONS FOR REFORM

Suggestions for reform are generally in one of three categories: systematic, procedural, or political. Systematic reforms are those which would exchange the whole system for something new. Some commentators, such as Robert M. Hutchins, have advocated a new constitutional convention to reexamine such matters as equal representation of all states in the Senate, the balance between security and order as provided for in the Bill of Rights, the electoral college, and the presidential or cabinet system of government as opposed to the parliamentary system. All of these issues affect Congress in some way, but it is extremely doubtful that wide agreement could be obtained in settling these fundamental questions if the existing system were scrapped. One of the most difficult —and most fundamental—changes would be to adopt a parliamentary system. As described in Chapter 3, under this system, the chief executive would be chosen by and responsible to the legislature. Although there

It seems to me that the drains on a congressman's energy for administrative and "representative" duties are very considerable, even assuming he has a fine staff and is able to delegate intelligently. Most people in comparable positions in business and executive life would not put up with the interruptions of their thought processes that are a necessary price of entry to this arena. It won't do to say that under a properly organized executive branch all constituents will receive their just dues merely by applying to the executive. Until philosophers become kings you are going to need an outside needling force. I think everyone here would agree that but for us far greater injustices would occur. I honestly can see no way of changing the system. Outside intervention such as ours is needed and I see no appreciably better way of organizing the workload if we are to undertake it. I find it burdensome, but I am glad to do it.

Statement by Congressman appearing in Charles L. Clapp, *The Congressman: His Work as He Sees It* (Washington, D.C.: The Brookings Institution, 1963), p. 57.

are a number of weaknesses in the presidential form of government, it must be noted in its behalf that the vast majority of citizens accept it and are satisfied with it.

Procedural changes are those which would keep the existing branches of government but try to improve their operation. Often it is suggested that this be done by setting up special agencies or committees to handle relations among the existing branches of government more smoothly and more efficiently. For example, there is the suggestion that all committees of Congress be made joint. Such consolidation would avoid the needless duplication of hearings, discussion, and testimony which now has to flow through identical committees in each house of Congress. Another suggestion would be a joint committee for overall policy formulation. Such a committee would make Congress more of a law-making body, instead of a rubber stamp to the President's policies, and would strengthen it in its relations with the executive branch. A third proposal is to establish a legislative-executive council which would include cabinet members and chairmen of congressional committees. Such a council would coordinate policy making by bringing administrative department heads and committee chairmen into constant contact. It would facilitate the information flow from the executive to the legislature and vice versa.

In addition to the procedural changes mentioned above, which would add to existing structures in order to improve procedure, there are other suggestions for reform which could be achieved within the existing structures. It is periodically suggested, for example, that the jurisdiction of the standing committees of Congress be made even more clear-cut so that precious time and effort would not be lost in jurisdictional squabbles. This clarification would mean greater efficiency; a particular bill by its very content would go to the proper committee without any political decision having to be made as to where it stood the greatest chance for passage. This change would, however, increase the power of committee chairmen, who would then have a virtual monopoly over all legislation in their domain. Proposals such as this, which tend to augment the chairmen's power, are often coupled with suggestions to make chairmen more responsive to the majority. A greater degree of responsiveness could be accomplished by further modifying the seniority system of choosing chairmen. Machinery could be set up for democratically electing chairmen at the beginning of each new session of Congress. The efforts to curtail the power of the House Rules Committee have already been noted—a reform which has been attempted several times but which has not been fully accomplished. Likewise, there is always some sentiment in favor of abolishing or at least limiting the filibuster in the Senate. But senators guard very jealously their right to speak whenever they wish on whatever subject they choose, even though some may occasionally abuse this right. So the filibuster, like the House Rules Committee, seems likely to survive for the foreseeable future. The other means for blocking majority action in the Senate also seem likely to remain.

"Man, If You Want To Stay In This Game, You'd Better Get In Shape"

Copyright 1972 by Herblock in The Washington Post

One of the most workable and least controversial possiblities for reform is to improve the quality and quantity of assistance to legislators. While the president has thousands of highly paid experts and advisers to help him make the crucial decisions he must face daily, Congress moves slowly along with only a few hundred such experts. If congressmen and senators wanted to professionalize the legislative process and introduce a higher degree of expertise, it would be a relatively simple matter to provide by law for a first-rate body of congressional experts. Both the House and the Senate have, over the years, increased their clerical and professional staffs; but much more could be, and needs to be, done along these lines.

The political impetus for congressional reform has occurred in two rather different ways. First, some reforms were attempted during the period of lopsided Democratic majorities and cooperation between the president and Congress: 1964 to 1966. As long-range solutions to the basic weaknesses of Congress, however, these efforts were not notably successful. The beginnings of a more fundamental attempt at reform came on the heels of the Watergate break-in and coverup in 1973. The impetus then was also political, but in an almost opposite way.

There is almost always a degree of institutional rivalry between the president and Congress. The expansion of presidential power at the expense of congressional power in recent decades has heightened this sense of competition. And among those members of Congress who did not share some of the president's general policy goals, especially on the Vietnam war, there was a sense not only of competition but of frustration and despair. Perhaps it was inevitable that when the president's grip on power weakened the leaders of Congress would seize the opportunity to enhance their own power.

In 1972 and 1973 several issues concerning this president–Congress rivalry came to a head, largely because of the Watergate scandal. First, on the Vietnam war itself, antiwar members of Congress had tried and failed for years to exert some pressure on the president to bring it to a conclusion. Not until March of 1973—at the very moment when the most damning revelations about President Nixon's 1972 reelection campaign were made—did Congress pass legislation restricting the president's ability to pursue the war in Indochina.[7] Furthermore, in November 1973 Congress overrode the president's veto of legislation limiting his war powers.

[7] In January, 1973, the Paris Peace Agreement was signed formally ending the Vietnam war. However, the Nixon Administration continued massive bombing in Cambodia and Laos for several months after the Peace Agreement was signed. It was this action that was the target of war critics—and majorities in both houses of Congress.

"Don't feel superior about Watergate, Democrats—there's public disenchantment with both parties!"

Cartoon by Frank Interlandi; © 1973 The Los Angeles Times, reprinted with permission.

Second, President Nixon had expanded the prerogative exercised by many of his predecessors to *impound* (not spend) funds appropriated by Congress. In 1972 there were several unsuccessful attempts to force him to spend money which had been impounded. But in 1973, during the Watergate investigation, sufficient political support was found in Congress to pass legislation that severely limited the president's right to impound funds.

The third instance of Congressional reassertion of independence has to do with executive privilege (discussed more fully in Chapter 5). Suffice it to note here that President Nixon's attempt to extend executive privilege to members of his staff to be used as a sort of shield against investigation into their connection to the Watergate break-in and 1972 campaign law violations did not work. In spite of early attempts to deny to Congress the right or power to subpoena members of the White House staff, they were called and they did testify.

What can be seen in each of these areas of presidential-congressional political maneuver during the crucial 1972-1973 period is a halting, tentative reassertion of the power of Congress—at the expense of a besieged president. Whether Congress would have been able to mobilize itself to recapture some of its former power without the Watergate affair is an open question. In any event, this series of developments points up how highly political congressional reform can be.

GLOSSARY

Closure or cloture A motion in the Senate to end debate (especially a filibuster), requiring a two-thirds vote of the members voting to pass.

Conference committee Nonpermanent joint committee of senators and congressmen set up to iron out differences in similar bills passed in each house.

Congressional Record Daily account of the proceedings of both houses.

Constituency Residents of an electoral unit; or the unit itself.

Filibuster A long series of speeches, often irrelevant, by an organized minority of the Senate aimed at preventing action on a bill they oppose.

Gerrymander To delineate electoral districts so as to favor one political party or group over others.

Multiple constituencies The residents of 435 congressional districts and 100 senate districts, because they change from election to election, and because they vote for both representatives and senators, constitute multiple constituencies.

Select committees Special nonpermanent committees created for a specific purpose.

Subcommittees Subdivisions of the standing committees of the House and Senate often having continuing or permanent assignments.

SUGGESTIONS FOR FURTHER READING

ABZUG, BELLA. *Ms. Abzug Goes to Washington.* New York: Saturday Review Press, 1972.

BAILEY, STEPHEN K. *Congress in the Seventies.* New York: St. Martin's, 1973.

BARTH, ALAN. *Government by Investigation.* New York: Viking, 1955.

BERMAN, DANIEL M. *A Bill Becomes a Law.* New York: Macmillan, 1966.

BOLLING, RICHARD. *House Out of Order.* New York: Dutton, 1965.

BURNS, JAMES MAC GREGOR. *The Deadlock of Democracy: Four-Party Politics in America.* Englewood Cliffs, N.J.: Prentice-Hall, 1963.

CLAPP, CHARLES L. *The Congressman: His Work as He Sees It.* Washington, D.C.: The Brookings Institution, 1963.

CLARK, JOSEPH S. *Congress: The Sapless Branch.* New York: Harper and Row, 1964.

FROMAN, LEWIS A., JR. *The Congressional Process.* Boston: Little, Brown, 1967.

GETZ, ROBERT S. *Congressional Ethics.* Princeton, N.J.: Van Nostrand, 1966.

GREEN, MARK, et al. *Who Runs Congress?* New York: Bantam, 1972.

POLSBY, NELSON W. *Congress and the Presidency.* Englewood Cliffs, N.J.: Prentice-Hall, 1965.

RIEGLE, DONALD O. *Congress.* New York: Doubleday, 1972.

ROBINSON, JAMES A. *Congress and Foreign Policy-Making.* Homewood, Ill.: Dorsey, 1962.

TAYLOR, T. *Grand Inquest: The Story of Congressional Investigations.* New York: Simon and Schuster, 1955.

TRUMAN, DAVID B. *The Congress and America's Future.* Englewood Cliffs, N.J.: Prentice-Hall, 1965.

TRUMAN, DAVID B. *The Congressional Party: A Case Study.* New York: Wiley, 1959.

WHITE, WILLIAM S. *The Citadel: The Story of the U.S. Senate.* New York: Harper and Row, 1957.

YOUNG, RONALD. *The American Congress.* New York: Harper and Row, 1958.

ZINN, CHARLES J. *How Our Laws Are Made.* Washington, D.C.: U.S. Government Printing Office, 1967.

Chapter 5
The Presidency

The kingpin of the American political system is the presidency. In establishing this office at the national level the Founding Fathers drew on their experience with the executives (governors) provided for in the thirteen state constitutions that antedated the federal constitution. But the lessons learned from this experience were more negative than positive. Many of the governors were made subservient to their state legislatures with the expectation that this arrangement would prevent the kind of executive tyranny that was typical of George III, King of England. In attempting to prevent such abuses, the state constitutions overcompensated; most of the governors were so weak that they were incapable of political maneuvering or of imaginative leadership. The framers of the federal Constitution were aware of these difficulties, and the vast majority of them wanted the American presidency to be a strong office capable of decisive action.

One state constitution in particular did not follow the pattern of the weak governor. The New York governor at this time was a very powerful figure; he was elected for a three-year term and could be reelected indefinitely. The chief executive in New York had the pardoning power, and he was designated the commander in chief of the state militia. Alexander Hamilton, who was from New York, pushed very hard at the constitutional convention for a federal chief executive on the pattern of the governor of New York. And as it turned out, many of the provisions relating to the presidency bore a striking resemblance to the Hamiltonian–New York model.

An equally important influence on the thinking of the Founding Fathers about the presidency were the theories of the seventeenth-century English political theorist John Locke. Locke is widely regarded as one of the most important democratic political thinkers. The men at Philadelphia were well read in the works of Locke, especially his second treatise, *Of Civil Government.* Thus the framers of the Constitution were familiar with Locke's ideas about executive power and the Lockean principle of *executive prerogative,* which refers to the right of the president, or executive, to use his own discretion in interpreting the powers given to him. According to this principle, he should take whatever actions he regards necessary to serve the public welfare, regardless of specific constitutional provisions.[1]

There was much debate at the constitutional convention concerning the nature and powers of the presidential office. Although many of the points discussed at the convention were resolved in the Constitution, the extent of presidential power was not. This vagueness on the question of presidential power allows—and even encourages—the incumbent president to interpret the power of his office as best suits the demands of the times and his own political philosophy. The result is that there have been almost as many different interpretations on the scope of presidential power as there have been men occupying the office.

THE CONSTITUTIONAL DUTIES OF THE PRESIDENT

The Constitution gives the president a number of specific functions—duties and powers—which he must take into account when shaping his

---

[1] Locke wrote: "The good of society requires that several things should be left to the discretion of him that has the executive power; for the legislators not being able to foresee and provide by laws for all that may be useful to the community, the executor of the laws, having the power in his hands, has by the common law of nature a right to make use of it for the good of society. . . . Many things there are which the law can by no means provide for; and those must necessarily be left to the discretion of him that has the executive power in his hands, to be ordered by him as the public good . . . shall require." Note that Locke is not suggesting that there are no limits to executive power. It should be remembered that he also said in the second treatise: "Who shall be the judge whether the prince or legislative act contrary to their trust? . . . To this I reply, The people shall be judge. . . ." The purpose in citing Locke at this point is to illustrate the sort of thinking about the proper scope of executive power which underlay the discussions at the constitutional convention.

own approach to the office. These constitutional powers or functions of the president include his role as commander in chief, chief of foreign policy, chief legislator, and chief administrator. His extraconstitutional roles (those not directly derived from constitutional provisions) will be discussed later in the chapter; they include his role as chief of state, chief of his party, and national leader, the latter in the context of the expansion of presidential power through crises.[2] The first four jobs of the president listed above are derived from specific constitutional provisions; the latter three, although they have also come to be very important presidential responsibilities, are derived from custom and usage and cannot be traced directly to the Constitution.

Commander in Chief

The appellation commander in chief refers to the president's job as the highest officer in the American military establishment. The president, and not any single military officer, has the final word regarding all matters of military policy. Occasionally, a politician or a columnist calls for a greater degree of independence for the military, for giving military leaders the right to rely on their own judgment in military matters. Fortunately, these complaints and suggestions have not succeeded in reducing this very important aspect of presidential power. The tradition of civilian predominance over the military is very old and very strong in the United States. The president, as a civilian,[3] is assumed to understand and to promote the national interests of the United States, the highly political concerns which the military establishment exists to serve.

In this country the military is not an end in itself; it exists only to serve the political needs of the nation as a whole, and these are determined by the national government, not by the military men themselves. If a president wants to ask their advice, he may, but he may overrule or disregard that advice if he chooses. Thus many high-ranking officers in the military had been advocating direct American air strikes against North Vietnam long before President Johnson authorized them in late 1964; but until he decided that it was in the national interest to do so, they were powerless to begin those bombing raids. The praise or

---

[2] This categorization, with a few minor changes, is taken from Clinton Rossiter, *The American Presidency* (New York: Harcourt Brace Jovanovich, 1956), pp. 16–43.

[3] A few presidents have been from the military; Dwight D. Eisenhower is the most recent example. But his rank as President of the United States, and thus as Commander in Chief of all the armed forces, supersedes his previous military rank in such a case. No President of the United States has ever ruled as a military dictator, as has happened in so many other countries.

blame for the wisdom of that decision will have to rest not with the commanders in the field, but with the commander in chief who made it.

Chief of Foreign Policy

The role of chief of foreign policy refers to the president's job as the chief diplomat for the United States. The president makes the crucial foreign-policy decisions which affect the United States' relations with other nations. Since one type of decision may be to use military means to achieve some goal, his role as commander in chief obviously overlaps his role as chief of foreign policy. But in addition to the power of calling out the troops, the Constitution gives the president two other seemingly minor powers which are, in fact, the very basis of his role as maker of foreign policy. These are the power to appoint and the power to receive ambassadors.

With the majority approval of the Senate, the president of the United States chooses those men who will represent this country abroad. This power of appointment also implies the right to instruct these representatives regarding the policies they will pursue, which means in effect that the president must make those policies. Similarly, the Constitution gives to the president alone the power to receive—or turn away—representatives sent to the United States by other nations. Suppose that some country with which the United States did not have diplomatic relations, such as Cuba, sent an ambassador to this country. If the president chose to receive that individual, he would by that act establish diplomatic relations with the Castro regime.

Chief Legislator

Chief legislator may be a somewhat misleading title. The president, unlike the chief executive in some other systems, for example, the Prime Minister of Great Britain, is not a member of the legislature. The Constitution does not allot him a seat in Congress, he cannot take part in its deliberations, and he cannot vote. But he plays a very important legislative role nonetheless. This role is derived from Section 3 of Article II:

> He shall from time to time give to the Congress Information of the State of the Union, and recommend to their Consideration such Measures as he shall judge necessary and expedient; he may, on extraordinary Occasions, convene both Houses . . .

This passage suggests that the president should have a legislative program, delivered at the time of his State of the Union address, that he may propose specific items to the Congress "from time to time," and that he may prod them in an effort to get his program adopted.

Beyond this constitutionally sanctioned legislative role, strong presidents have frequently offered the only effective source of congressional leadership. For the reasons noted in Chapter 4, Congress has often proved incapable of leading itself, so that the only alternative to legislative drift, indecision, and inaction is for the Congress to find a source of leadership outside itself—in the president. It should be noted here that the president's effectiveness as Chief Legislator depends a great deal on his effectiveness in fulfilling his other roles. For example, his success as National Leader or Chief of His Party, as well as his other roles, in part determines his ability to influence the shape of public policy. Indeed, President Johnson played such an active role in leading the 89th Congress (1965–1966) that critics of his handling of Congress referred to the latter as a "rubber stamp." This is an extreme example of the president acting as Chief Legislator.

Another legislative tool at the president's disposal is the power to veto bills passed by Congress, as mentioned in Chapter 4. But this weapon may be used in a positive manner as well as in the usual negative way. The president may threaten to veto legislation desired by key leaders in Congress (for example, "pork-barrel bills," which will pump federal money into their home districts in the form of new dams or post offices) unless action he favors is also taken (for example, on foreign aid). Used in this way, the threat of a veto may actually facilitate the legislative process, illustrating the president's role as chief legislator.

Chief Administrator

The title chief administrator refers to the president's function as head of all of the departments in the executive branch of the federal government. In comparison with the importance of his other constitutional functions, the president's administrative responsibilities might be considered minor—but only relatively speaking. These duties impose very heavy burdens on the American president. Knowing about, planning for, and taking charge of any *one* of the twelve executive departments in addition to the Executive Office (discussed below) is a job requiring much insight and skill.

To administrate means to manage, conduct, or direct. The president manages the affairs of the eleven departments which make up the executive branch of the federal government: Department of State, Department of the Treasury, Department of Defense, Department of Justice, Department of the Interior, Department of Agriculture, Department of Commerce, Department of Labor, Department of Health, Education, and Welfare, Department of Housing and Urban Development, and Department of Transportation.

Even with the help of thousands of bureaucrats, the President cannot possibly direct or manage the activities of all these departments. To aid him in this task, he appoints a head for each department, called secretary (or Attorney General in the case of the Department of Justice). These men, together with the United States Representative to the United Nations and the vice president, make up the president's cabinet. Although the Constitution does not specifically mention a cabinet, it does mention the appointment power of the heads of the executive departments, and the president's power to appoint ambassadors "and other public ministers," that is, public officials, including heads of departments.

The administrative departments have the primary responsibility for carrying out the laws of the federal government (see Figures 5-1 and 5-2). These duties are borne not only by the heads of these departments, but also by hundreds of thousands of civil servants. The federal employees—from Internal Revenue Service clerks to agents of the Federal Bureau of Investigation—implement policies formally enacted by Congress, but often originally designed and later elaborated by their chief executive, the president. The cabinet helps the president to formulate policy, but it is not his only source of assistance in policy making. In addition to the rather clear arrangement of the cabinet and the twelve administrative departments, each of which is subdivided (for example, sections within the Department of State for research on Latin American affairs and on the Chinese Communist regime), there is another group of presidential advisers and assistants known collectively as the Executive Office of the President. The Executive Office exists on two related, but distinct levels. These are the White House assistants, the president's close, personal advisers (also sometimes called the "Kitchen Cabinet"), and the staff agencies. The White House assistants are closer to the president and are more likely to give him instantaneous and off-the-cuff advice whenever he requests it. The staff agencies are more concerned with long-range planning and in-depth studies of problems; they are more likely to be professional or technical advisers than personal or political assistants.

The White House Assistants.   The number of White House Assistants and their titles vary with the particular president. President Johnson, for example, had twenty-six—ranging from nine Special Assistants through an Armed Forces Aide to a Chief Usher. A few of the more

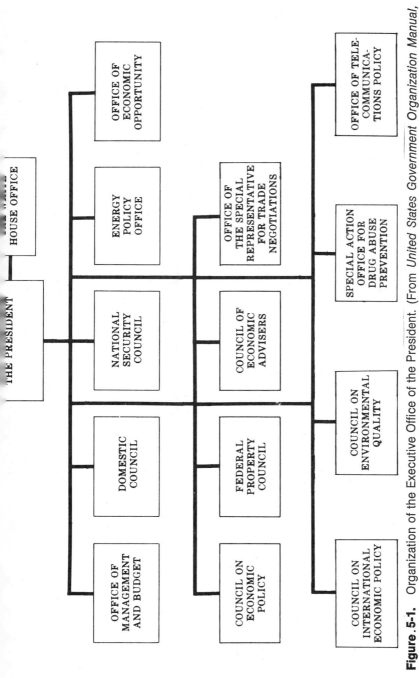

Figure. 5-1. Organization of the Executive Office of the President. (From *United States Government Organization Manual, 1972–73*, p. 68.)

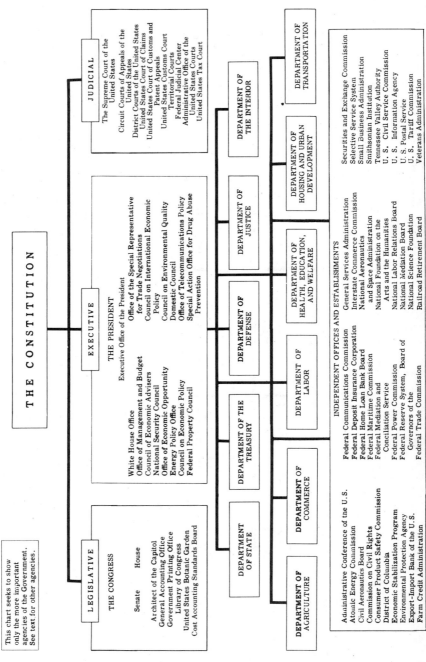

This chart seeks to show only the more important agencies of the Government. See text for other agencies.

THE CONSTITUTION

LEGISLATIVE

THE CONGRESS

Senate   House

Architect of the Capitol
General Accounting Office
Government Printing Office
Library of Congress
United States Botanic Garden
Cost Accounting Standards Board

EXECUTIVE

THE PRESIDENT

Executive Office of the President

White House Office
Office of Management and Budget
Council of Economic Advisers
National Security Council
Office of Economic Opportunity
Energy Policy Office
Council on Economic Policy
Federal Property Council

Office of the Special Representative
  for Trade Negotiations
Council on International Economic
  Policy
Council on Environmental Quality
Domestic Council
Office of Telecommunications Policy
Special Action Office for Drug Abuse
  Prevention

JUDICIAL

The Supreme Court of the
  United States
Circuit Courts of Appeals of the
  United States
District Courts of the United States
United States Court of Claims
United States Court of Customs and
  Patent Appeals
United States Customs Court
Territorial Courts
Federal Judicial Center
Administrative Office of the
  United States Courts
United States Tax Court

DEPARTMENT OF STATE

DEPARTMENT OF AGRICULTURE

DEPARTMENT OF COMMERCE

DEPARTMENT OF THE TREASURY

DEPARTMENT OF LABOR

DEPARTMENT OF DEFENSE

DEPARTMENT OF HEALTH, EDUCATION, AND WELFARE

DEPARTMENT OF JUSTICE

DEPARTMENT OF THE INTERIOR

DEPARTMENT OF HOUSING AND URBAN DEVELOPMENT

DEPARTMENT OF TRANSPORTATION

INDEPENDENT OFFICES AND ESTABLISHMENTS

Administrative Conference of the U. S.
Atomic Energy Commission
Civil Aeronautics Board
Commission on Civil Rights
Consumer Product Safety Commission
District of Columbia
Economic Stabilization Program
Environmental Protection Agency
Export-Import Bank of the U. S.
Farm Credit Administration

Federal Communications Commission
Federal Deposit Insurance Corporation
Federal Home Loan Bank Board
Federal Maritime Commission
Federal Mediation and
  Conciliation Service
Federal Power Commission
Federal Reserve System, Board of
  Governors of the
Federal Trade Commission

General Services Administration
Interstate Commerce Commission
National Aeronautics
  and Space Administration
National Foundation on the
  Arts and the Humanities
National Labor Relations Board
National Mediation Board
National Science Foundation
Railroad Retirement Board

Securities and Exchange Commission
Selective Service System
Small Business Administration
Smithsonian Institution
Tennessee Valley Authority
U. S. Civil Service Commission
U. S. Information Agency
U. S. Postal Service
U. S. Tariff Commission
Veterans Administration

Figure 5.2 Organization of the government of the United States. This chart shows the more important agencies of

important posts common to most presidents will be mentioned here. The special counsel is the president's personal lawyer. He advises the president on matters that require technical legal knowledge. Other special assistants serve as liaisons for the president in his relations with the Senate and the House of Representatives. Although the appointments secretary might seem like a relatively unimportant official, he carries the heavy burden of deciding who gets to see the president and for how long. The presidential press secretary keeps the news media posted on the president's activities and on any policy matters that the president sees fit to comment on to the press.

The president usually places confidence in a particular White House assistant, turning to him for advice much more often than to any of his other assistants. This individual under Dwight D. Eisenhower was Sherman Adams, who held the post of Assistant to the President. The post was abolished by John F. Kennedy. Kennedy's closest adviser was Theodore Sorensen, who held the position of Special Counsel. Under Lyndon B. Johnson, one of the closest relationships was between the president and Bill Moyers, his Special Assistant and Press Secretary from 1963 to 1967. During the first four years of the Nixon presidency, these roles were played by H. R. Haldeman and John Erlichman, his key White House aides. Because these men were deeply involved in the 1972 Watergate affair, particularly the attempted cover-up of the break-in, they were replaced in 1973. The entire character of the operation of the White House was changed as a result.

The Staff Agencies. The number and variety of agencies comprising the Executive Office of the President may be changed by legislation, establishing or transferring various divisions. Under President Johnson, for example, there were eight: Office of Management and the Budget, Council of Economic Advisers, National Security Council, Office of Economic Opportunity, Office of Emergency Planning, Office of Science and Technology, and Office of the Special Representative for Trade Negotiations.

The technical matters on which the staff agencies advise the president are all fairly obvious from the titles of the respective agencies. For example, the Office of Science and Technology keeps the president informed on the latest scientific research which might have military or international implications and which might require the expenditure of federal funds for research. The Office of Management and the Budget (OMB) is staffed by hundreds of experts who evaluate the budgetary requests of every government agency, board, or bureau. OMB whittles down or adds to the allocations for the upcoming fiscal year (a fiscal year runs from July 1 to June 30) and makes its recommendations to the president. In this process the Director of OMB is frequently called before Congress both to inform them of and to defend the president's recommendations. The three-member Council of Economic Advisers checks the pulse of the nation's economy and recommends remedial measures if the economy is slowing down or if it is expanding too rapidly and causing inflation and an upward surge in the cost of living. One of the most powerful and most secret of all government agencies is the National Security Council, discussed in Chapter 6. The president consults this body on vital matters of national defense. The Office of Emergency Planning, formerly known as the Office of Defense Mobilization, keeps available for the chief executive a number of contingency plans to deal with all conceivable types of emergencies from surprise nuclear attack to power failures over some region of the country.

THE EXTRACONSTITUTIONAL DUTIES OF THE PRESIDENT

In addition to his constitutional functions as commander in chief, chief of foreign policy, chief legislator, and chief administrator, the president fills a number of extraconstitutional roles. For the sake of clarity these are grouped below under three headings: chief of state, national leader, and chief of his party. These functions overlap to some extent the president's constitutional duties. But even so, they are sufficiently distinct to warrant separate consideration. That these functions are extraconstitutional should in no way be taken to mean that they are *un*constitutional. *Extra*constitutional simply implies that these jobs are not specifically provided for in the Constitution itself. They were either taken for granted, or have come to be important presidential duties as a result of custom and tradition.

Chief of State

The president's role as chief of state refers to the ceremonial functions he performs. In comparison to the jobs discussed above, the president's ceremonial duties seem minor or unimportant—but only relatively speaking. The president's ceremonial responsibilities demand a great deal of his time. Although the Founding Fathers must have expected that the president would be not only the pinnacle of the American political system, but also its figurehead, they did not make any provision for this role in the Constitution. Some high official has to receive foreign heads of state and dignitaries. But time has shown that even the antiaristocratic American people expect the chief of state to do even more than this.

The president pitches out the first baseball of the season, welcomes Boy Scout and Girl Scout delegations to the capital, proclaims National Brotherhood Week, and cuts ribbons when vital federal highway links are opened to traffic. He may be an honorary Navajo or Arapajo Indian; he is given a Red Cross membership card; and he may attend an annual prayer breakfast with a famous evangelist like Billy Graham. In short, the president is involved in all of the myriad ceremonies that seem to be an essential part of any political system. And although the American people in general are not given to much pomp and circumstance, when ceremony is called for, they expect the president to do the job. Indeed, some commentators have observed that the American presidency is in a way an "elective kingship." The president is expected to combine the democratic features of an elected executive with the pageantry and ceremony more characteristic of a king.

In most monarchical systems today, the chief of state is separate from the chief executive; one man performs the ceremonial functions, while another performs the executive or administrative tasks. In England, for example, the Queen is chief of state, while the Prime Minister is head of government. The important thing to note about the American president's duties as Chief of State is not the power which this function confers, for in fact it carries very little. Rather, it should be observed that this job is a tremendous drain on his time, a drain which other heads of government or chief executives usually do not have to face. This helps to explain why the burdens of the presidency are so great.

National Leader

Closely related to the president's role as chief of state is his job as national leader. Whereas many individuals may find one or all of the ceremonial responsibilities of the president irrelevant or unimportant, they are likely to pay a great deal of attention when he is acting as national leader. The president acts as national leader whenever he speaks to all the people or when he speaks for them, expressing America's feelings about some pressing world problem. Thus in his role as national leader he is both a voice of the people, moral spokesman for the country, and a world leader, moral spokesman for the "free world."

The president gives patriotic speeches on the Fourth of July and on other national holidays. He issues denunciations of un-American hate groups like the Ku Klux Klan or the American Nazi party. He is a major

---

The administrator of the future, for all his concern for policy, can never forget the other aspect of his job, which is to organize and coordinate a complex and dynamic system to carry out policy decisions that are made by others. We are in no danger of establishing an irresponsible bureaucracy, as long as the administrator is kept under the direction of responsible executives and is called to account by an independent Congress, for we do not really want administrative leadership: We want political leadership, which requires a strong administrative underpinning in order to be effective. The professional administrator must try to bridge the great gap between the way the scientists think and work and that of the politicians. He can never enjoy the luxury of the intellectual pride of the former, or the power of the latter. Through his professional skills, he must try to reconcile our technology with our democratic values. In this effort, the purpose of his profession is to carry, with a higher degree of concentrated responsibility, the moral burden that in a free society must be shared by all citizens.

Don K. Price, "Administrative Leadership," *Daedalus* (Fall 1961), p. 763.

---

influence on public opinion when he speaks on national issues such as air pollution or civil disobedience or extremism. The president speaks out forthrightly to the American people in a time of crisis—as did John F. Kennedy at the height of the Cuban missile crisis in October of 1962 and Richard Nixon on August 15, 1971, when he initiated the first peace-time wage and price controls in United States history. There is a tendency for a people to expect some national leader—in the United States, the president—to speak words of wisdom in a time of national emergency or on matters of urgency. Some have said that the president's role as national leader fills an emotional and psychological need. In this sense the president is the head of the "national family"; he satisfies the emotional need for a visible leader. When the image of the presidency is tarnished, as it was by the Watergate affair, discussed below, this emotional need will remain unfilled for many people.

Chief of His Party

As chief of state and as national leader, the president is the epitome of nonpartisanship. But at the same time, he is the undisputed head of one of the nation's two large political parties. He is as partisan in this role as he is nonpartisan when acting as national leader. The president may represent 51 percent of the people if his party holds a bare national majority, or he may reflect the views of less than 50 percent if he is not a "majority president." (Woodrow Wilson, Harry S. Truman, John F. Kennedy and Richard Nixon were all minority presidents when less than a majority voted for them in 1912, 1948, 1960, and 1968, respectively.)

Since World War II, when discussing whether a president enjoys majority support, public-opinion polls after the election are at least as important as the size of the popular vote received by the president when elected. President Johnson, for example, received more than 65 percent of the presidential vote in 1964, but by 1968 his popularity in the polls had slipped to 33 percent—one of the lowest ratings in recent history.[4] This fact may have contributed to his decision to withdraw from the 1968 presidential race. Similarly, Richard Nixon received over 60 percent of the vote in 1972, but his level of popular support as measured in successive opinion polls dropped steadily after the Watergate revelations in 1973.[5]

In his capacity as party chief, the president makes no pretense of nonpartisanship. When he makes ambassadorial appointments, appointments within the executive departments, and even when he appoints judges in the federal courts, he displays his partisanship—rewarding the party faithful and his own supporters. This practice, incidentally, is neither illegal nor dishonest—it is a necessary part of the patronage system. Patronage simply means the power to make appointments, and it is exercised in a highly partisan manner.

As chief of his party the president is also expected to give leadership to his party. He personally designates who the national chairman will be, and fills other key posts in the party. In addition, a strong party leader will be instrumental in shaping the party's platform, its goals, and its ideals.[6] During his tenure he will guide the party's destiny. Presidents are ranked not only on the basis of their ability to exert national leadership and to deal with foreign nations, but also on their capacity as a political leader. Thus a strong president or a successful president must, of necessity, be able to unite his party and to give it a sense of direction. Abraham Lincoln, Theodore Roosevelt, Woodrow Wilson, and Franklin D. Roosevelt—all ranked as great presidents—were highly partisan in their handling of the office. Indeed, a president who studiously avoids partisanship, who tries to stay out of the thick of politics, assures himself of a mediocre rank in comparison with the strong presidents. Conversely, a president who confuses his political opposition with the foreign

---

[4] A Gallup Poll in February 1968 showed 33 percent of those polled giving President Johnson's performance a "good" or "excellent" rating.

[5] A Gallup Poll in November, 1973, showed 27 percent rated Nixon's performance as "good" or "excellent."

[6] The president's role as party leader, particularly as it affects party strategy during the campaign, is discussed by Daniel M. Ogden, Jr., and Arthur L. Peterson, *Electing the President* (rev. ed.; New York and London: Chandler Publishing Company, 1968).

enemies of the United States will surely demean the office he holds and his own place in history.

THE EXPANSION OF PRESIDENTIAL POWER THROUGH CRISES

Whether one approves of presidential power or of the exercise of power by a particular president, that office undeniably has become the most powerful in the American political system and certainly one of the most powerful executive institutions in the world. The Constitution, as noted above, is somewhat vague on the question of presidential power. As a result, each president has interpreted the power of the office differently. Indeed, as Woodrow Wilson remarked: "In the twentieth century the presidency will be as big and as influential as the man who occupies it." And it happens that the nation has increasingly demanded that the man who occupies the office be aggressive, assertive, and dynamic—in short, that he be a strong leader. There are two reasons, basically, why the American presidency has come to be so powerful and why it has become accepted as such. To begin with, the expansion of presidential power can be linked to the national crisis that have occurred periodically within the American political system. This condition, in turn, has brought about the need for assertive and vigorous presidents.

There are a number of national crises which might be considered as having enhanced presidential power. The sections that follow will consider six of these crises: the Civil War, industrialization and monopolization, World War I, the Great Depression, World War II and the Cold War. Each of these national emergencies was met with decisive presidential leadership, and in each case the crisis provided the justification for the expansion of presidential power. But the crisis alone would not have resulted in enhancing the power of the presidency if an ambitious politician occupying the office had not boldly seized the opportunity.

A final crisis relating to the power of the presidency has had a negative impact. This refers to the long-range effects of the Watergate affair during the Nixon Administration. In this case we see a crisis of confidence which was beyond the president's control—a crisis which contributed to the diminution rather than the enhancement of presidential power.

The Civil War

The Civil War descended on the United States a few months after an obscure, backwoods Illinois politician by the name of Abraham

Lincoln assumed the nation's highest office. Lincoln met the challenge of the Civil War, in large part, by interpreting very broadly the president's role as commander in chief of the nation's armed forces. It is this power, more than any other, which has contributed to the president's dominant role in the American political system in modern times. And it was Abraham Lincoln, the sixteenth President of the United States, who first expanded this power to its full potential.

Fort Sumter fell to Confederate forces on April 14, 1861, barely one month after Lincoln's inauguration. In meeting this crisis, Lincoln took a number of steps which were without precedent in American history. And before adopting these measures, he was very careful to call for Congress to convene—on July 4, ten weeks away.

While waiting for Congress to come together, Lincoln took five unilateral steps which greatly enhanced his personal power and the power of the presidency. First, Lincoln called for a naval blockade of all southern ports. A naval blockade, it should be noted, is an act of war. According to the Constitution, only Congress can declare war, but President Lincoln's actions illustrated the fact that declaring war may be a mere formality as long as the president, using his power as commander in chief, can get the nation into a state of war without even consulting Congress. Second, Lincoln issued an executive order calling for 300,000 volunteers to augment the armed forces. Again, the Constitution gives Congress the power to "raise and support armies"; but by calling for *volunteers*, not actually violating the letter of the Constitution, Lincoln enhanced his own power. Third, he increased the size of the army and the navy, also by executive order and also without consulting Congress. Fourth, the president seized control of rail and telegraph lines from Washington, D.C., to Baltimore, Maryland, and later expanded the seizure all the way to Boston. These utilities, it should be noted, were privately owned. By executive order, and without consulting Congress, Lincoln seized these lines on the grounds that they were vital to national security. Finally, Lincoln ordered that the writ of habeas corpus, the cornerstone of Anglo-Saxon jurisprudence, be suspended along the seized rail and telegraph lines. What this meant in practice was that individuals suspected of aiding the Confederate forces could be arrested and thrown in jail without a trial and without any legal remedy.

Industrialization and Monopolization

A second crisis which was instrumental in expanding the scope of presidential power was the industrialization and monopolization of the American economy toward the end of the nineteenth century. This devel-

"The Grave of the Union," by "Zeke" (1864). This cartoon was occasioned by President Lincoln's proclamation of September 1862 ordering military trial of persons accused of interfering with the war effort. (From the New York Public Library collection.)

opment in the economy was more of a "creeping crisis" than an overt crisis like the Civil War. It did not "break out" at any given point in history, but rather built up to crisis level over a period of years. As business, industry, and commerce grew, the wealth of the country, or the gross national product (GNP), grew apace. What was lacking, generally speaking, was an equitable distribution of this newfound national wealth. More and more of the country's productive resources came to be controlled by a few giant monopolies—or trusts or cartels.

Whenever there was a slump in the economy, the small factories and the fledgling corporations were bought out by the giant monopolies. Sometimes the giants of an industry would artificially create a crisis by drastically lowering prices, thus making it impossible for their smaller competitors to make a profit. Either the small businesses would also lower their prices and sell goods below cost, or they would be shut out of the market because their goods would be overpriced. In either case, the small merchant was squeezed, the monopoly bought him out (at an unrealistically now price), and competition was thereby reduced or eliminated.

The crisis in the economy had reached a critical stage by the end of the nineteenth century. Large-scale monopolies or trusts controlled the petroleum, sugar, meat, steel, and other basic industries. Likewise, a few railroads, by a number of questionable practices, were able to buy out their competitors, so that in that industry as well competition had been effectively thwarted. Efforts to regulate these monopolies and trusts at the local and state levels had proved inadequate. So, as the result of mounting pressure to remedy this situation, Congress in 1890 passed the Sherman Antitrust Act. The Sherman Act is still the primary federal law having to do with trusts and monopolies. It forbids "every contract, combination, in the form of trust or otherwise, or conspiracy in the restraint of trade or commerce among the several states, or with foreign nations."

However, a comprehensive federal law was not enough. The problem posed by monopolies and trusts in the national economy required more than congressional enactments. It required decisive presidential action. And thus the Sherman Act lay virtually moribund from 1890 until Theodore Roosevelt became president, more than ten years later. Roosevelt for the first time vigorously enforced the Sherman Act, earning for himself the title "Trustbuster." During his tenure as president, twenty-five indictments were brought against some of the largest corportions in the country. Eighteen of these lawsuits were successfully prosecuted by the government in federal courts. This bold assertion of presidential power in insuring the health of the national economy was instrumental in earning a high rank for Theodore Roosevelt among American presidents and in enlarging the power of the office.

World War I

A third example of a national crisis calling for a bold assertion of presidential power was World War I. That war was the first to put to the test the vast resources of modern technology and the efficient industrial machine that had been built up in the United States. Although America was not one of the original belligerents, the victory of the Allied powers would have been impossible without American involvement. And because American industrial might was so important a part of that conflict, President Wilson felt that the successful prosecution of the war required a maximum effort on the part of American technology and industry. Further, he felt that this effort could be achieved only by imposing stringent government controls and regulations.

Wilson had Congress delegate extensive powers to him for the purpose of maximizing the American war effort. He had Congress create two government boards which were without precedent in American history. The War Industries Board, set up in 1916, had the power to require workers to put in extra hours in order to sustain the war effort. The second, the Committee on Public Information, was set up in 1917 in order to mold public opinion in support of the war. The Espionage Act of 1917 and the Sedition Act of 1918 made it a crime to make any statement whose intent was to interfere with military success or to discredit the American form of government. This second board gave the president the ability to regulate the public means of communication as long as the war lasted. These extraordinary powers claimed by Woodrow Wilson illustrated the fact that in modern wartime the president of the United States is commander in chief of almost everything.

The Great Depression

A fourth crisis which elicited a decisive presidential response was the Great Depression of the 1930s. Franklin D. Roosevelt was elected to the presidency in 1932 on a program that called for prompt and far-reaching action to counteract the economic depression which had hit the country. Unlike his predecessor, Herbert Hoover, a conservative and a strict constitutionalist, F.D.R. felt not only that the president could act in this situation, but also that he had a moral obligation to act. Roosevelt did not feel that the president was prevented from dealing with the economic collapse of the nation by the language of the Constitution. He showered Congress with bills designed to bring about economic recovery—legislation affecting industry, agriculture, commerce, and virtually every other segment of the American economy. The many proposals, considered as a package, are referred to as the New Deal—the name that F.D.R. gave to his economic recovery program.

Although there were many individual proposals in the New Deal package, they had two basic attributes in common: First, they called for the federal government to spend huge sums of money and, second, they advocated federal controls without precedent in peacetime. Franklin Roosevelt first began to implement the economic theory known as Keynesian economics, developed by the British political economist John Maynard Keynes. This theory was considered daringly radical at the time, but has since become economic orthodoxy. It holds that in times of economic recession or depression the government must spend more than it earns in order to get the economy back on an even keel. This method is known as "priming the pump," putting more money into circulation so that consumer demand will increase, production will increase, and eventually government revenues will catch up because of increased production and increased personal income which the government can then tax. But Roosevelt also felt that the economy should not be allowed to deteriorate further or to collapse again, and to that end he had Congress impose a number of regulations and restrictions which resulted in augmenting presidential power. A new crop of government agencies, independent boards, and regulatory commissions were established which in effect placed the president in charge of the nation's economy.

Although this power was limited and tempered, in theory, by congressional control of the pursestrings, this limitation is only intermittently used to deprive the president of his newfound powers. Indeed, many of the New Deal programs have lasted down to the present day. New institutions and programs which are designed to prevent a major economic disaster to the nation, and others which attempt to spare individuals the possibility of economic privation are known as welfare programs. These welfare programs have become permanent features in the American political system and important elements in the total picture of presidential power.

World War II

Even before the economic crisis—the Great Depression—had been solved, the United States faced a fifth national emergency, World War II. In the first place, F.D.R. took a number of steps in dealing with Japan and Germany which, for all practical purposes, committed the United States to war before the nation was legally at war with those countries. In paticular, there was the Lend-Lease Agreement with Great Britain by which the United States traded outmoded destroyers and other naval vessels for 99-year leases of British air and naval bases. This move was of invaluable help to the British, who were already at war with Germany in 1939. Technically, the agreement violated the principles of neutrality which the United States should have observed since it was not a war with Germany. It was presidential action, then, and not a declaration of war by Congress, which initially involved this country in World War II. The Korean and Vietnamese wars further illustrate the point that it is presidential action and presidential commitment which involve the country in war; a congressional declaration of war becomes, then, a mere formality. In the cases of Korea and Vietnam, Congress never did declare war.

During World War II, the Senate also to some extent forfeited to the president its power of advice and consent on treaties. Roosevelt felt that the normal treaty-making process, bathed in the glare of publicity, was not appropriate during a time of war. For this reason he preferred to enter into "executive agreements," secret arrangements with other heads of state, which left the Senate out of the process entirely. While executive agreements had been used on occasion earlier, it was F.D.R. who made extensive use of them. From 1940 to 1945, the United States entered into seventy-three executive agreements but only seven official treaties. Since that time presidents have relied even more heavily on executive agreements in place of treaties, thus bypassing the Senate.

The Cold War

World War II ushered in two revolutionary new developments which have contributed materially to the enlargement of the president's powers: the threat of Communist imperialism, and the advent of nuclear weapons. Immediately after the conclusion of World War II, Stalin's Red Army occupied most of Central and Eastern Europe—an area comprising East Germany, Poland, Hungary, Czechoslovakia, Bulgaria, and Rumania. In each of these countries, one by one, Stalin managed to impose Soviet-dominated puppet governments. In addition, Soviet troops or Soviet-backed rebels threatened the governments of Greece, Turkey, and Iran. This very tense situation in the late 1940s seemed to have the makings of World War II.

But the development of weapons of mass destruction prevented victory, in the conventional sense, by either side in what became known as the Cold War. The Cold War was prevented from becoming "hot" by what Winston Churchill called the "balance of terror." Neither side was willing to use its full military potential for fear of triggering an exchange of nuclear weapons that might spell an end to civilization itself. Thus the Cold War became a period of protracted tension between the world's two superpowers, the United States and the Soviet Union. The Cold War, of the crises considered in this chapter, shows the least signs of resolution. There has been a continuous state of crisis and the American president has become a perpetual commander in chief.

The Cold War has kept the United States involved in conflicts almost constantly since the end of World War II. Some of them have been "vest-pocket wars"—as in Greece, Korea, and Vietnam; others have been briefer confrontations—as the Berlin crises of 1958 and 1961, and the Cuban missile crisis of 1962. These recurrent crises have maintained the United States in a permanent state of war preparedness and have kept the world on the brink of thermonuclear war. Therefore, it is easily seen how the events of the past three decades have placed greater responsibility and more power in the hands of one man—the president of the United States—than ever before in human history.

Each of the six national crises discussed above reveals how histori-cal events and circumstances have steadily expanded presidential power. But there is another side to the coin. Each crisis which has faced the country has posed both a challenge and an opportunity. It has posed a challenge to the incumbent president to meet and overcome it, to defend the nation's security and its well-being. Each crisis has also posed an opportunity—an opportunity to expand both the president's own per-sonal power and the power of the office. And because, in each instance, a vigorous president who believed in the Lockean principle of executive prerogative seized the opportunity boldly, his own power was assured and the presidential office was made a stronger institution.

Lincoln in the Civil War, Theodore Roosevelt in the period of the giant trusts and monopolies, Wilson in World War I, Franklin Roosevelt in both the Great Depression and World War II—each of these men has left his imprint on the office and has left it a much stronger institution. In regard to the most recent challenge, the Cold War, not one man but five men have seized the opportunity to expand presidential power. Meeting the challenge of the Cold War, Truman, Eisenhower, Kennedy, Johnson, and Nixon have all acted vigorously to promote the national interest. This is not to say that every decision was a good one, or that they might not have done better; or that some of them were not stronger presidents than others. But it appears that the contemporary interna-tional situation demands a Lincoln–Theodore Roosevelt–Franklin Roosevelt kind of president rather than a passive man on the order of the Buchanan–Taft–Harding model. Challenging events have helped make the presidency the predominant institution in the American politi-cal system, but great men have helped to shape and meet the challenges.

The Watergate Scandal

It would be improper to consider the expansion of presidential power through crises without discussing a recent problem of American social life which has had a profound impact on the presidency. We refer, of course, to the Watergate scandal of 1972–73. Before analyzing how this crisis diminished the power of the presidency, we should briefly review three major aspects of the incident itself.

The Watergate is a plush apartment complex which during the elec-tion campaign of 1972 housed the Democratic National Committee staff office. In July, 1972, several men were caught burglarizing these head-quarters; it later came out that the Committee to Re-elect the President (CRP) had financed this bizarre act and had also been bugging the DNC for some time. Second, in the ensuing investigation it was learned that

"I don't hold with this new interpretation of ·
constitutional power!... Traditionally, executive
privilege meant only use of the executive washroom!"

"Grin and Bear It" by George Lichty; © Field Enterprises, Inc. 1973, courtesy of Publishers-Hall Syndicate

the CRP had been involved in an all-out effort to sabotage the process
of selecting a Democratic presidential nominee. False telegrams had been
sent, potential candidates had been smeared, purportedly by other Democrats, and slanderous accusations from presumably reliable sources had
been "leaked" to the press. Finally, there was a wholesale effort by the
CRP to circumvent the Campaign Financing Act that went into affect
in April, 1972. Testimony was heard by the Senate Select Committee
alleging corruption that included John Mitchell, formerly Attorney General, Maurice Stans, formerly Commerce Secretary, and H. R. Haldeman,
John Erlichman, and John Dean, III, Nixon's three top White House
aides. There was evidence of apparently illegal campaign contributions
totaling hundreds of thousands of dollars, secret bank accounts, myriad
spies and political saboteurs, the virtual selling of ambassadorships, and

a promise, in return for a secret campaign contribution of $250,000, not to pursue an investigation in a fraud case involving the Securities and Exchange Commission.

Needless to say, the magnitude of corruption, the number of activities involved, and the subversion of the electoral process shocked the nation and the world. The presidency was dealt a blow that compared with those it suffered from the corruption of the Grant Administration of the 1870s and the Teapot Dome scandal of the 1920s. The president's relations with Congress were soured, his credibility in international affairs, after four years of substantial achievement, was erased and the very foundations of our democratic system were shaken. For an entire generation of youngsters, the presidency would be symbolic of the graft and hypocrisy in politics. Many commentators at the time, however, found comfort in the fact the presidency *did* survive, and that our system was strong enough and stable enough to put into force self-corrective mechanisms. This, it was argued, attested to the vitality of the United States political system. If this interpretation was correct, Watergate was a very costly demonstration of the system's resiliency.

GLOSSARY

Cabinet A committee composed of the heads of all the executive departments, the president, the vice president, and two or three other top advisors appointed by the president.

Chief of state The ceremonial leader of a nation; in monarchies a king or queen, in the United States the president.

Commander in chief The president in his role of highest officer in the United States armed forces.

Executive A person who makes the policies, and directs others to implement them, of a nation, corporation, school, etc.

Extraconstitutional duties Responsibilities that are not specifically spelled out in the Constitution.

Executive agreements Arrangements made by the president with other heads of government, often secretly, which leave the Senate out of the treaty-making process.

Executive prerogative Right of the president (or other executive authority), to use his discretion in interpreting the powers given to him.

Minority president A president who received less than 50 percent of the popular vote.

Watergate The Watergate, an apartment complex in Washington, D.C., in 1972 housed the headquarters of the Democratic National Committee. The D.N.C. was burglarized by men hired by the Committee to Re-elect the President, supporters of President Nixon.

White House assistants The president's close, personal advisers.

SUGGESTIONS FOR FURTHER READING

BARBER, JAMES DAVID. *The Presidential Character: Predicting Performance in the White House.* Englewood Cliffs, N.J.: Prentice-Hall, 1972.

BINKLEY, WILFRED E. *The Man in the White House.* Baltimore: Johns Hopkins University Press, 1959.

BURNS, JAMES MC GREGOR. *Presidential Government.* Boston: Houghton Mifflin, 1966.

CORWIN, EDWARD S. *The President: Office and Powers.* New York: New York University Press, 1957.

FENNO, RICHARD F., JR. *The President's Cabinet.* Cambridge: Harvard University Press, 1959.

FINER, HERMAN. *The Presidency: Crisis and Regeneration.* Chicago: University of Chicago Press, 1960.

HUGHES, EMMET J. *The Ordeal of Power.* New York: Atheneum, 1963.

KOENIG, LOUIS W. *The Invisible Presidency.* New York: Holt, Rinehart and Winston, 1960.

LASKI, HAROLD J. *The American Presidency.* New York: Grosset & Dunlap, 1960.

MC CONNELL, GRANT. *Steel and the Presidency.* New York: Macmillan, 1966.

MC GINNISS, JOE. *The Selling of the President, 1968.* New York: Trident, 1969.

NEUSTADT, RICHARD E. *Presidential Power.* New York: Wiley, 1960.

POLSBY, NELSON W. and AARON B. WILDAVSKY. *Presidential Elections: Strategies of American Electoral Politics.* New York: Scribner's, 1972.

REEDY, GEORGE E. *The Twilight of the Presidency.* New York: World, 1970.

ROSSITER, CLINTON. *The American Presidency.* New York: Harcourt Brace Jovanovich, 1960.

SCHLESINGER, ARTHUR M., JR. *A Thousand Days.* New York: Macmillan, 1966.

WHITE, THEODORE H. *The Making of the President, 1972.* New York: Atheneum, 1973.

Chapter 6
The Judicial System

The judicial system of the United States is one of the most complex in the world, for three chief reasons. First is the courts' adherence to the key principle of common law, *stare decisis*, which means to be guided by previous decisions in similar cases. Second is the impact of federalism, resulting in an array of national, state, and local courts. Third is general acceptance—by the government at all levels and by the electorate—of the Supreme Court's power of judicial review: that is, the power to decide whether specific legislative or executive actions are allowed by the Constitution.

In each of these respects the legal system of the United States bears some similarity to other legal systems, but in its combination of all three features within the same system the United States is unique. There are other federal judicial systems—those of Canada, West Germany, India, and Brazil, for example—but in none of these does a national supreme court have the power of final judicial review in quite the same way that it does in the United States. Likewise there other systems that follow the principle of *stare decisis*—common-law systems such as those of Great Britain, Canada, Australia, India, and Nigeria—but the specifics of the common law as they have grown up in each of those systems necessarily are different. Finally, in its power of judicial review, the

Supreme Court of the United States is unique. For even those other systems which recognize a review power, as for instance the legal system of Argentina, have never had a high court as active in the political process as is the Supreme Court of the United States.

> To consider the Supreme Court of the United States strictly as a legal institution is to underestimate its significance in the American political system. For it is also a political institution, that is to say, for arriving at decisions on controversial questions of national policy. As a political institution, the Court is highly unusual, not least because Americans are not quite willing to accept the fact that it *is* a political institution, and not quite capable of denying it; so that frequently we take both positions at once. This is confusing to foreigners, amusing to logicians, and rewarding to ordinary Americans who thus manage to retain the best of both worlds.
>
> Robert A. Dahl, "Decision-Making in a Democracy: The Supreme Court as a National Policy-Maker," *The Journal of Public Law*, 6 (1957), 279.

COMMON LAW AND CODE LAW

Although the political role of the American courts has changed considerably, their form is substantially the same as it was in colonial times. The primary characteristic of American legal procedure still is adherence to the key principle of common law, *stare decisis*. This simply means that decisions must be guided by legal precedent, by decisions reached previously in similar cases. At the base of the American legal system, then, is the common law—judicial precedents regarded by all American courts as ordinarily binding. Legal precedents in a common-law system are as much "law" as are the legislatively enacted laws. In countries having a legal system based entirely on so-called code law, there is no such thing as a binding legal precedent. In those countries the courts merely enforce laws in the legal code, laws usually enacted by the legislature.

If a legal code is visualized as a Greek temple, consisting chiefly of a set of columns that may be replaced from time to time or even increased in number by the addition of a portico, law in the United States may be thought of as a group of pyramids. At the center is the huge federal pyramid, overshadowing fifty smaller yet sizable structures belonging to the states. The apex of the federal pyramid is the Constitution of the United States of America, and just below are "the Laws of the United States which shall be made in Pursuance thereof; and all Treaties made, or which shall be made, under the Authority of the

United States"—these three elements comprising the "supreme Law of the Land" according to Article VI of the Constitution. On the next tier down come orders of administrative agencies acting under authority of congressional statute or of presidential order when no congressional mandate is required. Forming the base of the pyramid is "judge-made," or common, law, a vast body of precedents in individual cases. Each state's legal structure likewise has a constitution at the top and common law at the base, with intermediary tiers of legislative enactments, agency regulations, county and municipal ordinances, and the like. When a portion of the law at a lower level conflicts with one above it, the higher one takes precedence. Decisions of the United States Supreme Court are superior to those of all other courts.

The social function of the law is twofold: to enforce codes of behavior supported by a majority of the electorate, through their chosen representatives, on all members of society; and to settle disputes. A criminal case requires a charge by a public prosecutor that a law has been violated. A civil case involves a dispute, usually about an alleged breach of contract or trust, or injury from a wrongful act (a tort), or probable injury. When a government agency is a party, it must hold that some public interest is at stake in the outcome. In a criminal case "the people" are the plaintiff and the accused is the defendant, and the government is obliged to protect the defendant's rights (see Chapter 9). In a civil case, the plaintiff may be either a private person or an agency of government; this also holds for the defendant. The plaintiff files a complaint against (or sues) the defendant.

A civil or criminal trial is an *adversary proceeding*, meaning that the plaintiff and the defendant—actually their attorneys, acting on their clients' behalf, in most cases—argue their case before an appropriate court, one that has *jurisdiction*. The judge has the responsibility for requiring facts to be presented according to the *rules of evidence*. Questions of law and procedure are decided by the judge, and questions of fact are decided by the jury if there is one (see Chapter 8 for the right to a trial by jury) or by the judge if there is no jury. When there is a jury, it delivers a verdict after being *charged* by the judge with a summary of the facts and relevant law; when there is no jury, the judge delivers the verdict. In a criminal trial the verdict sought is "guilty" or "not guilty," after which the judge dismisses the case or imposes a penalty (*delivers the sentence*) or places the defendant on probation. In a civil trial the verdict sought is a *remedy*, which often takes the form of a court order or an award of money *damages*. A court order may require the defendant to "cease and desist" from some action or may even "enjoin" him from taking some action (the latter type of order is called an _injunction_). In most jury trials a unanimous verdict is required, and occasionally a judge sets aside a jury's verdict. A verdict may be appealed to a higher court on the ground that it results from faulty law or procedure.

The advantage of common law over a strictly code-law approach is that it is very difficult for a legislature to anticipate every possible situation which might give rise to a lawsuit. Even though a legal code might be very logical and seemingly quite complete, it cannot provide in detail for every possible circumstance. These inevitable gaps are filled in the United States and in other common-law countries by the courts. When an unusual legal situation occurs, the court's decision is written down and kept for future reference by any lawyer or judge who might at some later date face a similar type of case. This kind of flexibility is not possible with code law; under that system the only way of filling a gap in the law is for the legislature to fill it. Such remedial legislation usually occurs only after a number of cases have arisen which cannot be disposed of under existing statute law.

The Flexibility of Common Law—A Case Study

An example of courts filling in the gaps in the law is the principle of "manufacturer's implied warranty" in present California law. Under the state code a defective product could be taken back to the store which sold it, but in the absence of an express _warranty_ (that is, a written statement of guarantee), the manufacturing company could not

---

The growth of the law inevitably reflects the forces and ideas which are transforming our society and world society. In one area after another, the law is going through natural processes of change—often of rapid change, corresponding to the violent rate of change in the world around us. New problems preoccupy the law, problems unknown a generation ago, or known in a different form, with a different degree of importance. Old problems take on new dimensions when seen in a setting that is steadily altered by the tide of events. As always in the evolution of law, the contemporary movement of change in law is also one of continuity. The law grows now, as it has in the past, around a firm axis of its own values.

Eugene V. Rostow, _The Sovereign Prerogative: The Supreme Court and the Quest for Law_ (New Haven, Conn.: Yale University Press, 1962), p. xv.

---

be held liable for injury caused by the defective product. Thus, suppose you bought an ice-cream cone with bits of glass in it and had to undergo abdominal surgery as a result. Under the old principle, you would have had to sue the store which sold you the ice cream in order to recover damages. In one case the court held that, since the law was not specific on the point of liability, the seller could not be held liable because he was not actually at fault (the situation with the ice-cream vendor in our example). The rather surprising result would have been, under the law as it was written, that it was technically impossible for the victim to sue anyone and that he would have to pay his own bills.

This situation seemed grossly unfair and not in keeping with the *spirit* of the written law, which was intended to give the innocent victim relief in such cases. Hence the court held that, since the manufacturer was guilty of purveying a defective product, he could be held responsible. The theory was that the manufacturer *implied* a warranty —implied that the product was free from defects—when it was sold. This precedent was followed and expanded in later California decisions, and a new legal rule was established. Such a development would have been unlikely under a strict code system of law, and innocent victims might still be paying their own hospital bills because of products which were defective but not explicitly warranted. This solution to the problem of manufacturer's liability, it should be noted, has not yet been adopted by all of the states.

Increasingly, though, common law has been codified in order to put it into a clearer and more orderly form, and some states have extensive legal codes. The Commission on Uniform State Laws has recommended various uniform acts, especially in the area of business law, some of which have been passed by all or most of the state legislatures. Thus disparities among the legal systems of the fifty states often are reduced or eliminated eventually. In the meantime, lawyers and political leaders have an opportunity to see how well differing legal rules work in solving similar types of problems. This is part of the genius of American federalism.

THE IMPACT OF FEDERALISM ON THE LAW

The second principal feature of the American legal system is federalism. Federalism was discussed in Chapter 3 in terms of the division of powers between federal and state governments. This division of power is complex enough regarding social services and the taxing power. But it is unbelievably complex in its application to the American system of law— or, more accurately, systems of law, for the United States has not one legal system but fifty-one. In addition to the federal court system, each of the fifty states has its own system of courts for guaranteeing order and justice—in compliance with state law, the constitution of the state, and the United States Constitution. The vast majority of laws which are broken are state laws, and most of the criminals in the United States are violators of state rather than federal laws. Likewise, the great bulk of civil disputes—such as those involving marriage, divorce, contracts, property, or torts—are covered by state laws, or by local laws made in pursuance of state constitutions.

Despite the great proliferation of state courts and state laws, Congress has acquired far-reaching authority to affect the lives of individual citizens, especially through its power to regulate interstate commerce. As a consquence, a number of types of dispute are adjudicated in federal courts. And although the federal court system is not as large as all the state courts combined, it is by far larger than that of any single state. Federal and state laws sometimes overlap, but it is generally possible to label a case as one which either (1) arises under a federal law or treaty or deals with some aspect of the federal government and hence will be tried in a federal court; or (2) arises under a state law or has to do with some aspect of state or local government and will be tried in a state court. There are a few cases which fall into a third category, known as *concurrent jurisdiction.* Cases which fall under concurrent jurisdiction may be tried in either a federal or a state court or both, depending on the nature of the case and the citizenship of the persons involved. The following is a list of typical kinds of cases under federal and state jurisdiction:

Federal Jurisdiction
1. Disputes between states.
2. Cases involving foreign diplomats.
3. Violations of federal law.
4. Admiralty or maritime cases (disputes arising from incidents on the high seas).
5. Cases arising under federal treaties.
6. Civil suits against the United States.

State Jurisdiction
1. Violations of state law.
2. Civil suits between citizens of the same state.
3. Civil suits between citizens of different states involving less than $10,000.
4. Civil suits against state government.

Civil suits between citizens of different states involving more than $10,000 are known as *diversity-of-citizenship cases.* The decision as to which state's court system to use in such cases is up to the plaintiff. Falling under the concurrent jurisdiction of state and federal courts are acts which involve the violation of both federal and state laws.

Certain courts, both state and federal, have only *appellate jurisdiction*; that is, they hear cases only on appeal. For example, the federal courts of appeal and most state supreme courts have only appellate jurisdiction. The most numerous courts are those which have only *original jurisdiction*; for example, United States district courts and most municipal courts. The jurisdiction of the United States Supreme Court is primarily appellate; the Court has original jurisdiction in disputes between states and in cases involving foreign diplomats.

In addition to the courts discussed above, there have been created a number of "special courts" in both the federal and the state system. Special federal courts are shown in Figure 6-1. Examples of special state courts are juvenile courts and, in some localities, traffic courts.

State court systems, typically, are organized into a supreme court (the court of last resort within the state system[1]), a number of intermediate courts of appeals, a larger number of superior courts or county courts, and finally the municipal courts or justice of the peace courts. The structure of the federal court system is approximately parallel: the Supreme Court of the United States is at the apex, followed by eleven circuit courts of appeals, and then the workhorses of the federal system —the federal district courts, currently numbering ninety-three.

There is a common but mistaken notion that all courts in the state system are automatically inferior to all federal courts. This simply is not the case. With a very few exceptions, the only point of contact between state and federal courts is from the state supreme court directly to the highest federal court, the Supreme Court of the United States. There is, ordinarily, no contact between lower state courts and lower federal courts.

In addition to the federal and state court systems, there are a number of administrative (regulatory) agencies which have quasi-judicial functions. For example, a person who feels that he has been the victim of unfair competitive practices in interstate commerce may bring his complaint to the Federal Trade Commission (FTC). Attorneys are retained, briefs are submitted, and arguments are heard. The FTC hands down a ruling which is much like a court decision. And if either party is dissatisfied, he may appeal the decision to the relevant circuit court of appeals, and, eventually, even to the Supreme Court. Other examples of quasi-judicial agencies are the Interstate Commerce Commission (ICC), the Federal Communications Commission (FCC), the

---

[1] In New York State, the trial courts of first instance (that is, the courts hearing most cases when they first arise) are called Supreme Courts, and the highest court in that state is called the Court of Appeals.

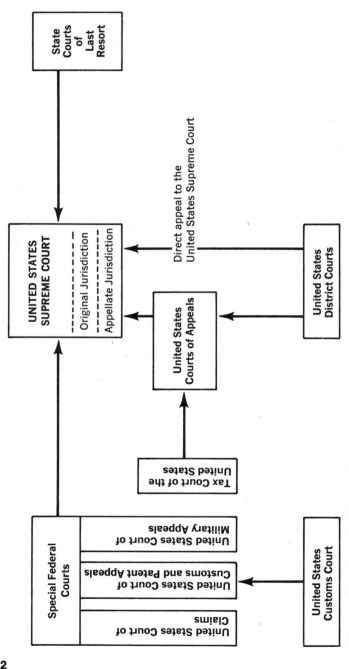

Figure 6-1. Organization and jurisdiction of the federal court system. (From Harold J. Spaeth, *An Introduction to Supreme Court Decision Making*, New York and London: Chandler Publishing Company, 1965, p. 3.)

National Labor Relations Board (NLRB), the Securities and Exchange Commission (SEC), and the Civil Aeronautics Board (CAB), to name the more important ones. Decisions by any of these agencies may be appealed to a circuit court of appeals. Incidentally, although these agencies have some of the attributes of a court, they are not made up of judges. Typically the commissioners, or members of the agency, are appointed for a specific term of office, such as fifteen years. Federal judges, on the other hand, are appointed for "good behavior," which, in practice, means until they retire or die.

JUDICIAL REVIEW

The third major principle of the American court system is the power of *judicial review*. Judicial review is a uniquely American contribution to the political process. It is the power of the judicial branch to determine whether acts of the legislative and executive branches (national, state, or local) are within the scope of the federal Constitution. Closely related to judicial review is the power of *statutory construction*, which is the courts' power to interpret legislative statutes and to decide whether executive regulations have legislative mandate. Thus the courts not only pass judgment on whether legislation of executive action is "constitutional" (that is, within the scope of the Constitution), but also define what legislative acts mean and what agents of the executive branch must do about them. Judges issue court orders compelling executive agencies to obey a constitutional or legislative mandate—either by taking appropriate action or by refraining from inappropriate action.

School Desegregation—A Case Study in Judicial Policy Making

The series of court decisions since World War II relating to school desegregation (discussed more fully in Chapter 4) provide a dramatic example of judicial review and statutory construction as they affect public policy. Groups of black children in four states—Kansas, South Carolina, Virginia, and Delaware—had brought suit to obtain enforcement of provisions for equal facilities in state constitutions and state statutes requiring or permitting (in Kansas it was the latter) segregation of black pupils in the public schools. In the first three cases, United States district courts held that separate schools can be "equal" under the Fourteenth Amendment to the Constitution and also ordered South Carolina and Virginia to rectify certain inequalities. In the Delaware case, the state courts ordered black pupils admitted to previously white schools and agreed to reconsider the constitutionality of segregation after equalization had been accomplished.

The United States Supreme Court, hearing appeals from the plaintiffs in the first three cases and the defendants in the fourth case, ruled that the plaintiffs and "others similarly situated" were "by reason of the segregation complained of, deprived of the equal protection of the laws guaranteed by the Fourteenth Amendment." A year later, in 1955, the Court remanded the cases to the district courts, instructing them "to take such proceedings and enter such orders and decrees consistent with this opinion as are necessary and proper to admit to public schools on a racially nondiscriminatory basis with all deliberate speed the parties to these cases."

Beginning with the 1954 *Brown* v. *Board of Education* case, as it was called, the judicial rather than the legislative branch made policy in a vital area of public education. The enactment by Congress of the Civil Rights Act of 1964 "provided some indication, however, that the burden of securing school desegregation might be shifted from the federal courts to federal administrative agencies."[2] Regulations implementing this act issued by the United States Office of Education in the spring of 1965 required a "good-faith substantial start" toward desegregation by the fall of that year on the part of every school district receiving federal funds. But the courts remain very much in the picture in two ways: first, in deciding suits relating to the question of whether state agencies are moving with "all deliberate speed" in providing "relief" to black pupils whose separate schooling has been found unconstitutional (judicial review); second, in deciding suits relating to the question of whether requirements by the United States for federal grants reflect the intent of Congress in passing the Civil Rights Act of 1964 (statutory construction).

The Historical Basis for Judicial Review

Establishment of the power of judicial review means that in practice the United States Supreme Court, as the court of final appeal, is the interpreter of the Constitution. There is nothing in the Constitution itself which gives the Court this power. The legislature, as in Great Britain, could be the guardian of the Constitution. It is even conceivable that the chief executive might perform this function. But partly by

---

[2] Harold J. Spaeth, *The Warren Court* (New York and London: Chandler Publishing Company, 1966), p. 131.

accident and partly by design the Supreme Court is the final arbiter of the Constitution, not Congress or the president.

It is clear that the Founding Fathers did intend the Court to have the power to declare state laws unconstitutional, but it is far from clear whether they intended it to have this same power over national laws or acts of the president. It is probably true that they favored some sort of Court power in interpreting the Constitution. In *The Federalist*, No. 78, Alexander Hamilton argued that in order for the judicial branch of government to balance the other two it would have to be strong and independent. In addition, several of the state courts after 1776 had dared to void several acts of state legislatures because the justices felt them to be in conflict with a "higher law." And in 1789 the first Congress adopted a Judiciary Act in which it was implied that the Supreme Court would not enforce acts of Congress which the justices believed to be unconstitutional. Despite these historical antecedents to the Court's power of judicial review, it remained for Chief Justice John Marshall, in a case decided in 1803, *Marbury* v. *Madison*, for the Court to claim for itself this formidable power.

Marbury v. *Madison* has to be regarded in the political context of the time in order to understand the reasoning behind the decision. By the year 1800, allegiances had polarized into two groups, the Federalists and the anti-Federalists (known after 1792 as the Democratic-Republicans). John Adams, a Federalist, was running for his second term as president in the 1800 election. He was opposed by Thomas Jefferson, the leader of the Democratic-Republicans. Adams lost his bid for the presidency, and the Federalists were also soundly defeated in most congressional races. Before turning the reins of government over to the Democratic-Republicans, the "lame-duck" Federalist Congress reformed the federal judicial structure, adding sixteen new circuit judgeships and forty-two justices of the peace for the District of Columbia. Lame-duck President Adams filled these new positions with loyal Federalists, including one William Marbury. At the same time, Adams appointed his trusted Secretary of State, John Marshall, to be Chief Justice several months before he had resigned as Secretary of State. Marshall, as Secretary of State, was given the job of delivering the commissions to the new appointees. Working late into the night of March 3, 1801—the night before Jefferson's inauguration—Marshall was unable to deliver all of the commissions. Jefferson and his Secretary of State, James Madison, decided to withhold the undelivered commissions; William Marbury was one of those appointed who did not receive his commission. Finally, Marbury asked the Supreme Court to issue a *writ of mandamus* ordering Madison to give him his commission.

Chief Justice Marshall was put in a very awkward position. If he issued the writ of mandamus that Marbury sought, President Jefferson in all probability would ignore it, thus seriously undermining the authority of the Supreme Court. On the other hand, if he declined to grant the writ, he would be hurting Marbury, his friend and political associate, and would be giving in to pressure from the president. The actual decision was a surprise to both sides: Marshall said that Marbury ought to be given his post, but that the Supreme Court did not have the authority to demand delivery of his commission. He said that the section of the Judiciary Act of 1789 giving the Supreme Court the power to issue writs of mandamus to public officers was unconstitutional! But in saying that the Court did not have the power to issue such a writ, Marshall assumed for the Court a vastly greater power: *judicial review*. He argued, in *Marbury* v. *Madison*, that if a law, like the particular section of the Judiciary Act in question, was contrary to the Constitution, it could not be enforced in federal courts. He further asserted that logically (the power cannot be found in the Constitution itself) the Supreme Court would have to decide which laws were in this category. Judicial review has come to be a vital element in the American system of checks and balances, and a crucial weapon of the Supreme Court.

Although Marshall had assumed a tremendous power for the Court, it was used very sparingly at first. It was fifty-four years before a subsequent Court decision found another act of Congress unconstitutional (*Dred Scott* v. *Sandford*, 1857). Indeed, since 1803, fewer than a hundred laws passed by Congress have been found unconstitutional by the Supreme Court. Nor does the Court often nullify an action of the president on constitutional grounds. That is why headlines were made by the decisions upsetting President Truman's seizure of the strikebound steel plants in 1952. Even the voiding of state laws under the federal Constitution has been relatively infrequent—less than twenty times between the first such decision in 1810 and the Civil War.

There are two interrelated reasons for the Supreme Court's restraint in exercising judicial review—a restraint reflected down through the lower federal courts and into the state courts. One is that the power of the judicial branch is limited both by the Constitution and by political realities (a point to be discussed later in this chapter). The other reason is that the Supreme Court has placed limits on its own power. For one thing, it restricts the number and nature of the cases it will hear on appeal (accepting a case is called granting *certiorari*). In addition, the Supreme Court usually observes what it calls *judicial restraint*. Although volumes have been written about this controversial legal doctrine, it can be summarized fairly accurately: A case will be decided on constitutional grounds only if there is no other way and only if there is a "clear" violation of the Constitution.

THE SUPREME COURT AS INNOVATOR

The Supreme Court, then, is often known as the protector of the Constitution—a guardian that uses its strength discreetly in its dealings with the president, the Congress, and the states. But even more important is the Court's role as innovator through its positive interpretation of the Constitution. The following three examples illustrate this type of innovation. One was the decision in *Brown* v. *Board of Education* (1954), in which the Court interpreted the Fourteenth Amendment to mean that states denied blacks the equal protection of the laws if they offered them only segregated schools. In a companion decision, *Bolling* v. *Sharpe*, the Court found segregated schools in the District of Columbia also to be unconstitutional. These landmark decisions attempted to commit the nation to a policy of racial equality—an area where Congress and the president had been unable or unwilling to act.

A second example of the Court as innovator through its interpretation of the Constitution was the *Baker* v. *Carr* decision in 1962, followed by *Wesberry* v. *Sanders* and *Reynolds* v. *Sims* (both in 1964). In these cases the Court declared that basic political rights were being denied where one person's vote was given substantially less weight than someone else's. This triad of decisions has led to the reapportionment of congressional districts and of the districts for upper houses of state legislatures.

Finally, in a series of cases including *Mapp* v. *Ohio* (1961), *Gideon* v. *Wainwright* (1963), *Escobedo* v. *Illinois* (1964), and *Miranda* v. *Arizona* (1966), the Court held that certain types of constitutional due process are required even in state court trials. In *Mapp*, the Court held that unconstitutionally seized evidence may not be used in a state prosecution. In *Gideon*, the Court held that a state must provide counsel for an indigent person accused of a major crime. In *Miranda*, the Court held that a constitutional right had been violated because a confession to a crime was used as evidence when the defendant had not been informed of his right to keep silent. The Court felt that its rule was the best way to insure that law-enforcement officers would never attempt to coerce a confession. Significantly, in none of these cases was the Court declaring acts of Congress unconstitutional; nor was it interpreting acts of Congress or acts of the president. It innovated by interpreting the Constitution so as to expand its meaning, in cases involving state and local laws or practices.

"And now, if I may, a special prayer for the Supreme Court."

Drawing by Alan Dunn: © 1962 The New Yorker Magazine, Inc.

STRICT CONSTRUCTIONISM

Strict constructionism is sometimes used as a synonym for judicial restraint. The basic notion is similar; cases should be decided according to the most literal interpretation of the Constitution; justices should not stray into a controversial policy-making role. In the 1960s conservatives complained that the liberal Warren Court, in cases such as those discussed above, had gone out of their way to clothe their own political

"BY GEORGE, THEY **HAVE** TAKEN A TURN TO THE RIGHT."

Drawing by Bill Mauldin; © 1972 Chicago Sun-Times, reproduced by courtesy of Wil-Jo Associates, Inc. and Bill Mauldin

and social views with the authority of the Constitution. Most of these controversial decisions would have been avoided, many felt, if the Court had applied the Constitution, as literally written, instead of the justices' private notion of what the law should be.

The Constitution, unfortunately, does not interpret itself. The First Amendment says, "Congress [and by extension state legislatures] shall make no law . . . abridging the freedom of speech or of the press. . . ." There is no qualifying phrase which says "except in cases involving obscenity or subversion." And yet some decisions, supported by so-called strict contructionists, have made just such exceptions.

Strict constructionists presumably would interpret very rigidly the Fourth Amendment prohibition against "unreasonable searches and seizures" of people "in their persons, houses, papers, and effects. . . ." But so-called strict constructionists in Congress supported the 1970 "no-knock" legislation that permits officers to break into a suspect's house without a warrant when he feels that the evidence would otherwise be lost.

Interestingly enough, President Nixon, who campaigned hard for strict constructionism in federal courts in 1968 and 1970, appointed more federal judges than any other president. He also managed to achieve a majority on the Supreme Court. Although claiming that his primary concern was with their judicial philosophy and their legal qualifications, the Nixon appointees are not notably superior to earlier appointees in either regard. In both Supreme Court nominations and federal court appointments Nixon has had more than his share of rejections because of poorly qualified candidates. Furthermore, there has been no clear "strict constructionist" application of the law by the Nixon appointees. In 1971 it was a federal judge in New York, appointed by President Nixon only one month earlier, who refused to go along with the Administration in suppressing the publication by the *New York Times* of the Pentagon Papers. Finally, Nixon's appointments appear to have been even more politically motivated (as opposed to philosophical choices) than is usual. All but a very few of his federal court appointees have been Republicans, many of them loyal party workers. There is no evidence that their judicial philosophy was routinely considered in making the appointment. There is considerable evidence that local party regulars were consulted, as is usually the custom, before the appointments were made.

Strict constructionism is what you make of it. The Constitution is too vague a document to admit of only one interpretation. Those who disagree with the decisions of a particular court will often accuse the Court of straying from the "correct" interpretation of the Constitution. Such charges, however, tend to be either naive or politically inspired. When the history of the Nixon (or Burger) Court is written, it will undoubtedly record a shift from the Warren Court in the general direction of conservatism. But it is unlikely that scholars will find that the Burger Court adhered more closely to the letter of the Constitution than any other.

In Chapter 9 the impact of Supreme Court decisions concerning civil rights and liberties is analyzed. Likewise in Chapters 3, 4, and 6, federalism, congressional powers, and presidential powers were shown to be influenced by decisions of the Supreme Court since the beginnings of the American political system. The courts, as was noted in Chapters 3 and 4, often play a profoundly political role—initiating major changes in national policy. It must be kept in mind that while the courts in the United States political system enjoy a high degree of independence from executive or legislative control, judges cannot completely disregard popular opinion on the major issues of national politics. Consequently, courts sometimes seem to be reacting to popular feelings on such issues. For example, in a case involving draft-card burning, decided in the spring of 1968, the Supreme Court upheld the conviction of the defendant. It is possible that this case could have been decided otherwise if public opinion against draft-card burning had not been so strongly expressed—and so consistently reflected in opinion polls. But even though judges cannot practically or politically avoid public opinion, it would be an exaggeration to suggest that they often decide cases on this basis.

GLOSSARY

Adversary proceeding Civil or criminal trial in which two opposed parties contest the facts or the law of a case or both.

Appellate jurisdiction The authority of a court to hear only cases already tried in a lower court and appealed to the higher court.

Certiorari An act of the Supreme Court in accepting a case (the name of a type of writ).

Concurrent jurisdiction Authority to hear a case held equally by federal or a state court.

Diversity-of-citizenship cases Civil suits between citizens of different states which involve more than $10,000.

Injunction A court order that requires a defendant to (or not to take) some action.

Judicial restraint A policy of the Supreme Court to decide cases on constitutional grounds only if there is no other way and only if there is a "clear" constitutional question.

Judicial review Power of the judicial branch to determine whether acts of the legislative or executive branches are within the scope of the federal Constitution.

Original jurisdiction Authority of a court to be the first to try a case.

Remedy The verdict sought in civil trial, usually taking the form of a court order or the award of money damages.

Stare decisis Key principle of common law that courts are guided by previous decisions in similar cases.

Statutory construction The power of courts to interpret statutes to decide whether executive regulations have a legislative mandate.

Strict constructionism The belief that by adhering to a literal interpretation of the Constitution the courts will avoid stamping their decisions with their own political and social values.

Warranty A written statement of guarantee.

SUGGESTIONS FOR FURTHER READING

ABRAHAM, HENRY J. *The Judicial Process.* New York: Oxford University Press, 1968.

BETH, LOREN P. *Politics, the Constitution and the Supreme Court.* New York: Harper and Row, 1962.

BICKEL, ALEXANDER M. *The Least Dangerous Branch: The Supreme Court at The Bar of Politics.* Indianapolis: Bobbs-Merrill, 1962.

BICKEL, ALEXANDER M. *The Supreme Court and the Idea of Progress.* New York: Harper and Row, 1970.

FREUND, PAUL A. *The Supreme Court of the United States: Its Business Purposes, and Performance.* New York: Meridian, 1961.

KURLAND, PHILLIP. *Politics, the Constitution and the Supreme Court.* Chicago: University of Chicago Press, 1970.

LEWIS, ANTHONY. *Gideon's Trumpet.* New York: Random House, 1964.

MASON, ALPHEUS T. *The Supreme Court in the American System of Government.* Ann Arbor: University of Michigan Press, 1963.

MC CLOSKEY, ROBERT G. *The American Supreme Court.* Chicago: University of Chicago Press, 1960.

MITAU, G. THEODORE. *Decade of Decision: The Supreme Court and the Constitutional Revolution, 1954–1964.* New York: Scribner's, 1967.

ROSTOW, EUGENE V. *The Sovereign Prerogative: The Supreme Court and the Quest of Law.* New Haven: Yale University Press, 1962.

SCHMIDHAUSER, JOHN R. *The Supreme Court: Its Politics, Personalities and Procedures.* New York: Holt, Rinehart and Winston, 1962.

SCIGLIANO, ROBERT. *The Supreme Court and the Presidency.* New York: Macmillan, 1971.

SCHUBERT, GLENDON A. *Constitutional Politics.* New York: Holt, Rinehart and Winston, 1960.

SCHUBERT, GLENDON A. *Judicial Policy-Making.* Chicago: Scott, Foresman, 1966.

SPAETH, HAROLD J. *An Introduction to Supreme Court Decision Making.* New York and London: Chandler, 1965.

SPAETH, HAROLD J. *The Warren Court: Cases and Commentary.* New York and London: Chandler, 1966.

Chapter 7
Federalism—
Intergovernmental Relations

National, state, and local governments have collaborated with each
other from the beginning of the American nation. Collaboration entails
both cooperation and conflict, which over time has evolved into a
system of governance encompassing diverse intergovernmental relationships. As the United States moves into the last quarter of the twentieth
century, two centralizing political forces are becoming dominant in the
American society; the nationalization of politics, and the preeminence
of the fiscal resources of the federal government.

The involvement of the federal government in urban affairs is
already so widespread and deep that problems and policies once considered local have now become national problems and policies. This
development should not be surprising since more than two-thirds of
the people of the United States now live in approximately 220 metropolitan areas covering less than 10 percent of the land area of the
country. A concentration of people means a concentration of voters
along with an intensification of the problems of maintaining the health
of the "little economies," of keeping up the physical plant, and of
making it possible for metropolitan dwellers to live and rear their
children in a world of equality, opportunity, health, and civic participation. The federal government and, increasingly, state governments are

involved in urban affairs because urban people have turned to them when they have been unable to get what they want from local governments.

It is clear from present trends that the domestic programs of the federal government are increasingly designed to serve people living in metropolitan areas. There is little indication, however, that such programs will be directly administered by the federal government. Instead, the traditional device of categorical grants-in-aid is being supplemented by block grants under revenue sharing to form the basis of new intergovernmental programs.

The entire direction of intergovernmental relations was changed by the ratification in 1913 of the Sixteenth Amendment to the Constitution of the United States authorizing Congress to levy an income tax. Since then, the national revenue system has been more easily administered and more responsive to changes in the economy than have state and local systems. For example, the Committee for Economic Development reports:

> The normal growth of the economy currently increases the annual yield of the existing federal income tax system by about $7 billion, and this would rise to about $11 billion (at 1965 prices) by 1975. This increase in the annual yield of federal income tax receipts is greater than the increase in national government expenditure for domestic services.[1]

It follows that if military spending were reduced or held constant, an increase in annual income tax yield of from $7 billion to $11 billion, without considering changing tax rates, would be available to support programs of social development and physical reconstruction of metropolitan areas. This fact alone, regardless of whether federal involvement takes the route of increased grants for particular programs or of a block grant to state and local governments, means that the national government will play a more important role in state and local affairs.

THE CONDITION OF FEDERALISM IN THE UNITED STATES

Periodically there is a great clamor about "states' rights," or "home rule," the idea that problems are better solved at the state and local level, that the federal government should provide for the common defense, regulate economic and political relations among the states,

---

[1] Committee for Economic Development, *A Fiscal Program for a Balanced Federalism* (June 1967), p. 43.

and do little else. Those committed to this approach tend to overlook the fact that the states are no more real entities, having rights or privileges, than is the United States government. Both are mere abstractions; the reality is the people who are governed by both. The main purpose of democratic government at any level is to deal with real human problems efficiently and fairly. When one group of people favors the solution at the state level of problems which they do not regard as national problems, then they advocate states' rights. But the very same people may favor federal action in some other area. For example, some individuals say that civil rights is a state problem whereas defense is a national one. Logically, the race issue is as national in scope as is the problem of defense.

Many Americans are alarmed over the growth of "big government." This growth is usually equated with an expansion in the size of the federal government which, they think, has developed at the expense of the states. However, much of this alleged federal growth is more apparent than real. As Table 7-1 and Figure 7-1 show, the federal budget from 1950 to 1972 expanded at a slower rate than did

Table 7-1. State and local expenditures versus federal expenditures, 1950–1972

	1950	1955	1960	1965	1970	1972
State and local expenditures (billion $)	22.8	33.7	51.9	74.5	131.3	175.0*
Increase over previous period	—	10.9	18.2	22.6	56.8	43.7
Percentage increase	—	48%	54%	44%	76%	34%
Federal expenditures (billion $)	42.4	67.3	91.3	118.5	197.2	231.6
Increase over previous period	—	24.9	24.0	27.2	78.7‡	34.4
Percentage increase	—	59%	36%	30%	66%	17%

* Estimated
‡ Federal budgets after 1968 included expenditures from certain trust funds, such as social security, which had not previously been included. This new basis for figuring the budget accounts for a large part of the increase between 1965 and 1970.
Source: Adapted from United States Bureau of the Census, *1972 Statistical Abstract of the U.S.*; pp. 386, 416.

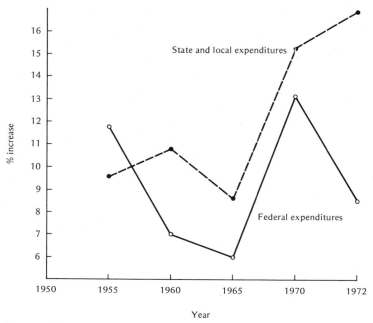

Figure 7-1. Average yearly increases in government expenditures: Federal versus State and Local. Source: Derived from data in Table 7-1.

state and local expenditures. This fact alone would seem to indicate the reverse of what is so often heard—in fact, it appears that state and local governments are growing more rapidly than the federal government.

What has expanded more than the relative size of the federal budget is the control exercised by the president and Congress over the economic and social life of the country. Although the growth in size of state government, seen in terms of budgets, has outpaced that of the federal government, the states have lost some measure of their autonomy. In case after case the states have adopted programs originated by the federal government but implemented by them. *Cooperative federalism* is a term applied to these shared federal–state programs by those who approve of the basic idea. In their execution they are state projects, but they must conform to federal standards in order to receive financial assistance from the federal government. One of the more obvious examples is welfare. Most states now have their own welfare systems; but in most cases they were not begun until federally sponsored welfare programs were initiated. Then, in order to get the federal government to share in the expense, the state programs conformed to the minimum federal standards. Some states, such as California and New York, have welfare programs that far surpass these minimum national standards; even so, they are careful to follow the federal guidelines so that they will not disqualify themselves for supplementary federal grants. The same pattern can be seen in such diverse areas as education, environmental protection, and highway construction. In each case, most of the initiative has come from the federal government although the program itself is primarily a state or local project. The result is that the national Congress has a great deal of power in setting the guidelines for these programs and in modifying them. This process is what is meant by *cooperative federalism.*

Why has this happened? Why has the power of the federal government over many programs grown at the expense of that of the states? There are a number of answers to this question. One rather obvious answer is that as problems have become more complex, as the government's role in the economy has become greater, the federal government was the more logical agency to offer leadership and innovation than were the state governments. But there are also factors at the state level which help to explain this process. An important ingredient in the decline of state power is the fact that the states have lagged far behind the federal government in the philosophy and techniques of government. Whereas the national government has gradually accommodated itself to the challenges and opportunities of the twentieth century, state governments for the most part have not. It has become increasingly difficult in recent years to find a national politician of any importance who seriously believes in the adage, "That government is best which governs least."[2] Most national politicians of both parties believe that government should play an active rather than passive role in society; the debates center not around the question of whether government should act, but rather how and when it should act.

The same cannot be said for the attitude toward government at the state level, however. There is a widespread feeling that state government should be passive rather than active. Ronald Reagan, the conservative Republican governor of California from 1966–1974, exemplified this attitude. Reagan was committed to a policy of less government. He said

[2] Although President Nixon committed himself in his second term to achieving an overall reduction in the scope of the federal government, he would not have agreed with the notion that big government in and of itself is evil, as implied in the adage. In fact, some activities of the federal government, such as environmental controls, increased significantly under Nixon's direction.

that government had done too much already, that the task at hand was to reduce its scope, not to move ahead but to stand still and figure out where we were. In his inaugural address he stated:

> The time has come to run a check and see if all the services government provides are in answer to demands, or just goodies dreamed up for our supposed betterment. The time has come to match outgo to income, instead of the other way round.

Few national politicians are so explicit in their distrust of the contemporary role of government.

STRUCTURAL DEFICIENCIES OF STATE AND LOCAL GOVERNMENT

The negative attitude toward government, which pervades so much of the thinking about state and local government, in many cases is embedded in state constitutions and in city and county charters. It is in part because of the archaic structural features of these basic documents that the states and local governments have had to look to the federal government for leadership on many matters that they might have solved by themselves. Despite constitutional reforms in some states, such as Michigan, and imaginative new structures like the city–county government of Dade County, Florida, most of the formal structures of government in the states remain woefully inadequate.

While the United States Constitution is an outstanding illustration of what a constitution ought to be, most state and local charters are examples of what a basic charter ought not to be. They contain thousands of extraneous provisions that more properly belong in statute law. Statute law, it should be noted, consists of those laws passed by a legislature— legislation on matters that are not fundamental to a system of government, issues that are likely to change over time. Constitutional provisions, on the other hand, ideally concern the bedrock issues, the basics of government. Unfortunately, this penchant for encrusting state constitutions with irrelevancies that should be left to legislative enactment is not confined to one or two states; it is widespread.

Many state constitutions are burdened with detailed provisions which go to great length in describing the precise limits of the power of the governor, legislature, counties, and cities. But these very provisions have often come into conflict with public demand that something be done by government in a particular situation. Consequently challenges arise which state or local officials are powerless to deal with. Interest groups, frustrated in their attempts to solve pressing problems within the existing structure of state government, then turn to the federal government for action.

The structure of local government, like that of state government, frustrates action on pressing problems. Local government in most states is a patchwork of overlapping municipalities, special districts, unincorporated areas, and counties. One of the greatest difficulties of local government is that of securing cooperation among these various units of government for common ends, replacing the conflict and competition which are so much more common. Most cities and counties were given their charters when the problems they faced were relatively simple compared to those of the 1970s. Their charters, in many cases, reflect the negative philosophy of government that characterizes most state constitutions, preventing local officials from acting decisively and imaginatively in dealing with problems.

One structural deficiency that still afflicts many city, county, and state governments is the dilution of executive power and authority. This deficiency is usually most pronounced at the county level. County boards of supervisors, typically, have no definable locus of authority and responsibility. Power is often distributed among a board of from five to twelve men. None of these supervisors is a chief executive. One of them may serve as chairman, but he seldom has any special powers or prerogatives. In addition to the plural executive arrangement on the board itself, there is often a dispersal of executive authority between the board of supervisors and other executive officers—for example, sheriff, coroner, treasurer, superintendent of county schools—all elected directly by the people rather than appointed by a chief executive. This dispersal of authority in most counties is more serious than it is in state governments although officials such as state treasurer, attorney general, and the like are often elected. City government, it should be noted, frequently suffers from the same type of dispersal of executive authority that exists at the state and county level.

Many of the structual problems of both county and city government can be solved by adopting a chief administrative officer form of government. This official is referred to as county manager, city manager, or chief administrative officer. He is chosen by and responsible to the county board of supervisors or, at the city level, the city council. He, in turn, chooses the heads of the various departments, who are directly responsible to him. This arrangement removes many of these offices from the ballot, thus reducing its length and making efficient, professional government possible. It is difficult for professionalism to develop in local government when county clerks, fire commissioners, county sheriffs, and the like are forced to play politician every two or four years in addition to their other duties. Sometimes it is objected that placing responsibility for overseeing all of the operations of county or city government into the hands of one individual creates the possibility of a one-man political empire, a sort of local dictator. This danger is more apparent than real, however, because the chief administrative officer is always responsible for his actions to an elected board or council. In short, the dangers of this solution seem to be minimal, and the advantages many. Such reform, however, presupposes overcoming public apathy and distrust which often characterize attitudes toward local government.

Those who distrust government, pardoxically, often prefer to have more rather than fewer levels of government. The underlying premise is probably that by diffusing responsibility it is somehow easier to prevent the concentration of too much power in too few hands. The large number of local governmental units (81,253 in the United States in 1967) and especially the proliferation of special districts seem to be illustrations of this attitude. Special districts perform some vital service in some area, such as in education. Indeed, school districts are such an important unit of local government that they are often considered separately from other special districts. Separate levels of government are organized for purposes such as flood control, water supply, air-pollution control, sewage disposal, or police and fire protection.

It would seem logical that many of these functions could be handled by larger, multipurpose districts; but there is a great deal of public indifference to suggestions for reform. In 1972 there were over 3,800 special districts in California. Each one of these special districts has its own boundaries, taxes the people who receive its services, and elects officials to govern itself. The remarkable thing is that, with so many overlapping levels of government, anything gets done at all; and that some voters, even though they are a tiny fraction of those eligible, continue to show an interest in special-district elections. But both public apathy and distrust of government have to be overcome in order to assign many of the functions of special districts to larger, multipurpose districts—or to the counties.

FINANCING STATE AND LOCAL GOVERNMENT

Another obstacle to good government at the state and local level is insufficient revenue to support necessary governmental activities. Any level of government experiences difficulty from time to time in paying for its programs, but these problems are particularly acute at the state and local levels. For although many of the vital services which are automatically associated with government, such as police protection, education, public health and welfare, roads, are state responsibilities, the states do not have the abundant resources of the federal government to pay for these things. This is not to say that states are without any sources of revenue, but often state and local taxes are resented even more bitterly than the more substantial federal levies. It should also be noted that local politicians often lack the courage to impose necessary taxes.

An illustration of this resentment of state taxes is the taxpayer's revolt which has caused the sharp increase in the number of local bond issues defeated across the country in the past several years. An alarming number of school districts have been forced to fire teachers and reduce education budgets because of the widespread defeat of local school bond elections. These defeats illustrate the fact that while the voters may feel that they do not have much impact on national fiscal policy, they can and do express themselves locally. This negative attitude to the expenses of state and local government has been one of the causes for the drift in power to Washington. There seems to be a feeling on the part of many people that if the federal government will pick up the tab for part or all of certain vital services, somehow they will get out of having to pay for it. Much of the cost is made up, of course, by rising federal taxes. Then, with federal direction of many programs, the complaint is heard that the national government is encroaching on the states, when in fact it is the states which have abdicated responsibility to the federal government.

A primary aspect of this state and local abdication of responsibility has to do with financing the costs of government. The federal government's income is made up largely of individual and corporate income tax, revenues which tend to keep ahead of the overall growth in the economy. Most states, on the other hand, have continued to rely on a combination of regressive taxes, such as the sales tax, and the federal government for their income. As the states rely more and more on federal grants-in-aid and revenue-sharing to pay their bills, their leadership possibilities are proportionately reduced. The point is that this role is more limited than it would be if there were more dynamic leadership in the states and more willingness to accept the responsibility for initiating and financing imaginative state and local programs of education, research, welfare, urban renewal, job retraining, and the like. And even though such leadership has been lacking at the state level, the states and localities do continue to provide the bulk of basic services, as Table 7-2 shows. Thus, state and local governments are still very much in the picture,

Table 7-2. Expenditures for selected program areas by level of government, 1970

	Federal	State	Local
Education	11%	39%	50%
Fire protection	1	1	98
Health and hospitals	31	36	33
Highways	20	57	23
Public welfare	34	44	22
Natural resources	76	19	5
Housing	55	2	43

Source: Adapted from U.S. Bureau of the Census, *Statistical Abstract of the United States, 1972*, p. 411.

and unless they abdicate responsibility completely, they are likely to remain so.

What about raising the money to pay the costs of services at the state and local levels? Where does the money come from? As can be seen from Table 7-3, most of these revenues come from taxes of various sorts. Although most states at one time depended on the property tax as their primary source of income, this tax today is used by the cities, counties, and special districts rather than state governments. As the table shows, local levels of government still derive more than $30 billion from property taxes, which remain for them the primary source of income. But there are several problems with continuing reliance on the property tax. After a certain point this becomes a regressive tax; it hurts the poor more than the wealthy, and it discourages people from owning or improving their property. Further, since property taxes are so immediate and painful—typically having to be paid in a lump sum once or twice a year—they are the focal point for "taxpayer revolts" mentioned above. Finally, there is a legal problem with this tax as with any local tax; it frequently requires a special election, or "tax override," to allow the rates to be raised, and the voters very often defeat such measures at the polls. Without other sources of revenue to tap, and without authority to raise the property tax rate, local governments find themselves in an unsolvable bind. Then they, like state governments, may turn to outside sources (in this case state and federal governments) for financial aid. In fiscal 1971, over $34 billion of local revenue came from the federal and state governments ($3.4 and $31.0 billion, respectively), accounting for over 37 percent of their total revenues. So cities, counties, and special districts are even more dependent on grants-in-aid than state governments.

Table 7-3. Governmental revenue, by source and level of government, 1970–1971 (in billions of dollars)

	All governments	Federal government	State and local governments		
			Total	State	Local
Total revenue[a]	342.5	202.5	198.1	97.2	100.9
Intergovernmental revenue	—	—	58.3	23.8	34.5
Revenue from own sources	342.5	202.5	139.9	73.4	66.5
Taxes, total	232.3	137.3	94.9	51.5	43.4
Personal Income	98.1	86.2	12.0	10.2	1.8
Corporate Income	30.2	26.8	3.4	3.4	—
Property	37.9	—	37.8	1.1	36.7
Customs duties	2.6	2.6	—	—	—
General sales	17.8	—	17.8	15.5	2.3
Selective sales[b]	32.3	16.8	15.4	14.1	1.3
Other taxes[c]	13.4	4.8	8.6	7.3	1.3
Charges and miscellaneous[d]	43.4	19.6	23.9	9.8	14.1
Current charges	29.3	12.4	16.9	7.1	9.8
All other	14.1	7.2	6.9	2.7	4.2
Utility revenue	7.3	—	8.1	.8	7.3
Liquor stores revenue	2.1	—	2.1	1.8	.3
Insurance trust revenue	57.5	45.7	11.8	10.3	1.5

[a] Net of duplicative intergovernmental transactions.
[b] Includes taxes on gasoline, alcohol, tobacco, and public utilities.
[c] Includes taxes on vehicles, operators' licenses, inheritance, and gifts.
[d] Income from international sales, postal services, hospitals, parks, and transportation facilities.

Source: Adapted from U.S. Bureau of the Census, *Government Finances in 1970–1971*, USGPO, 1972.

The sources of state revenue have become quite diverse, although a few generalizations can be made. Most states today rely to a large extent on a general sales tax ranging anywhere from 1 to 6 percent of the commodity price. Selective sales taxes on items such as gasoline, alcoholic beverages, tobacco, and public ultilities provide another major source of state income. Taken together, these sales taxes, amounting to some $42 billion in 1970, account for about one third of all revenues derived by the states from their own sources. Another form of state revenue which is gaining wider use is the personal and corporate income tax. In 1970 one dollar in seven collected by the states came from this

Table 7-4. Federal aid to state and local governments: 1972
(in millions of dollars; comprises federal funds and trust funds)

Type of aid, function, and major program		1972
Total Grants-In-Aid and shared revenue		39,080
Agriculture and rural development[1]		972
Removal of surplus commodities	638	
Rural water and waste disposal facilities	53	
Cooperative state research service	75	
Cooperative agricultural extension work	150	
Natural resources and environment[1]		1,450
Watershed protection and flood prevention	87	
National forest and grassland shared revenue	58	
Waste treatment works and pollution control	965	
Fish and wildlife restoration and management	62	
Land and water conservation fund	110	
Commerce and transportation[1]		5,605
Economic development	167	
Highway programs	4,742	
Urban transportation	261	
Federal-aid airport program	131	
Appalachian development	279	
Community development and housing[1]		3,229
Community action programs	656	
Model city grants	439	
Water, sewer, and neighborhood facilities	165	
Low-rent public housing	845	
Urban renewal	1,000	
Urban planning and open space	119	
Education and manpower[1]		6,798
Office of Economic Opportunity	203	
Elementary and secondary education	1,872	
Assistance to schools in federally affected areas	473	
Higher education activities	223	
Vocational education	508	
Libraries and community services	77	
Manpower development and training activities	1,429	
Employment security programs	832	
Work incentive	187	
Emergency employment assistance	651	
Health[1]		5,672
Mental Health	224	
Health services planning and development	317	
Health services delivery	469	
Preventive health services	7	
Health manpower	252	
Medical assistance	4,401	

Table 7-4. (*continued*)

Type of aid, function, and major program		1972
Income security[1]		12,144
Income maintenance	7,197	
Social services	1,440	
Vocational rehabilitation	588	
Food stamps	2,002	
Child nutrition and special milk	749	
Law enforcement assistance		362
General revenue sharing		2,250

[1] Includes programs not shown separately.

Source: Adapted from U.S. Bureau of the Census, *Statistical Abstract of the United States, 1972* p. 413. Based on figures from U.S. Office of Management and Budget.

source. The state income tax parallels the federal income tax although from the income for computation of federal income tax. The federal income tax law, incidentally, has the effect of subsidizing the state governments since the amount of state income tax paid is deductible from the income for computation of federal income tax. The federal government is willing to forgo a portion of the federal income tax in deference to taxes collected by the state; so when a state raises its income tax, the federal government takes a smaller share from the incomes of persons and corporations in that state. Other lucrative state taxes include those on motor vehicles, inheritance, and gifts. In New York and New Hampshire, state lotteries have been set up to supplement other sources of income. The relative mix of these various revenues differs from state to state, with increasing reliance being placed on sales taxes and the income tax in the more populous states.

Revenue Sharing

A revolutionary new approach for helping to finance state and local government is *revenue sharing*. First proposed by President Nixon as early as 1969, it wasn't enacted by Congress until 1972. Several proposals similar to Nixon's revenue sharing have been debated for many years. One of them was the Heller Plan, named after its author, Walter W. Heller, chairman of the Council of Economic Advisers under Kennedy and Johnson. His proposal, in essence, would return a certain portion of revenues from the federal government's income tax to the states.[3] Nixon's plan is similar to Heller's except that the monies to be transferred come out of *all* revenue and are not put into a special trust fund before being distributed to states, counties, and localities. The basis for distribution is more complex than a straight per capita formula, also taking into account the state's effort to raise its own revenue and the special problems of states with lower income per capita. The Nixon propsal was initially opposed by several powerful members of Congress, such as Wilbur Mills (D.–Ark), Chairman of the House Ways and Means Committee, on the grounds that the level of government which raises the money ought to account for how it is spent (i.e., set up guidelines). The opposition of Mills and others was eventually overcome and revenue sharing was passed.

There has always been, however, some sharing of revenue among various levels of government. In fiscal 1970 as shown in Table 7-2, more than $72 billion of federal money was transferred to state and local governments. Being channeled through grants-in-aid programs of several types rather than bloc grants to states as in revenue sharing, this money constituted more than 16 percent of all state and local revenue. Revenue sharing, in addition to untying many of the strings of grants-in-aid, involves the transfer of increasingly large sums of money. In the initial revenue sharing bill passed in 1972 $30 billion was allotted for a five year period, 1973–78, in direct bloc grants to state and local units of government. At the present time it appears as though many grants-in-aid programs will continue as in the past, with federal money and federal guidelines, while bloc grants without strings under revenue sharing will increase in size and significance over the next several years.

STATE POLITICS VERSUS NATIONAL POLITICS

The feeling is often expressed that politics at the state and local level is somehow better and more democratic than national politics. The sad truth is, however, that most citizens know very little about the problems and issues of their state, county, or city. To the extent that there is a concern with local matters, many of the observations made in Chapter 8 about national public opinion would apply. Apathy, misinformation, and lack of involvement, which characterize national politics, are even more true of state and local politics. Moreover, in many states, apathy

---

[3] This plan is outlined in Professor Heller's book *New Dimensions of Political Economy* (Cambridge, Mass.: Harvard University Press, 1966).

is encouraged by the political system; for example, long ballots—or "bedsheet ballots," as they are often referred to—complicate the job of the voter in many states. In some states, for example, it is not unusual for the citizens to have to choose:

Federal	*State*	*Local*
President	State Assemblyman	County Supervisor
Vice President	State Senator	County Sheriff
U.S. Congressman	Governor	Tax Assessor
U.S. Senator	Lieutenant-Governor	Treasurer
	State Attorney	Coroner
	General	Surveyor
	Secretary of State	County Superinten-
	Treasurer	dent of Schools
	Controller	County Board of
	Superintendent of	Education Member
	Public Instruction	County Clerk
	Board of Equalization	County Recorder
	Member	Local Judges

In addition, he may have to vote on as many as twenty state propositions (constitutional amendments and statutory initiatives), along with county- and city-charter amendment proposals. No wonder it is referred to as the bedsheet ballot! This discouraging barrage of names and issues overcomes all but the most dedicated citizens. Others are likely to vote for the national candidates and perhaps a candidate for governor and let it go at that.

Apathy in politics at the state and local level is also encouraged by the restrictions on political organizations found in many state constitutions. A number of states put limitations on political parties which, although they might seem innocuous, have the effect of preventing the parties from exercising any real political power. A typical provision is that forbidding parties from endorsing candidates in primary elections or raising more than a certain amount of money for campaign activities. By allowing individuals to run in party primaries even though they may have little or no loyalty to the official party organization itself, the state constitution discourages unified and responsible political parties. What is the use in working for the party if it is powerless to get "its man" nominated? Note that this difficulty is much less apparent in national politics, for national politicians often sponsor or help a congressional or senatorial candidate to win his party's nomination. They may even use campaign funds of the national party organization for such a purpose.

But in state politics, the help of the party organization—at least in the primary—is useless in many states. Likewise the restrictions on campaign expenditures by the parties encourage candidates to look elsewhere for financial support, for example, to volunteer political organizations, further diluting the effectiveness and unity of the official parties.

Partisanship is generally less pronounced in state and local politics than it is at the national level. Consequently even though the voters usually make their choices of president, congressman, and United States senator predominantly on the basis of partisan consideration, they are less likely to do so in choosing state and local officials and in deciding on programs of state and local government. Nonrational factors, such as a candidate's name or his physical appearance, and arbitrary factors, such as a candidate's occupational designation, which is often quite misleading, are likely to play an ever greater role in state and local politics than in national. Likewise, the advantage of being an incumbent, which is substantial in national politics, is overwhelming in state and local politics. In addition, in many states elections are nonpartisan at some levels of government. County supervisors and city councilmen, for example, often run for office without party labels. This is even true for statewide constitutional officials in some states. In the past it was thought that this nonpartisan approach would induce people to look for factors other than party label, such as the candidate's qualifications, his experience, and so on. On the contrary, it has been shown that by removing the party label, the last vestige of rational choice has been removed, leaving the voter to choose among the candidates on completely nonrational grounds. It can be said in favor of partisanship that if the voter chooses on this basis, at least he will have some general idea about the politics of the man he selects even if he knows nothing else about him.

Political issues at the state level are very likely to center around urban versus rural interests. Thus it is not unusual in state legislatures to find urban Democrats and urban Republicans getting together in an attempt to deal with metropolitan problems and being confronted with rural Republicans and rural Democrats who oppose these efforts. A great deal of legislation favored by the urban majority in many states has for years been blocked by the rural minority. This deadlock was possible because of the malapportionment of one or both houses; a majority of legislators were elected from sparsely settled rural districts. This picture was decisively changed by two Supreme Court rulings mentioned in Chapters 4 and 6: *Baker* v. *Carr* (1962) and *Reynolds* v. *Sims* (1964). The struggle between urban and rural interests goes on, but by 1970 rural predominance had been replaced in most state legislatures by the predominance of representatives from the more populous urban and suburban districts. This profound change was the direct result of *federal* judicial intervention. State legislatures, for the first time responsive to the interests of the urban majority, have ceased to reflect the rural bias that has been their trademark for generations.

The Environment—A Case Study in Intergovernmental Relations

The political battle over the environment that has gone on since the mid 1960s illustrates much of what we have said about intergovernmental relations. First, state and local governments, with several notable exceptions, have not done very much to deal with the problem. When there has been local action it has often come about either because of lawsuits forcing localities to act or because of legislation passed by the initiative process. A classic example of a successful environmental lawsuit was the 1972 Friends of Mamouth decision in California. The California Supreme Court in that case ruled that under 1970 environmental (state) legislation all developers, public *and private*, would have to file environmental impact reports on any development of substantial scope. This decision clearly went beyond the intentions of the state lawmakers who, later that year, granted the building industry a reprieve by suspending the impact report requirement indefinitely.

Another example of privately initiated environmental political action was the passage of the Coastline Initiative in California in the 1972 election. After years of indifference, then inaction and stalemate by the legislature, outraged citizens wrote their own legislation to protect the endangered coastline. The problem with this sort of approach to solving environmental problems is that it is cumbersome and inefficient. Many crisis areas may not be dealt with at all, and in others the particular solution may not be a very balanced one—for instance restricting the building of new power plants along the coast without imposing any limits on such construction elsewhere in the state.

These faltering approaches to environmental protection highlight the inability or unwillingness of state and local governments to act on a vital problem. The reason for their inaction or even hostility to policies in this area is in large part a reflection of how these governments are chosen and who they are. There has always been in the politics of most cities what could be called the "Chamber of Commerce" bias. Local government tends to mystify most people, as attested to by the dismal voter turnout in most local elections—averaging around 25 percent of those eligible. Those who do vote tend to be people with property and business interests in the city. In general, they are not the people who are taking the lead in pressing the environmental issue. To put it differently the 25 percent of the people who participate in local politics are not a random sample of the whole electorate; their views are not representative of the entire community. The same kind of bias is often reflected in the statehouse, in spite of somewhat higher levels of citizen interest and involvement, because most statewide politicians are local politicians who have "moved up."

Many environmental groups have found a better reception by national leaders—both in Congress and in the executive bureaucracy—because these men and women are much more visible than state and local leaders. Also, national leaders are responsible to a different kind of constituency. Instead of the local business leaders who tend to control local and, to some extent state, politics, national politicians tend to be responsive to a broader coalition of interests. On environmental issues, as is often the case, the dividing lines are not strictly partisan. Even though Democrats control most statehouses, they have not been at the forefront on this issue. A major victory in the battle to save the environment was won by President Nixon, a Republican, with the passage of his Environmental Protection Act of 1970.

The Environment Protection Art further exemplifies the process of federal policy initiation and state implementation. Money is channeled to the states and local agencies of government for a whole range of pollution control and related activities. Here, as in other areas of government spending, the expenditures at the state and local levels have increased substantially but the initiative for and direction of the various aspects of the program is federal—primarily, in this case, from the Environmental Protection Agency.

Some of the federal assumption of responsibility on this question may have been inevitable. Some problems, and this may be one, are primarily national problems. On the matter of air pollution control devices for cars, the Detroit automobile makers have long insisted that they could not and should not be required to have to comply with different regulations in each state, let alone each local air pollution control district. While some critics accused the automakers of using this argument as an excuse to delay development of effective emission controls, one can see the impossibility of having to meet different emission standards in each state. This aspect of pollution control, then, shows one kind of pressure for a national program.

With regard to financing the battle to save the environment, the pattern is similar to that discussed above for federal–state–local finances in general. First, the federal government's revenue sources are clearly greater than those of states and localities. Second, money has gone to the states sometimes as direct grants and in other cases requiring matching funds. Third, state and local expenditures (including monies received from the federal government) on the environment are increasing more rapidly than what the federal government spends through its own agencies. Overall spending for environmental protection by the federal government increased more than fourfold from 1969 to 1973, from $52 million to over $315 million.

Fourth, the president's programs on environmental protection have often seen the federal government stepping into what had been state problems when the states were either unwilling or unable to act. Because of federal action between 1969–1972: oil drilling was temporarily stopped in the Santa Barbara Channel in California, and later allowed to proceed under strict controls; a jetport proposed for the Florida Everglades was cancelled; a Cross-Florida Barge Canal was stopped; the use of DDT throughout the United States was almost entirely eliminated; and commercial whaling has been completely halted.

Finally, the willingness and ability of the President and Congress to act where governors and state legislatures did not in part reflects the structural flexibility of the national government. In some states and localities bitter, and often losing, battles have been fought to impose controls on pollution and developments which would drastically alter the environment. At the national level, President Nixon made environmental protection a major theme for his administration. Many of the actions taken did not require congressional approval. Others, such as the passage in 1970 of the National Environmental Policy Act which established the powerful Environmental Protection Agency, brought about a major structural change through legislation rather than constitutional amendment. In many states this would not have been possible; in most cities and metropolitan areas the formation of such an agency would require a charter amendment or an entirely new layer of government.

GLOSSARY

Bloc grants   Lump sum payments by the federal government to the states based on population, tax effort, and other factors. States may use the money on any programs they choose.

Chamber of Commerce bias   The domination of local politics by businessmen and property oriented people.

Chief administrative officer   Local government official appointed by and responsible to an elected body such as a city council or a county board of supervisors.

Cooperative federalism The process by which state and local projects are initiated by and financed by the federal government.

Grants-in-aid Federal money given to the states for specific programs (also called categorical grants-in-aid or functional grants).

Environmentalist A person who places a higher priority on saving natural physical surroundings than on development or economic growth.

Nonpartisanship A feature of political life in many local elections which prohibits participation by formal party organizations.

Revenue sharing A program of bloc grants from the federal government to the states first begun in 1972.

States' rights Rights and powers claimed for the various state governments (especially in the areas of health, education, and welfare programs), with the implication that the federal government should not be involved.

SUGGESTIONS FOR FURTHER READING

ADRIAN, CHARLES R. *Governing Our Fifty States and their Communities.* New York: McGraw-Hill, 1972.

ANDERSON, WILLIAM. *The Nation and the States: Rivals of Partners?* Minneapolis: University of Minnesota Press, 1955.

BANFIELD, EDWARD C., and JAMES Q. WILSON. *City Politics.* Cambridge: Harvard University Press, 1963.

BANFIELD, EDWARD C. *The Unheavenly City.* Boston: Little, Brown, 1970.

BOLLENS, JOHN C. *Special District Government in the United States.* Berkeley: University of California Press, 1957.

DAHL, ROBERT A. *Who Governs?* New Haven: Yale University Press, 1961.

GULICK, LUTHER H. *The Metropolitan Problem and American Ideals.* New York: Knopf, 1962.

KEY, V. O., JR. *American State Politics.* New York: Knopf, 1956.

MAIER, HENRY W. *Challenge to the Cities.* New York: Random House, 1966.

MUMFORD, LEWIS *The City in History.* New York: Harcourt, Brace, 1961.

RANSOME, COLEMAN B., JR. *The Office of Governor in the United States.* University, Ala.: University of Alabama Press, 1956.

RIKER, WILLIAM. *Federalism: Origin, Operation, Significance.* Boston: Little, Brown, 1964.

ROCKEFELLER, NELSON A. *The Future of Federalism.* Cambridge: Harvard University Press, 1962.

REAGAN, MICHAEL D. *The New Federalism.* New York: Oxford University Press, 1973.

SCOTT, STANLEY. *Streamlining State Legislatures.* Berkeley: University of California Press, 1956.

Chapter 8
Parties and Pressure Groups

Political parties are essential to democracy. They provide ideas, programs, and personnel for the orderly and responsible process of government. Clinton Rossiter quite properly maintains that the "primary function of a political party in a democracy such as ours is to control and direct the struggle for power."[1] In other words, politics is a contest, or a struggle, between groups contending for the voters' favor by making certain promises or by offering certain solutions to problems that require governmental action.

Political parties are a relatively modern phenomenon, having existed for less than two centuries; their arrival on the political scene roughly corresponds with the development of modern democracy. As Rossiter suggests: "Parties and democracy arose together; they have lived and prospered in a closely symbiotic relationship; and if one should weaken and die, the other would die with it."[2] Political factions developed in England in the latter part of the seventeenth century. At

---

[1] *Parties and Politics in America* (Ithaca, N.Y.: Cornell University Press, 1960), p. 39.
[2] *Parties and Politics in America*, p. 67.

that time the king, for financial purposes primarily, began to organize his supporters into a coherent coalition. Those who opposed the king's· demands also banded together to form a more effective opposition. The groups were soon labeled Tories and Whigs. The tendency of political forces to polarize into two major parties has remained in England to this day. At first, these English factions were not genuine political parties. They were not interested in nor capable of developing comprehensive programs and electing officials to public office. Their functions were more like those of today's interest or pressure groups, which are discussed in the second part of this chapter.

In the United States, political divisions assumed form early in the history of the nation. It has been suggested (as quoted in Chapter 3) that American political parties were born during the constitutional convention at Philadelphia in 1787. There, two groups emerged: one, the Federalists, supported a constitution favoring a strong central government; the other group, the anti-Federalists, insisted on a weak and decentralized authority. On the other hand, as Professor Rossiter indicates, political tendencies like those in England existed in the American colonies even before the debates and arguments over the Constitution. Yet genuine political parties had their birth in the 1790s and early 1800s —in spite of efforts by prominent early Americans, including George Washington, to dissuade their fellow countrymen from following what were considered the destructive tendencies of political division.

How can one define the term *political party*? As with much else in politics, a precise definition is virtually impossible. Yet there are two qualities or attributes that seem to characterize all political parties. The primary reason for the existence of a political party is to elect some of its members or followers to public office. From this, another feature of political parties arises. Political parties in democratic societies are interested in taking control and running the government for a certain period of time. It can be said, therefore, that the true purpose of political parties is leading and controlling the struggle for political power, to use Rossiter's terms.

THE MAIN FEATURES OF AMERICAN POLITICAL PARTIES

Historically, three features in particular have characterized the party system of the United States: (1) lack of ideology; (2) two major parties alternating in power; (3) decentralization and lack of party discipline. These three lasting characteristics require closer examination.

Lack of Ideology

Political scientists generally agree that modern political parties fall into two broad categories: those based on a set of ideological principles or designs, and those that appeal to the electorate with a general program. American political parties usually fall into the second category. This is not to suggest that they always adhere to a program. The fact is that American politics has been largely devoid of ideology. Moreover, it can be demonstrated that whenever ideology attempted to enter the American political process, it was rejected. The term *ideology* is used here as defined in Chapter 1: an all-encompassing system of belief.

There are several notable examples of the failure of ideology in American politics. One was the Populist movement of the 1890s. It was a federation of the Farmers' Alliance and the Knights of Labor. These groups founded the Peoples' Party in 1892 and supported the Democratic nominee for the presidency, William Jennings Bryan, in 1896. Populism failed to attract a widespread following, and eventually disappeared from the political scene, its members finding a home in one of the two major parties. It reached its high-water mark in 1894 with the election of six senators and seven representatives to Congress.

Another attempt at an ideological party occurred in 1912. Then the so-called Progressives followed former President Theodore Roosevelt when he left the Republican National Convention. Troubled by concentrations of economic and political power, the Progressives were attracted by T.R.'s exaggerated reputation as a trust-buster and foe of political bosses. Although Roosevelt as the Progressive candidate polled more votes than the regular Republican Taft, the split in the opposition brought victory to Democratic candidate Woodrow Wilson. The Progressives continued to be a factor in national politics through 1924, but after that they were absorbed by the two major parties.

In 1948 the Democratic presidential candidate, Harry S. Truman, faced challengers from both the right and left wings of his party. Senator Strom Thurmond, nominated by the Dixiecrats, and former Vice President Henry A. Wallace, nominated by a new Progressive Party. Although each of the "ideological candidates" polled well over a million votes, President Truman defeated his Republican opponent.

Senator Barry Goldwater tried, in 1964, to imbue the Republican party and the nation with the spirit and force of a "conservative" ideology. Although he gained enough devoted followers to secure the Republican presidential nomination, he lost the election by a landslide. In 1972, the Democrats nominated Senator George McGovern who was branded a "radical" and therefore "ideological" candidate. He received 38 percent of the national vote while President Nixon's total was 61 percent. The implications from such examples are clear: American voters seem to prefer somewhat vague and ambiguous party programs or platforms to the demands and rigors of political ideology.

Two-Party System

A second important feature of the American party system is its propensity to maintain the two-party structure. From the early days of the Republic, two political groupings emerged, beginning with the Federalists and the anti-Federalists, and two major parties have alternated in power to the present, when the contest for political power is waged between the Republicans and the Democrats. While third and fourth parties have appeared from time to time, and continue to appear, they have been conspicuous by their inability to attract voters in large enough numbers to enable them to assume political power. In most cases, these minor parties were assimilated by the larger two or just faded away never to be heard of again. In most instances, the system reverted to its dual pattern. There are three exception to this dual pattern:

1. In one-party states and districts, mentioned in Chapter 1 in connection with committee chairmanships in Congress, factions within the dominant party may serve the role of opposition. In addition, since 1964 there appears to be a resurgence of Republican strength in the South.
2. The number of voters who consider themselves "independent" has increased markedly in recent years (see Fig. 8-1).
3. In a few states, third parties have long played an important role in state politics. For example, in New York the Liberal party and in Minnesota the Farm-Labor party have on occasion held the balance of power between the two major parties.

One of the most persistent questions in American politics is the one demanding an explanation for the two-party system. Political scientists, however, have been unable to provide a completely satisfactory explanation for the existence and the persistence of the dualism in American political parties. Although no single explanation for the American two-party system has been empirically validated, various hypotheses have been offered, of which several will be examined below.

As has been indicated, American political parties emerged during and immediately following the constitutional convention, when those who supported the new constitutional order were divided about what should be its scope. One political scientist has suggested that the Constitution split the nation into two camps, a condition retained to this day inasmuch as "Human institutions have an impressive capacity to perpetuate themselves or at least to preserve their form."[3]

Observers of the American political scene, both foreign and domestic, note that among the factors which aid the two-party system, or at least discourage the development of a multiparty system, the single-member constituency with plurality elections is one of the most obvious. The United States, as noted in Chapter 3, is divided into 435 congressional districts. Each district sends a representative to Congress. Each state is allocated seats in the House of Representatives on the basis of its population at the time of the last federal census, which is taken at ten-year intervals. Every state has a minimum of one representative in Congress, while the maximum number representing it depends on its population relative to that of other states. In a few states, some congressmen are elected "at large." This means that the entire voting population of the state chooses the "at large" congressman; the entire state becomes his constituency. In addition, each state, large or small, has two senators in Washington. From each of the 435 congressional districts, only one person is elected even though any number of candidates may appear on the ballot. If, as an example, four candidates are on the ballot, the one who receives the most votes is elected. The winner does not have to receive more than half of the total vote, that is, a majority; a simple plurality will do.

This method of congressional election handicaps third parties inasmuch as the established parties and their candidates are given both a legal and a psychological advantage. Most people vote for a candidate who, they think, has a chance to win; in voting for a hopeful candidate of a minor party, typical voters feel that they are wasting their votes. Thus third parties in an established two-party system have a rather slim chance for success.

The low intensity of the American political contest is offered as another hypothesis for the two-party system. It has been suggested, and empirical voting studies have shown, that the vast majority of American voters are not interested in the issues that divide political parties; they are even less interested in the nuances that separate them. Instead, a large number of people believe that the difference between one party and the other is not especially significant. This situation arises from the fact

[3] V. O. Key, Jr., *Politics, Parties, and Pressure Groups* (New York: Crowell, 1964), p. 207.

that the individual voter normally does not feel that he will be personally affected by the election outcome. In other words, a vast majority do not consider victory by their party vital to the maintenance of a livelihood. There have been notable exceptions to this generalization; for example, the "white backlash" of voters who feel that their jobs or their property values are threatened by blacks. Politicians, under these conditions, have learned to refrain from taking rigid positions that might cost them votes, and most campaign oratory is shallow and very general. When there is widespread popular concern about an issue—such as there was about the war in Vietnam—the established parties usually produce candidates who meet that concern, at least on a verbal level. As long as both major political parties offer to confront the problems and to provide for the needs of society, third and fourth parties will seem unnecessary.

Lack of Party Discipline

The third characteristic feature of American political parties—one which upsets many political scientists and some political leaders—is the undisciplined nature of the parties. This feature is directly attributable to the nonexistence of strong, central party organizations. The federal structure of government and the diversity of America make it possible for individual politicians to build their own political power base without regard to the policies or programs of the national party organizations. Since a congressman, and to a lesser degree, a senator, is sent to Washington to represent the interests of his district or state, rather than the interests of the nation as a whole, it follows that so long as he does an adequate job in that respect his prospects for reelection are good. Thus it is not at all unusual for individual congressmen and senators to be elected under a party label and to vote against the party's programs in Congress. Senator Jacob Javits, Republican of New York, votes with the Democrats more often than with his own party. Similarly, Senator James Eastland, Democrat of Mississippi, has a voting record which is more in line with conservative Republican attitudes than with Democratic party stands.

In Great Britain, where political parties are highly centralized and strongly disciplined, neither Javits nor Eastland would have much of a chance for reelection. The respective party organizations and leadership would not support them, and without central party support a British candidate is as good as defeated. In the United States, individual political figures are able to develop their own base of support and thus can disregard the desires of their party.

Students of the American political process have shown concern for the condition of party politics, especially for the apparent lack of discipline in the two major parties. This lack of discipline, it is suggested, leads to party irresponsibility insofar as party leaders are not bound to adhere to platform planks and carry out campaign promises.

In 1950, the Committee on Political Parties of the American Political Science Association published the results of an exhaustive study of American political parties and offered suggestions for reforms that would lead, as the title of the study indicates, *Toward a More Responsible Two-Party System.*[4] The committee made several recommendations for reforms which, had they been followed, would have contributed toward making parties in the United States more responsive to the popular will. One of the suggestions, for instance, was to emulate the British system and make a party's programs binding on all those elected under the party's label. Needless to say, suggestions such as this have largely fallen on deaf ears. But there still may be some hope. Parties and politicians are inclined to respond to the desires of the majority whenever these desires are apparent and easily identifiable—which is true only at infrequent intervals. The passage of a vast array of "Great Society" legislation in the years 1964–1966 provides ample testimony of what can be done.

HOW AMERICANS VOTE—DEMOCRATIC THEORY VERSUS AMERICAN PRACTICE

In 1948, three social scientists undertook a detailed study of the voting behavior of 1000 voters in the city of Elmira, New York.[5] Their findings shed light on some of the factors that determine the voting habits of the American electorate. Religious affiliation, socioeconomic class, ethnic background, and age were among the various categories that proved to be predictive of voting behavior. In some instances, the Elmira study confirmed certain popular notions about the American voter. For example, relatively recent immigrant groups (such as Italian-Americans) and minority groups (such as blacks) voted predominantly Democratic. The study also found that religious affiliation played an important role as a determinant of American voting behavior, despite popular notions to the contrary. Catholics, for example, no matter what their class status, professional identification, or ideological orientation in a conservative-liberal spectrum, were more likely to vote Democratic than were Protestants in similar circumstances.

---

[4] New York: Holt, Rinehart and Winston, 1950.
[5] Bernard Berelson et al., *Voting: A Study of Opinion Formation in a Presidential Campaign* (Chicago: University of Chicago Press, 1954).

Berelson and his colleagues also examined and exposed the myths and the realities of American political behavior.[6] The generalizations they drew indicated a wide chasm between democratic political theory and actual political practice. Traditional political theorists, among them Aristotle, Locke, Jefferson, and John Stuart Mill, have written that democratic man is expected to fulfill certain obligations and responsibilities toward the system or society in which he lives. Classical democratic theory, then, assumes that the "typical" citizen of a democracy must take an active interest in the politics of his society. He must know the issues confronting him and his fellow men; he must know how political power is wielded; and he must choose wisely and prudently among alternative policies or courses of action. How do the findings in Berelson's study stack up to these expectations? In order to illustrate the discrepancy between theory and practice, the five qualities considered by classical political theorists as essential to the health and vitality of the democratic process will be discussed: interest, discussion, motivation, knowledge, and principle.[7]

INTEREST

Democratic Theory

The democratic individual is supposed to be interested and to participate in the affairs of his community (be it his city, state, or nation). This he does by contributing money to candidates or political parties, by arguing politics, and by voting.

American Practice

Berelson and his colleagues write that "the majority of the people vote, but in general they do not give evidence of sustained interest. Many vote without real involvement in the election, and even the party workers are not typically motivated by ideological concerns or plain civic duty."

DISCUSSION

Democratic Theory

The democratic citizen is expected to discuss and debate the issues with his family, friends, and co-workers.

American Practice

The Elmira study found that "there was little true discussion between the candidates, little in the newspaper commentary, little between the voters and the official party representatives, some within the electorate. On the grass-roots level there was more talk than debate."

[6] *Voting,* Chapter 14, "Democratic Practice and Democratic Theory."
[7] *Voting,* pp. 307–309.

MOTIVATION

Democratic Theory

There is an assumption that the citizen is strongly motivated for participation in the politics of his community.

American Practice

The Elmira research discovered that "for large numbers of people motivation is weak if not almost absent . . . The ballot is cast, and for most people that is the end of it. If their side is defeated, it doesn't really matter."

KNOWLEDGE

Democratic Theory

The citizen of a democracy is expected to be well informed on the issues affecting the life of his community.

American Practice

The Elmira study showed: "The citizen is not highly informed on details of the campaign, nor does he avoid a certain misconception of the political situation when it is to his psychological advantage to do so. The electorate's perception of what goes on in the campaign is colored by emotional feeling toward one or the other issue, candidate, party, or social group."

PRINCIPLE

Democratic Theory

There is an assumption that citizens will cast their vote on the basis of principle and after careful consideration of all the alternatives; that their decision will be rational rather than impulsive or emotional.

American Practice

The Elmira researchers conclude: "Many voters vote not for principle in the usual sense but 'for' a group to which they are attached— their group . . . The ordinary voter, bewildered by the complexity of modern political problems, unable to determine clearly what the consequences are of alternative lines of action, remote from the arena, and incapable of bringing information to bear on principle, votes the way trusted people around him are voting."

The foregoing is intended to demonstrate that the difference between democratic theory and practice in American politics may be significant; some argue that any discrepancy is frightening and potentially harmful to the political system. Critical commentators on American politics often decry the fact that a sizable portion of the electorate—as much as 35 percent in typical presidential elections and more than half in local contests—either cannot or do not exercise their voting privilege. How, their argument goes, can majority rule prevail when so many of those eligible to vote never bother to go to the polls? On the other hand, political scientists point out that, while the number of voters does not meet the classical requirements for majority rule, the system as a whole has shown a remarkable ability to continue, and in many regards to prosper, despite the apparent insufficiency of interest. Social scientists have argued that the political system might in fact suffer, because of misinformation, if all those eligible to vote took part in elections.

Eligibility to vote is determined by the states, under the Constitution, though certain amendments limit the restrictions that states may impose. The Fifteenth Amendment (1870) provides that the right of citizens to vote "shall not be denied or abridged . . . on account of race, color, or previous condition of servitude." (The Fourteenth gave Congress power to reduce representation in the House proportionately for any denials of the franchise to males over twenty-one years of age, but this clause has never been invoked since it was ratified in 1868). The Nineteenth Amendment (1920), culminating a women's suffrage campaign begun in 1848, prohibits denial or abridgment of the right to vote on account of sex. All the states limit the right to vote to citizens, and all had requirements about age (usually twenty-one) until the adoption of the Twenty-sixth Amendment in 1971 which gave the right to vote to 18-year-olds, and length of residence (varying from six months to two years). Almost all states disqualify persons who have been convicted of certain crimes or who have been adjudged as mental incompetents. Before the Age of Jackson in the 1830s property-holding and taxpaying qualifications to vote were common, but these have largely disappeared.

Since World War II, concern about voting rights has focused on two large groups who have been disfranchised by requirements about registration to vote: members of social and ethnic minorities, especially blacks, and persons forced to change their residences in an increasingly mobile society. After the 1960 presidential election the public-opinion analyst Elmo Roper estimated that between 2.5 and 4 million citizens had been denied the right to vote because of racial or social discrimination, 3 million because they were out of the country, 5 million because of illness or disability, and 8 million because they had not established residence requirements in the states where they were living.[8]

---

[8] Elmo Roper, "How to Lose Your Vote," *Saturday Review*, March 18, 1961.

The most blatant trick for disenfranchising blacks, the "white primary," was upset by the Supreme Court in 1944, as will be seen in Chapter 9. Other devices for circumventing the Fifteenth Amendment, such as the discriminatory use of literacy tests, have been prohibited in civil-rights laws and in the Voting Rights Act of 1965. The Twenty-fourth Amendment (1964) forbids the denial of the right to vote in a federal election because of failure to pay "any poll tax or other tax." Although the problem of enfranchising ethnic and social minorities, including low-income whites, has not been solved completely, great progress has been made.

Less progress has been made in extending voting rights to the growing number of Americans on the move. State residency requirements prevent millions of citizens from registering—that is, getting on the voters' list which every state requires as a protection against fraudulent practices, once common, such as casting ballots for deceased, fictitious, or absent persons. Others are disenfranchised by inability to get to the polls because of travel or because of illness or disability. States vary in the amount of difficulty and inconvenience involved in registering to vote or in applying for an absentee ballot. Reforms designed to remove roadblocks against participation in elections are constantly being taken, at the urging of civic-minded groups, but a substantial fraction of the electorate undoubtedly would fail to vote regardless of how easy the process might be.

Although it is difficult to find justification for a lack of participation by a large part of the electorate in an essential phase of the democratic process, it has been argued that perhaps 10 to 15 percent of the total voting public might better not vote. Students of voting behavior describe as "cross-pressured" those persons whose psychological identifications conflict to the point that they tend to neutralize each other. An example is the upwardly mobile son of a factory worker born into a strong Democratic environment who completes his college education, gains a lucrative job, moves to the suburbs, and encounters new acquaintances with strong Republican sentiments. Some analysts argue that the cross-pressured voter may in fact be the most discriminating. Although he may be less decisive than others, his vote may be a more considered one than that of the person who votes the "straight party ticket"—not to mention the political illiterate, whose vote is wrung from him by the hand of an aggressive party worker. The phenomenon of the cross-pressured voter may be related to the recent sharp rise in the number of Americans who describe themselves as politically independent (discussed in the next section of this chapter). Whether cross-pressuring is more likely to lead to independence or to apathy is the question. Apathy may stem from a *lack* of interest—caused by ignorance, laziness, or selfishness—as well as from a conflict of interests. Whatever the source, when one considers that political contests are sometimes very close (John F. Kennedy won the Presidency in 1960 by approximately 113,000 votes of nearly 70 million cast and Richard Nixon won in 1968 by a margin of 325,000 of 72 million votes cast), the possibility for harm by the completely uninterested and "cross-pressured" becomes apparent. But Berelson and his colleagues conclude:

> The apathetic segment of America probably has helped to hold the system together and cushioned the shock of disagreement, adjustment, and change. But that is not to say that we can stand apathy without limit.[9]

THE SOCIAL BASES OF AMERICAN POLITICS

While public-opinion surveys usually show that there are some American voters who call themselves "independent," the majority are committed to one of the two major parties. In fact, people quite often do not hesitate to divulge their party affiliation even to strangers. One might say, moreover, that most Americans were "born" either Republicans or Democrats. This means simply that for most people the family is a powerful determinant of voting preference. Sociologists describe the

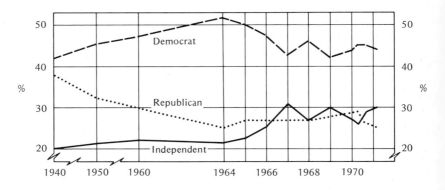

Figure 8-1.   Party affiliation: 1940–1971. In 1971 44 percent of all adults described themselves as Democrats, 26 percent as Republicans, and 30 percent called themselves independents. (From *The Gallup Report*, September, 1971.)

[9] *Voting*, p. 322.

family as the source of the most pervasive primary (face-to-face) group influence upon the individual.

Registration figures in states which require that the voter declare his party affiliation show that Democrats outnumber Republicans by a ratio of approximately 5 to 4. In October, 1971, the American Institute of Public Opinion (Gallup Poll) published the following figures concerning party affiliation: Democratic, 44 percent; Republican, 26 percent; Independent, 30 percent. The number of voters who identify themselves as Republicans has declined steadily since 1940. Conversely, the number of those who label themselves Independent has risen markedly in the same period. As of 1971 the Republican registration nationally was only 26 percent while independents constituted 30 percent. This does not mean that all those who are registered as Democrats always vote for Democratic candidates. If that were the case, very few Republicans would have a chance to be elected. It has been demonstrated that voters do not hesitate to cross party lines whenever it appears advantageous to do so. In 1952 and 1956, Dwight D. Eisenhower was elected president by near landslide majorities. In 1966, Ronald Reagan was elected governor of California by a plurality of almost 1 million votes over the incumbent Edmund G. Brown. In 1972, President Nixon's reelection assumed landslide proportions when one-third of the registered Democrats crossed party lines to support his candidacy. In all three instances, large numbers of Democrats were willing to cross party lines and vote for the candidate of the Republican party. Contemporary political scientists have classified elections such as these as "deviating." In other words, the personality of the candidate and/or the prevailing political mood caused voters to "deviate" from their declared party preference.

The 1972 congressional elections are more or less indicative of the strength of the two major parties in the American system. While the Republicans retained control of the presidency, the Democrats still outnumbered them 244 to 191 in the House of Representatives and 57 to 43 in the United States Senate.

WHO SUPPORTS WHOM

Although it is impossible to say with any degree of certainty that a particular group belongs to either the Democratic party or the Republican party, over the years certain group tendencies have become apparent.

Table 8-1. Party registrations. *Question: "If you had to register again today, would you register as a Democrat or as a Republican?"*

	July 15–18, 1971		
	Democrat	Republican	Don't Know
	%	%	%
National	44	30	26
Sex			
Male	46	30	24
Female	43	30	27
Race			
White	43	31	26
Nonwhite	67	11	22
Education			
College	38	38	24
High School	46	27	27
Grade School	50	26	24
Occupation			
Prof. & Bus.	38	37	25
White Collar	43	30	27
Farmers	39	45	16
Manual	49	23	28
Age			
18–20 years	38	26	36
21–29 years	45	24	31
30–49 years	47	29	24
50 & over	45	33	22
Politics			
Republican	4	86	10
Democrat	88	1	11
Independent	20	18	62
Region			
East	41	34	25
Midwest	42	32	26
South	53	24	23
West	42	27	31
Income			
$15,000 & over	40	38	22
$10,000–$14,999	42	31	27
$ 7,000–$ 9,999	45	29	26
$ 5,000–$ 6,999	45	26	29
$ 3,000–$ 4,999	44	26	30
Under $3,000	55	28	17
Community size			
1,000,000 over	43	23	34
500,000–999,999	49	22	29
50,000–499,999	47	30	23
2,500–49,999	42	35	23
Under 2,500 (rural)	43	33	24

Source: *Gallup Opinion Index*, September 1971.

Few will disagree, for example, with the assertion that the preponderant majority of blacks now support the Democratic party. But American political behavior is never clearcut and definitive. What may seem true today could very well change tomorrow. Until the election of Franklin D. Roosevelt in 1932, for example, most blacks voted consistently for the Republican party, which they associated with Lincoln and the Emancipation Proclamation. But since 1932 the Democratic party has claimed the overwhelming support of the black minority. With this reservation, Table 8-1 shows some of the most obvious traits of party affiliation.

PRESSURE GROUPS IN AMERICAN POLITICS

It goes without saying that the making of public policy in a complex society is a complicated matter. Policy making requires the interaction of many elements, groups, associations, and individuals. It also requires, in the end, a good deal of compromise and accommodation. One of the methods available for influencing the development and execution of government policy in a democracy is the application of organized pressure.

The application of pressure on government is something taken for granted in the American system. Groups and individuals have a variety of ways they can exert pressure and attempt to influence government policy. They may, for one thing, express approval of a government decision or policy by letters and other communications to elected officials and bureaucrats. Congressmen and administrators receive massive amounts of mail from organized pressure groups and from individuals. People may attempt to exercise influence by signing petitions which are then sent to those who make and execute policy; they may also write letters to editors of newspapers and magazines. All this activity implies that access to government policy in a democratic system is available to those who govern and to political parties and that it is possible for individuals and groups to exercise influence on public policy by the methods cited above. It is a recognized fact, however, that an organized pressure group can exert influence much more effectively than can isolated individuals.

The existence of groups with special interests in the American system of politics has been recognized from the early days of the Republic. In 1787, Madison wrote in *The Federalist*, No. 10, that groups with different interests (factions, he called them) would develop in the American system because they are inherent in the nature of man. Madison saw nothing terribly wrong in this development so long as there existed a variety of factions in the system in competition with each other. He felt that the most important task of government would be the regula-

NEW NATIONAL ANTHEM

Fitzpatrick in the St. Louis Post-Dispatch

tion of the competing interests of these groups. When the astute French nobleman and historian Alexis de Tocqueville visited the United States early in the nineteenth century, he was greatly impressed with what he considered a peculiarly American quality. As a people, he wrote in *Democracy in America,* Americans are characterized by a desire to form and belong to many different types of groups and associations. While de Tocqueville may have overstated the case, there are some characteristics of group behavior in American politics which bear examination.

The Objectives of Pressure Groups

Why do people organize into special-interest or pressure groups? There are many answers to this question, and they reflect the infinite variety of human desires, needs, aspirations, biases, and preferences. People have organized for political reasons, for economic purposes, along religious lines, on the basis of sex, by occupation or profession, by race, and so on. Pressure groups, in other words, reflect the great diversity or pluralism of American society. Thus the press reports how the American Federation of Labor–Congress of Industrial Organizations (AFL-CIO) pressured the government to increase the minimum wage and to extend the coverage of workers. There are also constant references to the work of such organizations as the National Association for the Advancement of Colored People in advancing the cause of civil rights. For twenty years after World War II, the American Medical Association (AMA)—an organization representing most of the nation's medical doctors—waged a campaign of pressure against passage of a medicare program, which was at last enacted by Congress in 1965. And there are groups like the League of Women Voters and Common Cause that are motivated primarily by an unselfish interest in better government. These are some examples of pressure-group activity from among the great number and variety of organized pressure groups operating within the American political system.

The Methods of Pressure Groups

The methods employed by organized pressure groups are many. Some are easily discernible; others are hidden beneath the surface of pressure-group activity. Generally, however, influence is exerted in three distinct ways. First, pressure groups work toward influencing public opinion. Second, they exert pressure on elected officials at all levels of government from the lowest (the city council) to the highest (the Congress of the United States). Finally, pressure groups attempt to influence those who are involved with the day-to-day operation of public policy, that is, administrators and bureaucrats.

Since politics in a democracy derives its strength from popular support, public opinion and how it forms and changes is of great interest to pressure groups. The ability to manipulate public opinion in a certain direction may mean success or failure of a particular program or policy supported or opposed by a pressure group. Organized pressure groups spend great amounts of money and put a good deal of effort into the process of opinion formation. The avenues for public-opinion manipulation available to a well-financed pressure group are innumerable. The press, radio, and television are the most obvious media through which pressure groups may reach the public. But there are other, much more subtle methods used. During its antimedicare campaign, for example, the AMA distributed to its members throughout the United States material on the "evils of socialized medicine." Many doctors made this material available to their patients by placing it conspicuously in waiting rooms; some printed matter even found its way in monthly statements to patients.[10]

Virtually all organized pressure groups maintain public-relation departments or hire public-relations agencies. Some pressure groups also maintain speakers' bureaus which are always glad to furnish speakers to all types of clubs, schools, and fraternal organizations. Such methods have one end in view: the persuasion and perhaps manipulation of public opinion.

Pressure groups realize that influence must be exerted where it is likely to have the greatest effect. Thus, as Key writes, they "are most conspicuous in their activities in support or in opposition to legislative proposals."[11] Most national pressure groups maintain offices in Washington, and those with interests at the state level have offices in state capitals. Persons employed by pressure groups to influence legislation are most commonly known as lobbyists. They know their way around the halls of Congress and the state legislatures; some are former legislators, while the rest are often able to develop strong and influential acquaintances within the nation's legislative institutions. The term *lobbyist* gained an unfavorable connotation in the past because some of the practitioners of this "'gentle art of persuasion" were quite unscrupulous. Thus, when reference to lobbying is made, many people conjure up images of outright coercion and corruption. However, most legislators argue that they consider lobbyists essential to the legislative process. All public issues are at least two-sided, and it is not uncommon for legislators to seek the opinion of groups for and against pending decisions. During the committee stage in the legislative process, for instance, lobbyists or other spokesmen for pressure groups are invited to appear before

---

[10] See Eugene Feingold, *Medicare: Policy and Politics* (New York and London: Chandler Publishing Company, 1966).

[11] *Politics, Parties, and Pressure Groups*, p. 132.

congressional committees to present testimony—one-sided and biased testimony, to be sure—which will aid the committee's deliberations. As one observer of pressure-group politics writes:

> Committee hearings provide the various organizations with opportunities to present their arguments and also to show how strongly the members of the group favor or oppose a given proposal.[12]

Sometimes pressure groups attempt to influence the legislative process by financial assistance to cooperative candidates for public office or by publicizing an uncooperative candidate's record. The labor unions, for example, have a long history of support for candidates friendly to labor and opposition to those who are considered enemies of the labor movement. The principle of "rewards for friends, punishment for enemies" costs organized labor millions of dollars during congressional and presidential campaigns. Other groups such as the National Association of Manufacturers and the AMA also spend considerable sums of money supporting particular candidates or political parties at election time. Some groups make contributions to both political parties in order to be on the safe side, just in case.

When Madison made reference to the fact that one of government's main activities would be to regulate and arbitrate disputes between factions, he made a prophecy that has come true. A society as diverse and as complex as that of the United States requires a good deal of regulation in many regards. This governmental regulation, intended to preserve the smooth functioning of society, has given the government formidable powers. One of the undisputed facts of modern political life is the expansion of governmental power. And with the growth of government, the power of the executive branch has grown much more than has the power of the other branches of government, the legislature and the courts. Chapters 4 and 5 have mentioned the tendency of Congress to grant considerable administrative discretion to executive departments and agencies, under the Commerce Clause of the Constitution, and Chapter 6 has noted the quasi-judicial nature of regulatory bodies. A glance at the organization chart of the executive branch in Chapter 5, with its "independent offices and establishments" ranging from the Atomic Energy Commission to the Veterans Administration, highlights the impact of the executive branch on almost every phase of daily life.

---

[12] Henry A. Turner, "How Pressure Groups Operate," *Annals of the American Academy of Political and Social Science* (September, 1958), p. 66.

Leaders of pressure groups are aware that the power of administrators and bureaucrats is substantial. As a consequence, lobbyists have shown an inclination in recent years to use their persuasive tactics on administrative officials. They have often met with success for a number of reasons. For one thing, they find it easier to persuade an individual who has the authority to make a decision of interest to an interest group, rather than depending on a legislator who, unless he is in a very powerful position, can be only of limited use. And as has been noted, the legislative branch, primarily because it lacks both time and expertise, has tended to grant the administrative agencies broad powers of discretion in regard to the execution of programs and policies. In other words, the way a policy is put into effect is largely left to the discretion of bureaucrats. The power to enforce the decisions of the legislature is in the hands of another branch, the executive, which wishes to guard its prerogatives and thus can be either vigorous or passive. Finally, those who administer the government's policies in the United States are appointed to their positions and are responsible to the people only indirectly, through the president who appoints them. It can be assumed, therefore, that pressure groups find it easier to influence those who do not rely on the ballot for their position. Henry Turner puts it this way:

> Pressure organizations with friends in top administrative positions have advantages not available to other groups in securing permits, licenses, contracts, subsidies, favorable adjustments of tax problems and anti-trust suits, and various other types of privileges and favors.[13]

The Effectiveness of Pressure Groups

What factors are involved in the effectiveness of pressure groups? What makes one group more effective than another? What makes politicians, administrators, and the public listen to the propaganda of a particular pressure group? Social scientists for the most part have been unable to provide concrete criteria for measuring pressure-group effectiveness. Attempts at such measurement have been made by political scientists E. E. Schattschneider and Harry M. Scoble. For instance, Scoble estimates that "the net gain of the Democratic Party in Presidential elections as a consequence of the existence of unions is perhaps as much as 2.8 million votes."[14] Schattschneider's earlier estimate was just

[13] "How Pressure Groups Operate," p. 67.
[14] Harry M. Scoble, *Ideology and Electoral Action* (New York and London: Chandler Publishing Company, 1967), p. 161.

under a million votes.[15] Nonetheless certain characteristics of pressure-group strength have emerged. It is generally agreed, for example, that the most important measure of pressure-group effectiveness is goal achievement; that is, the ability of a pressure organization to attain its desired goals, whatever they may be. In this regard three attributes are most likely to lead toward a successful effort: *size* (numbers of members), *money*, and *purpose*.

An important, if not the most important, ingredient in pressure-group strength and effectiveness is size. The larger the group, the more important its influence is likely to be—especially if its appeal is directed toward elected officials. It is obviously difficult for one who owes his position to the electorate, for instance, to disregard the desires of such groups as the labor unions and the farmers. These groups represent millions of members who can, if united behind one party or candidate for the presidency, make the difference between success and failure. Size alone, however, without the benefits of leadership and organization, will not work. If one considers the black community in the United States as a pressure group, for example, it can be said that this group was largely ineffective, until recent years, because it lacked a united purpose and organization even though in terms of size it has always been most impressive. Consequently, when a leader like Stokely Carmichael of the Student Nonviolent Co-ordinating Committee (SNCC) shouted the slogan "Black Power," it is conceivable that he wanted to organize blacks to act more and more like a pressure group and thus by their political strength "reward friends and punish enemies."

To a pressure organization, money may mean the difference between attainment of goals and futility. A pressure group's effectiveness is often determined by the amount of money at its disposal. High-powered lobbyists, legal counsel, and public-relations firms are expensive; the maintenance of offices in Washington and in state capitals costs money; advertising in large newspapers, on television and radio, and in national magazines is a very costly proposition; the printing and mailing of organization propaganda in large volumes is expensive; the "rewarding of friends and punishment of enemies" at election time also costs money. In short, a pressure group without money is lacking one of the essential prerequisites to goal accomplishment. Among the most powerful pressure groups in American politics are those representing the professions (doctors, dentists, lawyers) and the industrialists (the

[15] E. E. Schattschneider, *The Semi-Sovereign People* (New York: Holt, Rinehart and Winston, 1960), pp. 49–52.

National Association of Manufacturers and the Chamber of Commerce). These groups are also the most wealthy. But they enjoy something else which proves extremely beneficial to their efforts: These groups enjoy the respect of the community. In other words, their professional status and commercial success make them prestigious in the eyes of the public. In turn, this prestige can be translated into effectiveness when it is necessary. It should be noted that in actual size these groups are small; however, the influence they are able to exert is great. It could be argued that this disproportionate influence is another undemocratic factor in American politics.

Finally, a pressure group will be effective if its message is emotionally appealing to a large segment of the community. There are certain things in the context of American politics that are considered almost sacred. For example, most people will support groups advocating such notions as morality and decency, patriotism and good government. It should be noted that these appeals to the emotions of individuals are broad enough to cover almost any conceivable subject. If a pressure group, then, can successfully associate its campaign with either morality or patriotism, it is automatically assured of a large following. A good case in point is the AMA's effort to defeat the government's proposal to establish the medicare program. For almost twenty years the AMA was successful in stalling passage of medicare legislation by organizing a massive campaign to discredit the program as one step closer to "socialized medicine." The AMA appealed to public opinion with a purposeful argument—the argument supporting, both implicitly and explicitly, the "American way of life" by opposing such notions as medicare as "un-American." In other words, supporting the AMA position was a patriotic thing to do, and by inference also moral; while the opposition was painted as unpatriotic and, also inferentially, immoral.

THE DIFFERENCE BETWEEN PARTIES AND PRESSURE GROUPS

David B. Truman indicates that political parties and pressure groups in the American political system perform similar functions. Both are unofficial agencies of the political system and attempt to influence the decision-making process by acting "through or upon any of the institutions of government."[16] The similarity, however, ends here. The differ-

[16] David B. Truman, *The Governmental Process* (New York: Knopf, 1961), p. 37.

ences between political parties and pressure groups are more significant than are their similarities.

There are two factors which distinguish a political party from a pressure group: *purpose* and *tactics*. In most cases, the main purpose of a pressure group is to influence a specific public policy. On the other hand, a political party's primary reason for existence is to take over and control the entire decision-making apparatus, thus influencing the whole spectrum of governmental activity. The tactics employed by pressure organizations and political parties also differ substantially. A political party is interested in winning elections. To win control of the government, a political party must nominate and support candidates for election to public office. Conversely, a pressure group almost never submits its own candidates for election although it might support candidates of one of the existing political parties.

Occasionally, a pressure group will enter the political arena with candidates of its own for public office, local, state, or national. Once that is done, however, and if the pressure group is successful in electing persons to office, it loses its pressure-group characteristics and becomes a genuine political party. It can be argued, for example, that the Farm-Labor party in Minnesota, presently allied with the Democratic party, was originally a pressure group, a coalition of farmers and workers. It became a political party when it became able to elect local and state officials. Also groups calling themselves political parties without being able to elect candidates to public office (there are several in American politics) are political parties in name only; in truth, they are pressure groups.

GLOSSARY

Cross-pressured Belonging in part to several different categories of voters whose ideals tend to cancel one another out in their political effects.

Disenfranchised Being denied the right to vote, often by some administrative gimmick.

Independent A citizen voter who does not affiliate himself with any major political party.

Lobbyist A person employed by an organization to influence legislation and, on occasion, administrative action.

Minority groups Groups of Americans who are not male, white, Anglo-Saxon, and Protestant.

Party discipline Mechanisms by which party leaders see that office-holders vote in accordance with the party's programs, a feature notably lacking in American parties.

Plurality elections Elections won by the candidate who takes more votes than any of his opponents, not necessarily a majority of the votes cast.

Political party An organization which strives to elect public officials in order to control governmental power.

Pressure group Any organization that actively seeks to influence public policy by direct persuasion of policy makers.

Two-party system A system of electoral politics in which only two parties, not more, commonly contest elections; in the United States, the predominance of the Democratic and Republican parties is characteristic of our two-party system.

Women's suffrage The right of women to vote.

SUGGESTIONS FOR FURTHER READING

BERELSON, BERNARD, et al. *Voting: A Study of Opinion Formation in a Presidential Campaign.* Chicago: University of Chicago Press, 1954.

BINKLEY, WILFRED E. *American Political Parties: Their Natural History.* New York: Knopf, 1958.

BONE, HUGH A. *American Politics and the Party System.* New York: McGraw-Hill, 1965.

CAMPBELL, ANGUS, et al. *The American Voter,* New York: Wiley, 1960.

DOMHOFF, G. WILLIAM. *Fat Cats and Democrats.* Englewood Cliffs, N.J.: Prentice Hall, 1972.

DUVERGER, MAURICE. *Political Parties: Their Organizations and Activities in the Modern State.* New York: Wiley, 1956.

ELDERSVELD, SAMUEL J. *Political Parties: A Behavioral Analysis.* Chicago: Rand McNally, 1964.

FEINGOLD, EUGENE. *Medicare: Policy and Politics.* New York and London: Chandler, 1966.

FENTON, JOHN H. *People and Parties in Politics.* Chicago: Scott, Foresman, 1966.

GOLDMAN, RALPH M. *The Democratic Party in American Politics.* New York: Macmillan, 1966.

HERRING, PENDLETON. *The Politics of Democracy.* Reissue; New York: Norton, 1966.

HOFSTADTER, RICHARD. *The Idea of a Party System.* Berkeley: University of California Press, 1969.

JONES, CHARLES O. *The Republican Party in American Politics.* New York: Macmillan, 1966.

KEY, V. O., JR. *Politics, Parties and Pressure Groups.* New York: Crowell, 1964.

LANE, EDGAR. *Lobbying and the Law.* Berkeley: University of California Press, 1964.

LAWTON, KAY. *Political Parties and Democracy in the United States.* New York: Scribner's, 1968.

PHILLIPS, KEVIN P. *The Emerging Republican Majority.* New York: Arlington House, 1969.

ROSSITER, CLINTON. *Parties and Politics in America.* Ithaca, N.Y.: Cornell University Press, 1960.

SCAMMON, RICHARD M., and BEN J. WATTENBERG. *The Real Majority.* New York: Coward-McCann, 1970.

SCOBLE, HARRY M. *Ideology and Electoral Action: A Comparative Case Study of the National Committee for an Effective Congress.* New York and London: Chandler, 1967.

TRUMAN, DAVID B. *The Governmental Process.* New York: Knopf, 1951.

ZEIGLER, HARMON. *Interest Groups in American Society.* Englewood Cliffs, N.J.: Prentice Hall, 1964.

Chapter 9
Civil Rights and Civil Liberties

The terms *civil rights* and *civil liberties* are often used interchangeably, but the former is now used most commonly to refer to guarantees of equality despite "accidental differences"—race, sex, age, national origin —whereas the latter term usually refers to an individual's chosen behavior. Civil liberties involve the right of the individual to enjoy certain freedoms, especially in the realms of expression and political participation, and certain protections against violations of privacy[1] and personal security by organs of the state such as the police, the judiciary, the military, and administrative agencies. In general, civil rights and liberties reflect the assertion in the Declaration of Independence "that all men are created equal, that they are endowed by their Creator with certain unalienable rights."

A democratic society is characterized by the rights and liberties afforded to its citizens as well as by the methods used to protect public

[1] While this chapter deals primarily with cases involving freedom of speech, freedom of religion, and race relations, there is more and more concern with the Court's role as protector of the citizen's right to privacy. An example of this concern is the 1973 case *Roe* v. *Wade*, in which the Supreme Court ruled that the decision to have an abortion rests basically with the woman and her doctor— and that the state should not interfere.

order and stability. Moreover, a democratic society is judged by how it treats individuals and groups that belong to political, religious, racial, and philosophical minorities. Even though the majority often disagrees with the demands of one or several minorities, it does not have either the legal or the moral right to disregard them. As has been stressed elsewhere in this book, the survival of democracy depends on the willingness of the majority to accommodate the minority. By the same token, one of the main assumptions of democratic politics is that the majority has the right to rule so long as the rights and interests of the minority are given consideration. Democracy in the United States is based on the theory that all citizens are equal before the law. This theory was put quite succinctly by the late Supreme Court Justice Hugo Black, who once noted that in the American system of government "even the worst citizen" is fully protected under the law and must be afforded all the benefits of due process under the Constitution. But what are these rights?

CONSTITUTIONAL GUARANTEES—THE BILL OF RIGHTS

The United States Constitution prohibits the government from intruding into the personal and private affairs of individuals. Persons living in the United States have the right to think, believe, worship, and advocate almost anything, so long as the thoughts, beliefs, religious practices, and causes advocated are not offensively contrary to the basic mores of society as a whole. As the Declaration of Independence makes clear, free people must have the right to life, liberty, and the pursuit of happiness without governmental interference. Such rights, in short, are to be enjoyed by everyone in the United States regardless of his skin color, his religious, political, or philosophical convictions, or his national origin. These rights are guaranteed in a number of places in the body of the United States Constitution. They are, however, most conspicuously guaranteed by the Bill of Rights, the first ten amendments, and by the Due Process Clause of the Fourteenth Amendment, which makes most of the Bill of Rights applicable to the States. The Constitution further guarantees certain protections to the individual insofar as he acts or speaks in a *public* capacity. These prohibitions and protections, public and private, are often lumped together and called civil rights and civil liberties.

The first three amendments are concerned with freedom of expression and religion, the right to bear arms, and the quartering of troops; the Ninth Amendment makes clear that unspecified rights (freedom to travel abroad, for example) are not denied to the people; and the Tenth

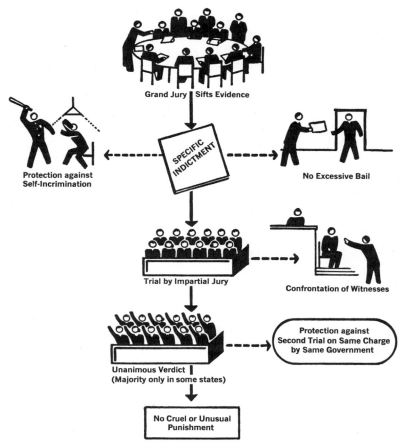

Figure 9-1. Protection of the accused. (From Robert E. Cushman, *Our Constitutional Freedoms*, New York: Public Affairs Committee, Inc., 1944, p. 19.)

Amendment "reserves" to the states and the people those rights not delegated to the United States. Almost all the other civil rights and liberties defined in the Constitution relate to *due process of law*. Article I, for instance, forbids Congress to pass *bills of attainder* (laws directed against particular persons or groups) and *ex post facto laws* (laws imposing penalties for actions not unlawful at the time committed, or increasing penalties after the fact). Article III carefully limits the definition of treason. The Fourth Amendment prohibits unreasonable searches and seizures, and the Fifth prohibits the taking of private property for public use without just compensation. Other articles spell out protections of the accused in criminal actions (see Figure 9-1).

The rights of the accused deserve special mention since they clearly reflect the spirit of Anglo-American law. This law has evolved to protect the people, both individually and collectively—rather than to serve the interests of a ruler or a ruling class or an abstraction called "the state." For that reason, crime is by definition an offense against the people, as Chapter 6 has noted; and in accusing and trying an individual the people must protect *his* rights too. Thus the accused is presumed innocent until proven guilty and is given every reasonable opportunity to defend himself. He has the privilege of refusing to testify against himself, of consulting counsel, of being released on bail pending trial, of confronting witnesses against him, and of being tried by a jury (a party to a civil suit involving more than $20 also has the right to a jury trial under the Seventh Amendment). Buttressing the other rights of the accused is the *writ of habeas corpus* which is guaranteed except "in Cases of Rebellion or Invasion" by Article I. The legal historian Zechariah Chafee, Jr., called habeas corpus "the most important human right in the Constitution."

POLITICAL RIGHTS—PRIVILEGES OF GOOD CITIZENSHIP

So-called political rights might more meaningfully be considered *privileges* than rights. They involve, for example, the right to hold public office and to vote at election time. Convicted criminals do not have the right to vote or to hold public office. In other words, society has withdrawn that privilege from such persons. The Nineteenth Amendment, extending the suffrage to women; the Twenty-third, allowing residents of the District of Columbia to vote for president and vice president; and the Twenty-fourth, making it illegal for states to demand the payment of a poll tax in order to vote for national officials; and the Twenty-sixth, giving 18-year-olds the franchise, are examples of constitutional provisions extending the political rights of American citizens. According to Anglo-American legal and constitutional theory, civil rights and liberties are inherent in United States citizenship; and they cannot be arbitrarily revoked by government and ought not be impaired, even by constitutional amendment. By contrast, political rights are the rewards society gives those who abide by its rules and, under certain conditions, can be withdrawn. Another constitutional amendment, for example, could once again disfranchise women or the residents of the District of Columbia.

Throughout this book the terms *people, persons,* and *citizens* are used interchangeably with respect to civil rights and liberties, whereas only the term *citizens* normally is used with respect to political rights. This usage reflects that of the Constitution. Noncitizens as well as citizens under the jurisdiction of the United States enjoy equal rights of free expression, association, privacy, and due process of law. (Indeed, most civil rights and liberties extend to corporations, which the courts treat as *legal persons.*) On the other hand, political rights, notably the right to hold office, are limited to citizens—and to *natural-born* citizens in the case of the presidency. The original Constitution, although it empowered Congress to "establish a uniform rule of naturalization," did not define citizenship. A definition awaited adoption of the Fourteenth Amendment (1868), which states: "All persons born or naturalized in the United States and subject to the jurisdiction thereof, are citizens of the United States and of the State wherein they reside."[2]

Noncitizens (aliens) lack one fundamental right of citizens: the right to enter the country and to stay. Congress has the power to exclude would-be immigrants or to deport them, in addition to prescribing the standards for gaining citizenship through *naturalization.* The first restrictive immigration law was passed in 1882, and a quota system (discrimination in favor of some nationalities and against others) was begun in 1921. Oriental immigrants were largely barred from 1882 to 1952, but now the quota for Asians is the same as for others. Deportation, though not technically a punishment and therefore not limited by constitutional guarantees, is used less harshly than it once was because of increasing public and judicial humaneness.

In the United States system of government, the institution which has the last word, which is the final arbiter, on questions of rights and liberties is the United States Supreme Court. Its decisions and precedents have established the foundations upon which the rights and liberties guaranteed in the Constitution are based. As Henry Abraham has written: "No other branch of our government is as qualified to draw lines between the rights of individuals and the rights of society as the Supreme Court of the United States."[3] Therefore, in the pages that follow, civil rights and liberties are examined from the perspective of the Supreme Court. Specifically, discussion of the freedoms fostered and guaranteed by the First Amendment—most particularly freedom of

---

[2] Offspring of United States citizens acquire citizenship at birth even if born outside United States territory.

[3] *Freedom and the Court: Civil Rights and Liberties in the United States* (New York: Oxford University Press, 1967), p. 167.

speech and religion—as well as freedom from discrimination, will be based on Supreme Court decisions and on principles established in those decisions.

FREEDOM OF SPEECH

A sentiment commonly expressed in the United States is that "It's a free country" and a person may say and do whatever he pleases. While the sentiment is not entirely unfounded, it would be far from realistic to accept it at face value. Even in a free and open society, there are limits to free speech since one person's freedom may well imperil another's. Moreover, although the First Amendment to the Constitution is quite clear in protecting the principle of free speech, it also entails a good deal of individual and collective responsibility. For example, society has the right and the obligation to protect itself from disintegration. Thus an individual may not incite violent disorders by insisting that he is merely exercising his freedom of speech. Nor is slander allowed on the argument that a citizen in a democratic society has the right to say anything he pleases. In other words, freedom of speech, like all other freedoms, is relative rather than absolute. To illustrate the point with a classic example: A person is free to shout "Fire!" in a crowded theater if there is a fire. But if there is no fire he does not have the right to yell that there is one, thus causing panic and perhaps mental and physical injury; that would be license, not freedom. By the same token, in *Yates* v. *United States* (1957), the Supreme Court held that a person may think about and *theoretically* advocate the overthrow of the United States government. But once such a theory is overtly translated into action, the advocate is liable for prosecution, and no court would stand in the way of his being punished in accordance with laws duly passed by Congress.

The "Clear and Present Danger" Doctrine: *Schenck v. United States*

In a case decided in 1919, *Schenck* v. *United States*, the United States Supreme Court, through one of its most illustrious members, Oliver Wendell Holmes, Jr., established a principle which has been one of the cornerstones of cases involving freedom of expression ever since. Although modified on several occasions since 1919, the "clear and present danger" test has served as a precedent in court actions in the area of free expression and seems likely to guide federal courts in decid-

Publishers-Hall Syndicate, 1973

THE MILWAUKEE JOURNAL

'Now you can go back to telling mature adults
what they cannot see or read!'

Drawing by Bill Sanders courtesy of Publishers-Hall Syndicate

ing cases of individuals involved in activities critical of United States
policies in Southeast Asia or elsewhere.

As Secretary of the Socialist party, Charles T. Schenck in 1917 sent
to about 15,000 prospective draftees a pamphlet urging them not to
serve in the armed forces. Under the Espionage Act of 1917, which prohibited such activities, Schenck and some of his associates were indicted
by the federal government and convicted of (1) conspiring to cause

insubordination in the armed forces of the United States, and (2) using the mails to transmit matter which was declared nonmailable by the Espionage Act. Schenck and his associates argued that the sections of the Espionage Act under which they were convicted were unconstitutional because they restricted freedom of speech and of the press; they took their case to the Supreme Court for final disposition.

The Court unanimously rejected Schenck's contention that portions of the Espionage Act of 1917 were unconstitutional. And in a widely quoted passage the Court, through Justice Holmes, drew the line between the rights of the individual and the rights of society to take precautions when the danger to it was "clear and present." This, the Court said, is especially true in time of war. Holmes put it this way:

> We admit that in many places and in ordinary times the defendants in saying all that was said in the circular would have been within their constitutional rights. But *the character of every act depends upon the circumstances in which it is done* . . . The most stringent protection of free speech would not protect a man in falsely shouting fire in a theater and causing panic. . . . The question in every case is whether the words used are used in such circumstances and are of such a nature as to create a *clear and present danger* that they will bring about the substantive evils that Congress has a right to prevent. . . . When a nation is at war many things that might be said in time of peace are such a hindrance to its effort that their utterance will not be endured so long as men fight and that no Court would regard them as being protected by any constitutional right.[4]

The "Bad Tendency" Test: *Gitlow v. New York*

Quite obviously the "clear and present danger" test is difficult to apply. At what point, for example, does a particular speech constitute a "clear and present danger" to the safety and welfare of society? Moreover, is it not possible that the government will utilize the "clear and present danger" argument to suppress expressions it does not like? The United States has been confronted with this dilemma on numerous occasions since 1919. Most recently, some of those who openly criticized the government's policy in Vietnam were accused of committing treason against the United States by giving "aid and comfort" to the enemies of the United States through their critical speeches, statements, and publications. While such accusations are highly questionable, they were made, in some cases by high-ranking members of the government.

[4] *Schenck v. United States,* 249 U.S. 47 (1919), at 52 (emphasis added).

In 1925 the Supreme Court modified the "clear and present danger" doctrine with the "bad tendency" test. The latter was designed to prevent expression, in either speech or publication, which had a *tendency*, even a remote one, to bring about serious "disturbances of the public peace." In other words, the "bad tendency" test implied that the rights of society took precedence over the rights of individuals. Hence, society, in order to protect itself, could take steps to avoid being placed in jeopardy *before* any overt act against it occurred. It was over such a sweeping grant of power to the government that the originator of the "clear and present danger" doctrine, Justice Holmes, together with Justice Louis D. Brandeis, disagreed with the majority of their colleagues on the Court.

The "bad tendency" test was formulated in *Gitlow* v. *New York* (1925). Benjamin Gitlow was prosecuted under the New York Criminal Anarchy Act of 1902 for distributing a document called "The Left Wing Manifesto." It contained exhortations to overthrow the United States government by force and violence, among other things. In upholding Gitlow's conviction, the Supreme Court reiterated that First Amendment freedoms are not absolute. It went on to declare that the state should not be expected "to measure the danger from every such utterance in the nice balance of a jeweler's scale. . . . [The state] may, in the exercise of its judgment, suppress the threatened danger in its incipiency."[5]

Such a broad grant of power to the state went too far, according to Holmes and Brandeis. In a blistering dissenting opinion, Justice Holmes argued that Gitlow's manifesto constituted neither a "clear" nor a "present" danger to the government of the State of New York; it was, in fact, a purely theoretical argument, and not a very good one at that. Holmes wrote:

> It is said that this manifesto was more than a theory, that it was an incitement. *Every idea is an incitement.* It offers itself for belief and *if believed* it is acted on unless some other belief outweighs it or some failure of energy stifles the movement at its birth.[6]

National Security: *Dennis* v. *United States* and *Yates* v. *United States*

Three laws passed by Congress since 1940 were intended to curtail so-called subversive activities: the Smith Act of 1940, the Subversive Activities Control Act of 1950, and the Communist Activities Control

---

[5] *Gitlow* v. *New York,* 268 U.S. 652 (1925), at 669.
[6] *Gitlow* v. *New York,* 268 U.S. 652 (1925), at 673 (emphasis added).

Act of 1954. The last two are products of the Cold War, while the first was passed during World War II. In all three, Congress relied more heavily on the "bad tendency" test than on the "clear and present danger" doctrine. Legislative prescriptions such as these often create more problems than they solve. As Henry Abraham put it:

> The problem implicit in this legislation is, of course, where to draw the line between the individual's cherished right to espouse and express unpopular, even radical, causes and the right of the community to protect itself against the overthrow of government. As the courts have been called upon to demonstrate time and again, democratic society has the right and duty to maintain concurrently both freedom of expression and national security.[7]

The three "counter-subversion" laws have come in for close scrutiny by the courts. The cases briefly described below questioned congressional authority to restrict by legislation the free expression of ideas. As will be seen, Court attitudes have undergone changes since 1951.

The Smith Act of 1940, closely modeled on the New York Criminal Anarchy Act of 1902 discussed in relation to the *Gitlow* case above, was tested in the courts by *Dennis* v. *United States* (1951). In 1948, Eugene Dennis and ten other leaders of the American Communist party were indicted under the Smith Act for knowingly and willfully conspiring to advocate and teach the violent overthrow of the United States government. They were convicted in trial court; their conviction was upheld by the court of appeals; finally, they took their case to the United States Supreme Court for final determination. They argued that the Smith Act was unconstitutional because it restricted their right of free expression. They also contended that the vagueness of the Smith Act denied them due process of law as guaranteed by the Fifth Amendment.

The Supreme Court upheld the conviction of the eleven Communists by relying more heavily on the "bad tendency" test than on the "clear and present danger" principle. Chief Justice Vinson, speaking for the majority, pointed out that in cases of this type the danger to the government need not be imminent; it need not be "clear and present"; it is sufficient that it be "clear and *probable.*" The mere existence of the Communist Party as a conspiracy was justification enough to warrant curtailment of its members' activities, the majority claimed. A conspiracy to advocate the violent overthrow of the government cannot be distinguished from the advocacy itself, claimed the Court.

Dennis and his co-defendants were sent to prison. However, two members of the Court, Black and Douglas, strenuously objected to the

---

[7] Abraham, *Freedom and the Court,* p. 126.

opinion of the majority. But these were troubled times. The fear of Communist subversion was very strong; the Cold War was an undisputed reality; and McCarthyism was in the process of becoming a powerful and potentially destructive force in American politics. In his dissenting opinion, Justice Black—one of those jurists who believed that the freedoms guaranteed by the First Amendment are absolutely inviolable— caught the mood of the time quite poignantly:

> Public opinion being what it now is, few will protest the conviction of these Communist petitioners. There is hope, however, that in calmer times, when present pressures, passions and fears subside, this or some later Court will restore the First Amendment liberties to the high preferred place where they belong in a free society.[8]

The political atmosphere surrounding the *Dennis* case was conducive to the decision reached by the Court. Fear and anxiety were in the land, the fear and anxiety of Communist subversion. Individuals and groups within the United States were making all sorts of accusations against government officials, artists, performers, academicians, private groups, and government agencies. Essentially, these accusations revolved around the issue of loyalty to the United States versus adherence to a set of beliefs or principles which were believed to be inimical to United States interests and therefore "un-American."

By the middle 1950s the climate of opinion in the United States had undergone a rather remarkable change, primarily because of two factors. First, Joseph Stalin, who had ruled the Soviet Union with an iron hand for close to thirty years, died in 1953, and the new Soviet leadership showed signs of a desire to coexist with the capitalist world and more particularly with the United States. The bitter Cold War that had characterized East-West relations since 1945 was showing signs of a "thaw." This had a psychological impact on both sides of the Iron Curtain. Second, Senator Joseph McCarthy's domestic political influence was waning. He had made a reputation as a vigorous anti-Communist early in the 1950s, but was no longer in a position to exploit the fears and anxieties of the American public by claiming that Communists or their sympathizers were in positions of power and authority at virtually every level of government and in most of the nation's colleges and universities. By 1954, the senator from Wisconsin had gone a little further than his Senate colleagues could accept. His sensational investigations had uncovered little that was not already known to such agencies as the F.B.I. Meanwhile, the careers and reputations of countless individuals had been ruined. In the end, the United States Senate expressed its dis-

[8] *Dennis* v. *United States,* 341 U.S. 494 (1951), at 581.

pleasure with Senator McCarthy's tactics by voting to censure him. His conduct, a majority of the senators insisted, tended to bring the United States Senate into dishonor and disrepute. Senator McCarthy died in 1957, but his political influence and his irresponsible anti-Communism had died after his censure by the Senate in December of 1954. When the Supreme Court was given the opportunity to reexamine the Smith Act of 1940, the justices seized upon it to alter significantly some of the law's provisions. This change was accomplished through *Yates* v. *United States* (1957).

Most particularly, the Court stated that, although the constitutionality of the Smith Act was not at issue, clearly the federal government ought not be able to punish individuals like Oleta O'Connor Yates for holding or expressing the "abstract idea" or philosophical conviction that the United States government should be overthrown by force and violence. The Court held that the government, in cases brought before the courts under the Smith Act, had to show that the danger against it was "clear and present," not "probable." In other words, the Supreme Court affirmed that an individual living in a democracy may *believe* anything he likes so long as he does not attempt to put his beliefs into overt action intended to overthrow the government violently.

Public reaction to the *Yates* decision was largely unfavorable. Vociferous groups and commentators unleashed virulent attacks on the Court. Public-opinion polls showed that a large number of people were not convinced that the difference between the theoretical "advocacy" of a cause and overt "action" against the government was clearly defined. In any event, the *Yates* decision drastically modified the conclusion reached in the *Dennis* case. But this was by no means the end to litigation involving the Smith Act and its related legislative enactments, the Subversive Activities Control Act of 1950 and the Communist Activities Control Act of 1954.

Other Cases Related to Subversive Activities

Four years after the *Yates* decision, in *Scales* v. *United States* (1961), the Supreme Court reviewed the case of Junius Irving Scales and in a 5 to 4 decision upheld his conviction on the grounds that he had been an "active" member of the Communist party and as such was guilty of "knowingly" belonging to an organization engaged in illegally advocating the overthrow of the United States government by force and violence.

Also in 1961, in *Communist Party* v. *Subversive Activities Control Board* the requirement of the Subversive Activities Control Act of 1950 that any subversive "action" or "front" group register with the government was upheld as constitutional. In this instance, the Communist party was ordered to register by the Subversive Activities Control Board established by the Act. It refused on the basis that registration was a violation of the First and Fifth Amendments to the Constitution, but a 5 to 4 majority of the Court felt otherwise.

Under the provisions of the Subversive Activities Control Act, the Communist party was convicted in federal court for failure to register. In 1963, the United States court of appeals for the District of Columbia reversed the conviction. Since the Smith Act had declared the Communist party to be a criminal conspiracy, the court of appeals argued, its registration would be tantamount to compulsory self-incrimination, in violation of the Fifth Amendment. Thereupon, the government took the case to the Supreme Court, which refused to hear it and thus upheld the decision of the court of appeals, in *United States* v. *Communist Party* (1964).

On issues involving freedom of expression versus national security, the courts have not established consistent principles. The cases briefly described above illustrate the difficulties inherent in such efforts. While the courts have dealt repeatedly with the problem, they have been unable to finally resolve the basic dilemma of individual rights as opposed to the right of society to maintain order and stability. Courts do not make decisions in a vacuum. Even though the Anglo-American system of law emphasizes the independence of the judiciary, court benches are occupied by humans who live in a particular environment and whose biases, political views, and personal anxieties often find their way into court decisions.

FREEDOM OF RELIGION

Many of the early settlers in what is now the United States had made the dangerous journey across the Atlantic to escape religious and political persecution and maltreatment. Yet often these new settlers of early America did not hesitate to establish their own religious orthodoxy, at least in some segments of the New World. In the Massachusetts Bay Colony, for example, an official Puritan church was established. It was supported by taxes, and membership in the church was a mandatory prerequisite for voting. Dissenters were banished from the colony; the most famous of these was Roger Williams, founder of Rhode Island, who was forced to leave Massachusetts because he called for the toleration of all religious beliefs in the New World. The Anglican church became the official church of Virginia. "The English church in Virginia was given legal monopoly; all competition among other producing and consuming units of religious persuasion was prohibited."[9] Some colonies, however, notably Pennsylvania and Maryland, were founded on the principle of religious toleration.

This principle was not one, in other words, that all the settlers of early America brought with them from across the sea. But as time passed, new immigrants to the colonies brought with them diverse religious beliefs. Thus the established churches found it difficult to maintain absolute control over religious beliefs and practices. The new arrivals were anxious to exercise their religious freedom while, at the same time, demanding popular government. And with the idea of popular government entrenched in most of the colonies, the established churches found it almost impossible to acquire financial support through state-imposed taxes. As Grimes wrote:

> It was one thing for a colony to impose a tax to support an established church when it was presumed that the church represented the views of the majority; however, it was clearly insufferable to those not of the faith when they constituted a majority to be taxed to support views that they did not endorse.[10]

The road to religious freedom has not been without its problems and difficulties, even in the United States. Until the election of John F. Kennedy to the presidency in 1960, one of the unwritten rules of American politics was that no Catholic could be elected President of the United States. And even Kennedy had to submit to the embarrassment of a modern-day inquisition when he appeared before the Greater Houston Ministerial Association during the 1960 campaign to reassure Protestant American ministers that he was not going to take orders from the Pope. The United States, nevertheless, has moved further toward religious toleration than most other societies. In fact, the American experiment with religious freedom has been copied by a number of other societies.

The United States Constitution, in Article VI and the First Amendment, insists on a clear separation between church and state—between spiritual and temporal affairs. This does not mean that the political system established by that Constitution is hostile to religion. Quite the contrary. The United States government not only tolerates the religious convictions of everyone so long as they do not cause harm to others in the community, but also has encouraged religion in a number of ways: Church property and income are not subject to state and federal taxes;

---

[9] Alan P. Grimes, *Equality in America: Religion, Race, and the Urban Majority* (New York: Oxford University Press, 1964), p. 13.

[10] *Equality in America*, p. 21.

the currency of the United States carries the motto "In God We Trust"; the Bible is used for court oaths; the armed forces are supplied with chaplains; the sessions of each house of Congress open with the chaplain praying for divine guidance; each session of the Supreme Court is opened with the clerk intoning: "God save the United States and this Honorable Court." Indeed, the great variety of religious practices in the United States is testimony to the fact that the government encourages such practices.

In the body of the United States Constitution, in the third paragraph of Article VI, the Founding Fathers were very explicit about religious liberty: ". . . no religious Test shall ever be required as a Qualification to any Office or public Trust under the United States." Furthermore, the First Amendment to the Constitution opens with these words: "Congress shall make no law respecting an establishment of religion, or prohibiting the free exercise thereof." Such prohibition, however, applied only to the federal government and not to the individual states. Although ratification of the Fourteenth Amendment following the Civil War eventually made the Bill of Rights applicable to the states through its famous Due Process Clause, the courts did not concern themselves with the great issues of religious liberty until the 1930s. As with free expression, the attitudes of the courts toward religious freedom will be examined through significant Supreme Court decisions.

Freedom of Belief and Illegal Behavior: *Reynolds v. United States*

In the 1870s, Congress passed an act which prohibited the practice of polygamy. Reynolds, a Mormon living in the territory of Utah, was convicted under this act. He took his case to the Supreme Court on the issue that the act was unconstitutional since it prohibited the free exercise of religion. The Mormon church, Reynolds argued, not only allowed polygamy, it encouraged it. While the Court declared that the Constitution clearly established a "wall of separation" between church and state, it held that Congress was within its constitutional rights in enacting the legislation outlawing polygamy. Thus, in 1879, the Court distinguished between freedom of belief and illegal behavior in the name of religion.

Obligation versus Privilege: *Hamilton v. Regents of University of California*

As a student at the University of California, Hamilton was required to take military training. He refused, on religious grounds, to receive such training and was expelled from the university. The case reached the

United States Supreme Court on appeal, and the university's expulsion of Hamilton was upheld. Although Hamilton's religious beliefs were fully protected by the Constitution, the Court held in 1934, his attendance at the university was not compulsory—it was not an obligation but a privilege. And if Hamilton did not like the unversity's requirement concerning military training, he could go elsewhere or he could refrain from attending college altogether.

The Flag Salute Cases: *West Virginia Board of Education* v. *Barnette*

During the late 1930s and early 1940s, a religious sect known as Jehovah's Witnesses caused to be brought before the courts a number of cases involving issues of religious freedom. The resulting decisions by the Supreme Court clarified greatly the meaning of religious liberty in the United States. Several cases involved the unwillingness of children of this sect attending public schools to salute the flag: these are known collectively as "The Flag Salute Cases." The most important of these, important because it put an end to the controversy, is the *Barnette* case of 1943.

In 1942 the West Virginia Board of Education ordered the salute to the flag to be "a regular part of the program of public schools." Refusal to salute the flag would be regarded as "insubordination and [would] be dealt with accordingly." Jehovah's Witnesses, including the Barnettes, refused to allow their children to salute the flag. Consequently, the children were expelled from school, and their parents were prosecuted in the courts. The Barnettes argued that saluting the flag violated the First Commandment and therefore inhibited their free exercise of religion.

The Supreme Court, in a 6 to 3 decision, upheld the right of the Barnette children and their coreligionists to refuse to salute the flag on religious grounds. Justice Jackson delivered the majority opinion for the Court, and his language is a moving reaffirmation of the principle of religious freedom.

> To believe that patriotism will not flourish if patriotic ceremonies are voluntary and spontaneous instead of a compulsory routine is to make an unflattering estimate of the appeal of our institutions to free minds. . . . If there is any fixed star in our constitutional constellation, it is that no official, high or petty, can prescribe what shall be orthodox in politics, nationalism, religion, or other matters of opinion or force citizens to confess by word or act their faith therein.[11]

[11] *West Virginia Board of Education* v. *Barnette* 319 U.S. 624 (1943), at 642.

Transportation to Parochial Schools: *Everson* v. *Board of Education*

This case tested a New Jersey law permitting free bus transportation for school children of parochial and private schools. Everson, as a taxpayer, filed suit in state court challenging the effects of the law. He contended that the state law, and his city's compliance with it, violated the separation of church and state principle of both the New Jersey and United States constitutions. The Supreme Court, however, decided that public safety and the welfare of the children gave the state the right to provide free public transportation to school children of all denominations, no matter whether they attended public or private school. The state of New Jersey, the Court concluded in 1947, had not breached the "wall of separation" between church and state

Released Time: *McCollum* v. *Board of Education*

In this case of 1948 and in *Zorach* v. *Clauson* (1952), the Supreme Court considered the problem of "released time" for religious instruction of public-school students. In 1940, interested members of the three major faiths—Jewish, Catholic, Protestant—in the city of Champaign, Illinois, agreed to form an association called the Champaign Council on Religious Education. They asked the local board of education for permission to offer religious instruction to public-school children in grades 4 to 9; permission was granted. Mrs. McCollum, as a taxpayer and parent, filed suit against the Champaign Board of Education. She argued that she did not want her child exposed to religious instruction; nor did she want him to go through the embarrassment of being sent to another place while the rest of his classmates received religious instruction.

The Supreme Court upheld Mrs. McCollum's contention that the board's action violated the separation of church and state and was, therefore, unconstitutional. Justice Black, speaking for the Court, referred to the "wall of separation" idea and pointed out that tax-supported property must not be used for any kind of religious instruction.

In the second case dealing with the issue of "released time" (*Zorach* v. *Clauson*), the Supreme Court reached a different, and surprising, decision. New York permitted school children to be released during the school day to go to religious centers for instruction. The law was challenged in the courts as "respecting an establishment of religion." The Supreme Court, through Justice William O. Douglas, stated that while the separation between church and state must be complete and unequivocal, the actions of New York were within the limits of the Constitution.

Public school facilities were not used for religious instruction, and public funds were not expended; the school authorities merely accommodated those students whose parents approved their receiving religious education. This was in the best traditions of the United States, Justice Douglas emphasized.

The School Prayer Case: *Engel* v. *Vitale*

Controversy and a most heated debate followed the Supreme Court's decision in this case in 1962, widely known as "The School Prayer Case." The controversy is not yet over and the debate is continuing. Some groups and certain congressmen and senators have called for the passage of a constitutional amendment to prohibit the Supreme Court from deciding cases involving state educational policies. Spokesmen for the major denominations, however, have welcomed the "school prayer" decision. The government, they insist, should maintain its benevolent neutrality toward religious training and the exercise of religion.

The New York State Board of Regents, the body that sets educational policy in the state, had approved a short "nondenominational" prayer to be recited daily in New York public schools. Pupils who did not wish to participate in the exercise could remain silent or would be excused from the classroom while the prayer was being recited. The Supreme Court held that an officially sanctioned prayer in public schools constituted a violation of the "establishment" and "free exercise" clause of the First Amendment.

Some General Conclusions

Religious liberty is a firmly established and accepted principle in the United States. But, like all other liberties, it is not absolute. A person may not commit murder in the name of religion, explaining that his faith calls for human sacrifice as part of the ritual. In the United States, the individual is free to express and exercise his religious convictions— he is encouraged to do so—as long as he does not encroach upon the rights of others or the safety and welfare of the general community.

From the cases briefly described above, the reader should be aware that public attitudes and court actions involving issues of religious freedom are at best in a state of flux. Who could have predicted, for instance, that four years after the *McCollum* decision the Supreme Court would decide in favor of New York's "dismissed-time" program for religious instruction? And who could have imagined that Congress, after failing to pass similar bills in the past, would approve in 1965 President

Johnson's Aid to Education Act, which included provisions for aid to parochial-school students? What may seem paradoxical about this outcome is that John F. Kennedy, a Catholic, argued in 1961 that federal aid to church schools was a violation of the First Amendment. But Lyndon B. Johnson, a Protestant, obviously felt otherwise. And as of 1972 the Supreme Court had not yet dealt with a case challenging the constitutionality of this legislation.

This section concludes with a reminder that, while the United States Constitution insists on the separation of church and state and on the freedom of religion, it has not established a policy based on freedom from religion. Church membership and attendance are, in fact, higher in the United States than in some countries where there is no separation of church and state.

RACE RELATIONS IN THE UNITED STATES

The final chapter of this book examines some of the problems associated with what is now popularly called the "Black Revolution." In this section the roots of the race problem will be analyzed. As with freedom of speech and religion, court actions are cited to shed light on the black struggle to attain equality of treatment in a society based on the assumption that all men are born free and equal before the law. It would not be just to maintain that progress toward the attainment of the ideal of equality has not been made. It has. The election of Edward W. Brooke of Massachusetts to the United States Senate—the first black to be elected to the Senate since the days of Reconstruction—and the 1967 appointment of Thurgood Marshall, whose grandfather was a slave, to the United States Supreme Court testify to the tremendous changes that have occurred. In the 1970s blacks were elected as mayors in major U.S. cities such as Newark, Los Angeles, Atlanta, and Detroit.

Yet it would be dishonest to insist that the time has come when a man's color no longer determines the opportunities open to him. After all, Senator Brooke and Justice Marshall and a few black mayors are conspicuous examples of qualified blacks who have reached the pinnacle of achievement in the United States. But the black population in the United States numbers over 20 million. Moreover, even though this is the last quarter of the twentieth century, an era characterized by immense success in conquering problems that even a decade ago were in the realm of science fiction, such as the moon landing, there are persons who still believe that blacks are inherently inferior to whites; and this in spite of scientific evidence to the contrary. In 1952, for example, the

United Nations Educational, Scientific, and Cultural Organization (UNESCO) assembled a distinguished committee of internationally prominent scientists to examine questions of racial differences. They drafted a statement which, among other things, includes the following:

> Available scientific knowledge provides no basis for believing that the groups of mankind differ in their innate capacity for intellectual and emotional development. . . . It is now generally recognized that intelligence tests do not in themselves enable us to differentiate safely between what is due to innate capacity and what is the result of environmental influences, training and education. Wherever it has been possible to make allowances for differences in environmental opportunities, the tests have shown essential similarity in mental characters among all human groups.

There is little doubt that the black man today is better off than his brother of a generation or even ten years ago. At least on paper, his position has improved and some statistics prove it. The rate of illiteracy among blacks has decreased markedly and so has the rate of infant mortality, two criteria often cited to prove the contention that black accomplishments have been impressive. But if such arguments are followed to their logical conclusion, both the illiteracy rate and infant-mortality rate are still three times as high for blacks as for white Americans. And if other criteria are used, such as number of school dropouts, divorce or abandonment cases, welfare recipients, unemployed teenagers, the rate for blacks is truly staggering. A few 1970 Census statistics will help make the point. The unemployment rate for blacks was twice as high as for whites. Almost one out of three black families was fatherless as against about one out of ten white families (28.9 percent of black families and 9.4 percent of white families were headed by women). As of 1969, of all blacks over twenty-five living in the nation's twelve largest metropolitan areas, 57 percent had not finished high school; among whites 39 percent had not done so. The median income of black families in 1970 was 40 percent less than for white families ($10,216 for white families and $6,278 for black families).[12]

The Dilemma in Perspective

Blacks were first brought to the New World from Africa as slaves. The plantation economy of the South depended very heavily on slave labor, and the fear that the slaves would be freed was one of the reasons

---

[12] United States Department of Commerce, Bureau of the Census, *The Social and Economic Status of Negroes in the United States, 1970* (July, 1971).

for the outbreak of the Civil War. The *Dred Scott* decision in 1857 held that slaves were property and therefore could not become citizens—indeed, that Congress had an obligation to protect the property rights of slave-owners. Chief Justice Taney's opinion sharpened the conflict that culminated in President Lincoln's Emancipation Proclamation of 1863. Immediately after the Civil War, Congress passed a number of laws requiring the southern states to guarantee the newly freed Negroes their constitutional rights. In 1868, the Fourteenth Amendment defined citizenship to include the former slaves, and by 1871 the Fifteenth Amendment expressly guaranteed their voting rights. But by the turn of the century, all of the former Confederate states had been able to place the black man into a position of second-class citizenship by using a variety of methods to deny him access to political power. Such openly discriminatory devices as poll taxes, unfair literacy tests, and the white primary election were used; and the federal government, including the courts, showed little inclination until recently to challenge southern practices. Thus for almost a century after the slaves were emancipated and constitutionally enfranchised, the southern states found ways and means to keep blacks "in their place."

The Civil Rights Cases

In 1875 Congress passed a civil-rights act designed to give blacks access to certain public accommodations. This act made it a criminal offense for any owner or operator of a theater, hotel, or public conveyance to deny its use to individuals on the basis of race or color. Nevertheless, blacks were denied the use of such accommodations throughout the South, and a number of them brought suits under the provisions of the Civil Rights Act. The United States Supreme Court heard several of these cases in 1883 and gave them the collective title of "The Civil Rights Cases."

The Court declared the Civil Rights Act of 1875 unconstitutional. A majority of 8 to 1 held that Congress did not have the authority to forbid individuals from discriminating against other individuals, in spite of the fact that the discrimination illegalized by the act applied to enterprises of public accommodation licensed, in most cases, by the state. In any event, leaders in the southern states, according to Professor Abraham, took a cue from this decision and "in the four year period between 1887 and 1891 alone, eight of them enacted legislation *requiring* railroads, for example, to maintain *separate* facilities for whites and Negroes."[13]

[13] *Freedom and the Court*, p. 225.

The "Separate but Equal" Doctrine: *Plessy v. Ferguson*

The action of the Supreme Court in The Civil Rights Cases was followed in 1896 by the decision in the case of *Plessy v. Ferguson*. The facts of this case are fascinating. Following the example of other states of the old Confederacy, the Louisiana legislature passed an act (appropriately known as the "Jim Crow Car Act of 1890") requiring the railroads to maintain separate facilities for whites and blacks. Homer A. Plessy was seven-eighths white and one-eighth black. He was selected by a group of blacks to test the validity of the state law, and one day he boarded a train in New Orleans and went into a coach reserved for whites. The conductor asked him to move to the section of the train reserved for blacks. Plessy refused and was promptly arrested for violating the Jim Crow Act of 1890. He appealed his conviction to the United States Supreme Court on the grounds that his arrest constituted a violation of the Thirteenth and Fourteenth Amendments—especially the latter's Equal Protection of the Laws Clause.

The Supreme Court, in a 7 to 1 opinion, decided that Jim Crow legislation such as that passed by the state of Louisiana was constitutional. In the process, the Court established the famous "separate but equal" doctrine, insisting that so long as facilities for blacks were equal to those provided for whites they could be separate. In a fine example of convoluted logic, the Court found that separate facilities discriminated as much against whites as against blacks!

The Plessy decision gave southern states an excuse to discriminate further against blacks. Such actions, according to C. Vann Woodward, author of the classic *The Strange Career of Jim Crow*, granted the South "permission to hate," and southern legislatures moved at breakneck speed to make certain that virtually all public facilities, from toilets to cemeteries, were segregated.

Changes in the "Separate but Equal" Doctrine

Changes in the doctrine were inevitable, and they came. Some changes were instigated by executive action in the late 1930s and early 1940s, when President Roosevelt by Executive Order created a Civil Liberties Unit within the Department of Justice, and later the Fair Employment Practices Commission (FEPC), to work toward the elimination of discriminatory employment practices.

Furthermore, many authorities feel that a 1938 Supreme Court decision, *Missouri ex rel. Gaines v. Canada*, contributed a great deal to changing the "separate but equal" doctrine. Lloyd Gaines, a black resident of Missouri and a graduate of the segregated Lincoln University, applied for admission to the School of Law of the University of Missouri. He was scholastically qualified, but Canada, the registrar at the University of Missouri, pointed out to Gaines that, according to state law, the two races were to be educated in "separate but equal" facilities. Moreover, Canada pointed out, the state law provided that funds could be available to qualified blacks like Gaines if they wanted to receive a legal education in neighboring states with unsegregated law schools. With NAACP prodding and financing, Gaines took his case to court, ultimately reaching the United States Supreme Court.

In a 7 to 2 decision, the Court held that Gaines had been denied the "equal protection of the laws" as guaranteed by the Fourteenth Amendment. The state of Missouri, the Court argued, was obligated to furnish equal, albeit separate, facilities for the legal education of its black citizens. Since no such facilities existed in Missouri, the state had violated Gaines' civil rights. Although the "separate but equal" doctrine was not seriously challenged by this decision, a significant dent was made on its surface.

More substantial improvements toward equality were made during the presidency of Harry S. Truman after World War II. In 1945, 1947, and 1949, the House of Representatives passed legislation that abolished the poll tax, an old standby of discrimination in voting. The Senate, however, refused to go along with the House, and the proposals were never enacted into law. But President Truman, aware of the seriousness of the problem and familiar with Gunnar Myrdal's monumental *An American Dilemma*, published in 1944, decided to do something about it. In 1946 he appointed a 15-member "blue-ribbon" committee to investigate the problems of racial discrimination and to make recommendations for executive and legislative action. In 1947, the committee published its report under the title *To Secure These Rights*. The report contained numerous recommendations for the achievement of racial equality in the United States. To his credit, President Truman made these recommendations part of his campaign platform during the 1948 election; he promised to work toward the implementation of the committee's suggestions. This stand led a large number of southern Democrats to revolt against the national Democratic party and to support Senator Strom Thurmond for the presidency.

When Congress passed the Selective Act of 1948, it failed to include a Truman-backed provision eliminating racial discrimination and segregation in the armed forces. However, Truman resorted to the Executive Order once again. In a brief but strongly worded passage, he banned the practice of racial segregation in the armed forces of the

United States. Many consider this action one of Truman's most important domestic achievements. The "separate but equal" doctrine was dying, and two 1950 Supreme Court decisions, *Sweatt* v. *Painter* and *McLaurin* v. *Oklahoma State Regents*, speeded its demise.

Sweatt had applied for admission to the University of Texas Law School in February 1946. His application was rejected solely because he was black. At the time, Texas had no law school for blacks, but the authorities promised the state court to which Sweatt first took his case they would build one, and one was, indeed, opened the following February. Sweatt, however, refused to attend the new segregated law school. He appealed his case, contending that although the new law school was "separate" it was by no means "equal" to that of the University of Texas. The state's action, Sweatt argued, denied him the "equal protection of the laws."

The Supreme Court upheld Sweatt's contention that the separate facilities of the segregated law school were not equal to those of the state university. The opinion contained several passages pointing out that the number and quality of faculty, the library facilities, the personal contacts so essential to the successful practice of law, plus the obvious stigma of segregation made the new law school for blacks explicitly unequal to the University of Texas law school. Sweatt's exclusion, therefore, from the recognized law school of the state university was unconstitutional.

The facts and circumstances in *McLaurin* v. *Oklahoma State Regents* are even more interesting than those surrounding the *Sweatt* case. In addition, they make vividly clear the near pathological desire of southern legislatures to keep blacks segregated from the white community; the devices they were forced to invent were ingenious, and very often ludicrous.

McLaurin, a black educator, decided to work toward a doctorate in education and applied to the University of Oklahoma for graduate study. The Oklahoma legislature had passed a law authorizing the university administration to admit Negroes for graduate study on a segregated basis. The state legislature went on to define what was meant by "segregated basis." It meant instruction in separate classrooms or at separate times. McLaurin, however, was in a unique position: he was the only black working toward the doctorate in education. But the university authorities wanted to comply with the law. In so doing they simply emphasized the sheer absurdity of the "separate but equal" doctrine.

Instead of providing separate—in this case, it would have been private—instruction, the university required McLaurin to sit apart from the white students in a hallway so that he could see and hear his professor. Later he was brought into the classroom proper but was placed in a roped-off section clearly designated for blacks only. Still later, when the case was being decided by the courts, he was assigned a seat in the classroom in a row specified for black students. In the library McLaurin was assigned a specific desk, and his movements in the building were restricted. In the cafeteria he was assigned a special table and was required to eat at a time when other students were not using the facilities. This kind of treatment, the Supreme Court unanimously held, was not only degrading and silly, it was also unconstitutional. The university was ordered to admit McLaurin to full student privileges forthwith.

The Final Blow to the "Separate but Equal" Doctrine: *Brown* v. *Board of Education*

The early 1950s brought to the forefront the realization that there was something radically wrong with a society that required black soldiers to fight and die alongside white Americans in Korea, to protect the United States and the "free world" from communism, and upon returning home, in some sections of the country, to be subjected to the indignities and mistreatment of second-class citizenship. The liberal element, and concerned Americans whose ideological orientation was not necessarily well defined, were clamoring louder than ever before for the attainment of the cherished ideal of equal treatment. Large segments of the white community began giving greater support—moral and financial—to such organizations as the NAACP, the Congress of Racial Equality (CORE), and the Urban League. At the NAACP, a group of lawyers under the leadership of Thurgood Marshall (later appointed to the United States Supreme Court by President Johnson) were hard at work getting more cases before the courts.

In 1952 the NAACP lawyers took to the Supreme Court five cases dealing with problems of public-school segregation in five different states. The Court agreed to hear arguments and decided to combine the five cases into one. This was to be the celebrated landmark case of *Brown* v. *Board of Education*. Marshall and his legal team contended that segregated education was by its very nature unequal and, therefore, unconstitutional since it violated both the letter and the spirit of the equal protection of the laws clause of the Fourteenth Amendment.

The main facts and circumstances in these cases were discussed in Chapter 6. What is relevant here is that after more than a year of argument, reargument, and deliberation—and after having amassed a huge volume of evidence from many sources, including some of the nation's most distinguished and respected social scientists—the Supreme Court, under the leadership of Chief Justice Earl Warren, reached its decision on May 17, 1954. The Court's opinion in this case is unique in three respects. First, the decision was unanimous; it is comparatively rare for the Supreme Court's nine members to be in unanimous agreement. Second, the Court relied extensively on evidence supplied by social scientists, most of whom contended that the social and psychological effects of segregated education on children did incalculable damage. Finally, and most importantly, the *Brown* decision laid to rest the doctrine of "separate but equal" established in *Plessy* v. *Ferguson* in 1896. The Court accepted the NAACP contention that segregated education could not possibly be equal. In the words of the Court: "Separate educational facilities are inherently unequal."

A year after the 1954 decision in the *Brown* case, the Supreme Court announced its famous "implementation" decision. It should be kept in mind that the Supreme Court has no power of its own; it must depend on the executive arm of the government for the enforcement of its decisions. Nevertheless, in May 1955, the Supreme Court, again unanimously, decided to empower local *federal* courts to oversee the enforcement of the *Brown* decision. It urged that desegregation of public schools proceed "with all deliberate speed."

Most of the southern states reacted bitterly, and sometimes defiantly, against the Court after these decisions. Some of these states vowed to disregard the action of the courts and had to be forcibly made to desegregate their public school facilities. The federal government resorted to the use of federal marshals and army troops to force the desegregation of a high school in Little Rock, Arkansas. Moreover, the entire nation and most of the world became painfully aware as late as 1963 of the problems connected with the attempt to enroll a lone black student each at the University of Mississippi and the University of Alabama. In the late sixties and early seventies, the nationwide emotionalism surrounding the issue of "busing" indicated that the shockwaves from the *Brown* decision are likely to continue affecting American public opinion for some time. Long-established norms and patterns of behavior cannot be changed overnight; and the South's resistance to the efforts at nondiscriminatory education reenforces that truism. Yet change is occurring, even in the old South. The next generation may well look at the last two decades as a high-water mark in the transformation of American social attitudes and values, especially in the realm of race relations.

The problem of racial prejudice has not been eradicated. This chapter has dealt with the historical and legal aspects of racial inequality and with the efforts to reenforce the constitutional, legal, and moral bases for equality. The final chapter will examine some of the major challenges facing contemporary America. One of these is the issue of racial prejudice, still "an American dilemma." This issue has been brought to universal attention by the black revolution—the demand for full social and economic equality now—which is part of the global "revolution of rising expectations."

GLOSSARY

Aliens Visitors or residents in a country who are not nationals of that country.

Civil liberties Rights of individuals to enjoy certain freedoms, which in the United States include freedom of expression, political participation, and protections against violations of privacy by government agencies.

Civil rights Guaranteed equality of access to public facilities despite race, sex, age, or national origin.

Citizenship In the United States, U.S. nationality acquired by birth or naturalization, entitling the citizen to full rights, including the right to vote and hold public office.

Clear and present danger A legal doctrine that would not restrict freedom of expression of opposition to the United States unless such expression threatened the public safety.

Conspiracy Secret acts, or the planning of them.

Due process of law A right of individuals, stipulated in the Fourteenth Amendment, by which many of the guarantees of the Bill of Rights have been extended by limiting state and local government agencies.

Equal protection of the laws A right of individuals, stipulated in the Fourteenth Amendment, which has been used by the Supreme Court in several cases dealing with acts by states that discriminate against minority persons.

Freedom of speech (and press) The absence of arbitrary restrictions on what people say or publish.

Immigrants Aliens who are allowed to settle in the United States.

Separate but equal The doctrine that governed Supreme Court decisions on race relations from 1896 to 1954. States could provide separate facilities, such as schools, for blacks as long as they were equal to those provided for whites.

Separation of church and state A doctrine established by the Supreme Court applying the First Amendment's prohibition of any "establishment of religion" by Congress.

Subversive activities Activities which have as their ultimate object the overthrow of the government.

SUGGESTIONS FOR FURTHER READING

ABRAHAM, HENRY J. *Freedom and the Court: Civil Rights and Liberties in the United States.* New York: Oxford University Press, 1972.

CHAFEE, ZECHARIAH, JR. *Free Speech in the United States.* Cambridge: Harvard University Press, 1954.

COHEN, WILLIAM et al. *The Bill of Rights: A Handbook* and *The Bill of Rights: A Source Book.* New York: Benziger Brothers, 1968.

DRINAN, ROBERT F. *Religion, the Courts, and Public Policy.* New York: McGraw-Hill, 1963.

EDWARDS, T. BENTLEY, and FREDERICK M. WIRT. *School Desegregation in the North.* New York and London: Chandler, 1968.

FELLMAN, DAVID. *The Defendant's Rights.* New York: Holt, Rinehart and Winston, 1958.

FORTAS, ABE. *Concerning Dissent and Civil Disobedience.* New York: New American Library, 1968.

GRIMES, ALAN P. *Equality in America: Religion, Race, and the Urban Majority.* New York: Oxford University Press, 1964.

HOOK, SIDNEY. *The Paradoxes of Freedom.* Berkeley: University of California Press, 1962.

LEVIN, MURRAY B. *Political Hysteria in America.* New York: Basic Books, 1972.

MEIKLEJOHN, ALEXANDER. *Free Speech and Its Relation to Self-Government.* New York: Harper, 1948.

MILLER, LOREN. *The Petitioners.* New York: Pantheon, 1966.

NORTH, ARTHUR A. *The Supreme Court: Judicial Process and Judicial Politics.* New York: Appleton-Century-Crofts, 1966.

SCHUBERT, GLENDON A. *Judicial Policy-Making.* Chicago: Scott, Foresman, 1966.

STEDMAN, MURRAY S. *Religion and Politics in America.* New York: Harcourt Brace Jovanovich, 1964.

WIRT, FREDERICH M., and WILLIS D. HAWLEY. *New Dimensions of Freedom in America.* New York and London: Chandler, 1969.

WOODWARD, C. VANN. *The Strange Career of Jim Crow.* Revised ed.; New York: Oxford University Press, 1966.

PART THREE
FOREIGN POLICY AND DOMESTIC PROBLEMS

Chapter 10
The United States and the World

As in some of today's new nations, following independence the American people were quite apprehensive about outside interference in their domestic affairs. They scrupulously followed a policy of noninvolvement and neutrality. In fact most of America's leaders of the late eighteenth century and early nineteenth century spoke out forcefully in defense of the isolation of the United States.

FROM ISOLATION TO INVOLVEMENT—A BRIEF SURVEY

On retiring from the presidency and political life, George Washington advised his countrymen to maintain their isolation from the sordid politics of the Old World. Thomas Jefferson, whose background was cosmopolitan and whose political ideas had been influenced by European thinkers, did not hesitate to call on his fellow countrymen to avoid "entangling alliances" at all costs. Announcing a policy that has been emulated by leaders like Nehru, Nasser, and Tito, Jefferson said that the new American republic should seek "peace, commerce, and honest friendship with all nations; entangling alliances with none." In 1823, President Monroe, in his annual message to Congress, warned the European powers not to meddle in the affairs of the Western Hemisphere. At the same time, he made it clear that the United States had no desire to play a role in the politics of Europe. This brief statement of policy has been known ever since as the Monroe Doctrine.

There is a good deal of truth in the old maxim that history repeats itself. In the latter part of the eighteenth century, France and England were the two dominant powers in Europe. Already in the international stage, Europe was beginning to expand to encompass the world. France and England competed with each other for friends, allies, and satellites. The possibility of nonalignment under those conditions was not very great; therefore, many smaller powers fell in line and committed themselves to one of the two great power blocs. Conditions since 1945 are in many ways similar to those prevailing at the time of America's birth as a new nation. Instead of France and Great Britain dominating Europe, it is now the United States and the Soviet Union that predominate in the world. Around them, alliances are formed, friends gather, and satellites gravitate.

Just as the American people early in their history as a nation wanted to steer clear of involvement with either of the prevailing powers, most of the new and developing nations have attempted to do the same since 1945. They have succeeded, however, in only in a few cases. Many of the new nations simply do not enjoy the advantages of insularity—they are not separated from the centers of political power by two vast oceans—and do not possess the resources, natural and human, that allowed the United States to guard its neutrality and to defend its national integrity. At the same time, modern techniques of subversion coupled with modern developments in communications and transportation make it virtually impossible for genuine neutrality to exist.

The American leaders' reasons for desiring to remain outside the arena of European power politics were plain and understandable. Like any new nation, the infant American republic had domestic problems that had to be dealt with. Chief among these were (1) the building of a nation out of different regional, religious, political, social, and economic interests; (2) the fostering of domestic industries so that dependence on outsiders would be minimal; and (3) the extension of its frontiers from the Atlantic to the Pacific in order to fulfill its "manifest destiny." Referring to this period, Foster Rhea Dulles writes:

> To safeguard the future, it was only necessary to raise protective barriers that would enable the American people to go their own way, free of all foreign distractions and insulated from all alien influences.[1]

---

[1] *America's Rise to World Power: 1898–1954.* (New York: Harper and Row, 1955), p. 20.

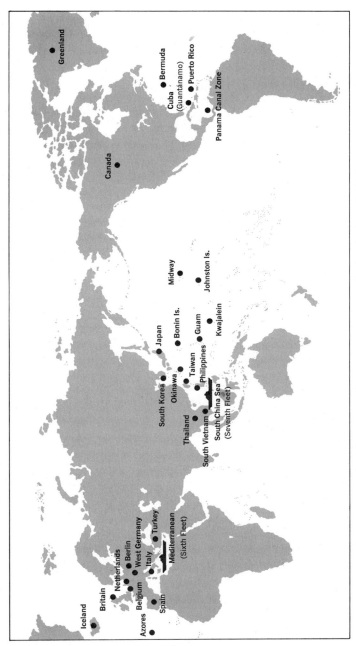

United States servicemen overseas at the beginning of 1974

Noninvolvement, however, did not mean that the United States should not have diplomatic relations with foreign nations. On the contrary, the diplomatic representation of the United States increased steadily after 1789. By the beginning of the twentieth century, America had diplomatic or consular officers in most countries of the world in order to pursue "peace, commerce, and honest friendship."

While the United States was determined to remain aloof and isolated from the political conflicts of European powers, the problems and controversies of the Old World would not stay away from the United States. So in spite of policies and principles laid down and followed by consecutive administrations, beginning with Washington's, America did finally become involved in the politics of Europe and of the world. Hence America is today a global power whose interests, obligations, and responsibilities extend to the four corners of the earth. This transformation from isolation to globalism is one of the most remarkable phenomena in modern history.

When did it all begin? When did the United States choose to become a world power? Most historians set the year 1898, marking the start of the Spanish-American War from which the United States emerged victorious and a first-rate power, as the beginning of the transformation of American foreign policy. In other words, it took the United States more than a hundred years to become secure enough at home to undertake international commitments. The Spanish-American War also marked the beginning of a new style or emphasis in international politics, and especially in the application of force. Up to that time, nations had gone to war either to defend their territorial integrity or to acquire more territory and thereby extend their influence and power. In simpler terms, wars were fought in order to advance or protect what has been called the "national interest."

Beginning in 1898, the United States changed all that by claiming that it had no territorial designs on any nation or people, but that it would fight for the purpose of extending to less privileged peoples the rights and liberties enjoyed by Americans. The argument, for example, during the Spanish-American War was that the United States was fighting to free the Cubans, the Filipinos, and the Puerto Ricans from Spanish oppression and misrule. It was a gallant but doubtful justification for a war that most historians have condemned as unnecessary. But such moral judgments are beside the point. In substance, the Spanish-American War set a pattern that has been followed by American foreign policy ever since. So whether it is World War I or World War II, the Korean conflict, or more recently the war in Vietnam, the aim or objective of the United States has been "to make the world safe for democracy."

Dean Rusk, Secretary of State in both the Kennedy and the Johnson administrations, once said that America has five major goals in foreign policy. Together, these goals constitute what may be broadly called America's effort "to make the world safe for democracy." As expressed by Secretary Rusk, America's foreign policy objectives are:

1. To deter or defeat aggression at any level, whether of nuclear attack or limited war or subversion and guerrilla tactics.
2. To bring about a closer association of the more industrialized democracies of Western Europe, North America, and Asia (specifically Japan) in promoting the prosperity and security of the entire free world.
3. To help the less developed areas of the world carry through their revolution of modernization without sacrificing their independence or their pursuit of democracy.
4. To assist in the gradual emergence of a genuine world community, based on cooperation and law, through the establishment and development of such organs as the United Nations, the World Court, the World Bank and Monetary Fund, and other global and regional institutions.
5. To strive tirelessly to end the arms race and reduce the risk of war, to narrow the areas of conflict with the Communist bloc, and to continue to spin the infinity of threads that bind peace together.[2]

Some critics of American foreign policy argue that in these goals there is too much emphasis on moralism or idealism and not enough on realism. These critics point out that the United States views the world as it would like to see it or as it ought to be, and not as it really is. Others point out that while America speaks in moralistic and legalistic terms, in practice she has most often behaved with substantial realism, always keep her national interest paramount. Both moralism and realism have in fact influenced the conduct of American foreign policy.

THE INSTITUTIONAL FRAMEWORK OF FOREIGN POLICY

As a sovereign nation with global interests and responsibilities, the United States has a foreign-policy establishment. There is a group of institutions and organizations that handle the diplomatic affairs of the United States. These different organizations deal with the formulation or execution of American foreign policy or with both. Before these organizations are discussed, it is necessary to dispel a popularly held, but false, assumption about foreign policy vis-à-vis democracy.

[2] *Department of State Bulletin*, October 15, 1962.

Since the beginning of America as a free nation, there has prevailed a popular notion that foreign policy, like domestic policy, is or should be under public control. This feeling has been reinforced by a number of political leaders who from time to time have intimated that foreign policy is in the hands of the people. This attitude is reflected, for instance, in the slogan "Power to the people."

The notion that control over foreign policy could or should be restored "to the people" is highly misleading. The people of the United States, or of any sovereign state for that matter, have never had control over the details of foreign policy. The Senate has assisted, in some cases, in the making of foreign policy, while the president and the Department of State have historically monopolized both its formulation and execution. But American foreign policy, as well as the foreign policy of any other independent nation, has been characterized by a lack of popular control. This is not to say that popular opinion does not have influence on the development of some foreign policies; it has. Yet there is a vast degree of difference between influence and control. Public opinion studies have shown that although the public's awareness of international affairs has grown tremendously in the past fifty years, there still remains a substantial degree of ignorance and misinformation in the general public's attitudes about specific issues of foreign policy. A close student of the foreign policy process has written:

> Decisions on foreign policy involve matters that are not of immediate and direct experience to many of us. . . . The decision of means to be employed in foreign policy is a terrifying demand to place on a citizen. One should be little astonished, therefore, if the citizen rejects the burden.[3]

The President

By constitutional mandate as well as by custom and tradition, the president of the United States is the individual most closely concerned with American relations with other nations. He is involved with both the formulation and the execution of foreign policy. Some presidents, in fact, have regarded their role in foreign affairs as unlimited. The president's role in the area of foreign policy will be illustrated by a brief examination of the attitudes and behavior of some recent presidents.

[3] Robert A. Dahl, *Congress and Foreign Policy* (New York: Norton, 1964), pp. 72–73, 78.

Woodrow Wilson, a political scientist as well as a practical politician, believed that in foreign policy the president's power was absolute. Ultimately, President Wilson discovered that his power was, in fact, limited. The president cannot disregard completely the wishes of the Congress (especially the Senate) and accomplish the ends he desires in foreign policy. Wilson's greatest failure as president was his inability to get the Senate to ratify United States participation in the League of Nations, an organization based largely on Wilson's idealism. So this noble attempt to create a body that would try to eliminate violence as a means of settling international disputes failed without the moral and material benefit of American participation. Historians have blamed President Wilson for his unwillingness to take into his confidence important members of the Senate establishment, led by Senator Lodge of Massachusetts, in the Paris negotiations leading to the creation of the League.

Both Presidents Roosevelt (Theodore and Franklin Delano) regarded the chief executive's power in foreign policy as virtually absolute. Both acted on many occasions with utter disregard of congressional sentiments and desires. Theodore Roosevelt did not hesitate to express contempt of Congress for allegedly acting too slowly in regard to questions involving the national interest. An anecdote illustrates his feelings toward the Senate. He once remarked to a visitor that he was so angered by the Senate that he often felt like unleashing a pack of lions in the Senate chamber. "But Mr. President," the startled visitor asked, "what if they ate the wrong Senators?" "They wouldn't," the president replied, "if they stayed long enough."

Franklin D. Roosevelt served as United States president during a period of great crises, the greatest of which was World War II. Throughout the war, President Roosevelt acted as though Congress had gone on vacation. He conducted diplomacy on a personal level, meeting Allied leaders in places like the mid-Atlantic, Teheran, Malta, Cairo, and Yalta to plan strategy and the conduct of the war. The decisions reached in those meetings had far-reaching implications for America; yet the Senate was rarely consulted—it was simply presented with an accomplished fact. Congress long ago acknowledged the power of the president to conduct foreign affairs by *executive agreement,* which is as binding as a treaty but does not require Senate ratification. During the war, Roosevelt made extensive use of this power, often committing the United States to policies and programs of significant consequences.

Harry S. Truman, in the straightforward midwestern style that characterized him, once remarked, "I make American foreign policy."

And so he did. Some of America's most important postwar foreign policies bear the Truman imprint. But Truman was a senator before he was F.D.R.'s vice president, and he knew the ways and idiosyncracies of the Senate. Although he felt that his power in foreign affairs was great indeed, he wanted to avoid committing Wilson's errors by not taking into consideration the wishes of the Senate leadership. Consequently, Truman made a determined effort to develop a genuinely bipartisan foreign policy supported by both Democrats and Republicans. And he succeeded. While the Republicans opposed most of Truman's domestic policies, in foreign affairs they helped create and supported such novel and far-reaching programs as the United Nations; the Marshall Plan (to help rebuild the destroyed economies of Europe); the Truman Doctrine (assisting Greece and Turkey to defend themselves against Communist subversion); the Berlin airlift of 1948 (which met Stalin's threat to starve the city into submission); the North Atlantic Treaty Organization (NATO); the Point Four Program (offering economic and technical assistance to former colonial areas achieving independence); and the unequivocal United States' response to the aggression by North Korea against South Korea—to mention the most important of his policies.

Dwight D. Eisenhower came to the presidency from a background of military leadership. As allied commander in Europe during World War II, he led into battle and to victory the forces of more than half a dozen nations. His position required great tact, and General Eisenhower apparently possessed diplomatic talent as well as personal charm and charisma. He needed these gifts in order to coordinate smoothly the activities of the tremendous forces comprising the "Grand Alliance."

As president, Eisenhower seemed to believe in personal diplomacy at the highest level—in what came to be known as "meetings at the summit." Despite opposition from many professional diplomats and foreign-service officers, who felt that summit meetings seldom succeed, he expressed the desire to go anywhere and meet with any leader in the cause of peace. In 1955 he went to Geneva, where he made his famous proposal to utilize atomic energy for peaceful purposes. In 1960 he went to Paris to meet with Nikita Khrushchev to discuss possible avenues to better cooperation for the sake of maintaining world peace. In the course of the meeting, Khrushchev disclosed that a high-flying U-2 spy plane had been brought down over Soviet territory, ending that summit meeting in humiliation and failure for Eisenhower and the United States.

Of the policies initiated by the Eisenhower administration, the most important were the Eisenhower Doctrine offering assistance to Middle East countries threatened by Communist subversion; the development of the theory of massive retaliation against the Soviet Union, which suggests that a Soviet attack anywhere would be met by American annihilation of the Soviet Union; the development of alliances on the periphery of the Soviet Union and China, such as SEATO (South-East Asia Treaty Organization), CENTO (Central Treaty Organization), the organization which commits the United States to the defense of the Middle East, ANZUS (Australia, New Zealand, United States), and several bilateral agreements. The initial commitment of the United States in South Vietnam also began during Eisenhower's term.

The man who succeeded Eisenhower to the presidency, John F. Kennedy, had his own ideas about foreign policy. As an accomplished historian and refined politician, Kennedy realized that international politics in the age of thermonuclear weapons required imagination, patience, and a great sense of the possible. When appointments to the cabinet were announced early in 1961, many observers felt that Kennedy's choice of Dean Rusk as Secretary of State was indicative of the fact that Kennedy, like F.D.R., wanted to take personal charge of foreign policy. Arthur M. Schlesinger, the history professor who served as an assistant to the president, confirms that feeling in his memoirs of the Kennedy presidency, *A Thousand Days*. Kennedy allowed Dean Rusk to handle the day-to-day administrative tasks of the vast State Department bureaucracy while he personally dealt with the great issues of foreign policy.

In foreign affairs, as on domestic issues, Kennedy brought a new style and vitality. In the relatively short period of two years, he gained the respect and admiration of people in all corners of the globe and the confidence of such leaders as Charles de Gaulle of France, Konrad Adenauer of West Germany, and Nikita Khrushchev of the Soviet Union. A number of foreign policies were instigated under Kennedy's leadership. In particular, four stand out: the imaginative Alliance for Progress in Latin America; the conclusion and ratification of the Nuclear Test Ban Agreement; the Laotian neutrality agreement; and the quick and decisive response to the missile threat from Cuba. On the negative side, Kennedy must be held responsible for beginning the escalation of the United States involvement in Vietnam.

President Johnson's contributions to foreign policy remain controversial. Most observers agree that Lyndon B. Johnson was least skillful in the area of foreign affairs. However, he can be given credit for the treaties on nuclear nonproliferation and on cooperation in outer space, the United States–Soviet Union consular treaty, the opening of an air link between New York and Moscow, and an overall interest in the easing of tensions between the United States and the Soviet Union. All of the above and a large number of domestic accomplishments, however, will be dwarfed by Lyndon B. Johnson's massive and very unpopular response to the conflict in Vietnam.

The boldest moves in recent United States foreign policy have been made by a Republican president, Richard Nixon. During his first term, 1969–1973, Nixon presided over the winding down and conclusion of the Vietnam War, the end of the draft, and a major arms limitation agreement with the Soviet Union. In 1971, he unilaterally imposed a 10 percent surcharge on United States imports, which had the effect of pressuring other nations into a basic restructuring of the international monetary system. But his boldest stroke of all was his decision to visit personally America's two archenemies, China and the Soviet Union, in February and May of 1972. It was the first time an American president had ever visited China, and only the second time for the Soviet Union (Roosevelt was there in 1945). Moreover, formal relations, just short of diplomatic recognition, were established with China in 1973, bringing to an end 24 years of extreme hostility. But at this writing it is too early to tell whether President Nixon's achievements in foreign policy during his first term would be overshadowed by the scandal of Watergate during his second.

What has been said above is illustrative of the point that the president's role in foreign policy, if not absolute, is very large. American foreign policy at any given time is likely to reflect not only the president's foreign policy views but also the stamp of his personality.

The Congress

The Constitution affords the Congress, the Senate in particular, a substantial role in foreign policy. According to the Constitution, treaties concluded between the United States and other nations must be ratified by the Senate. Moreover, the Senate must give its consent to presidential appointments to high diplomatic posts. In its advisory capacity, the Senate also contributes significantly to the making of foreign policy. One of the most prestigious committees is the Senate Committee on Foreign Relations currently headed by J. William Fulbright, Democrat from Arkansas. Senator Fulbright has come in for both praise and criticism in the past several years for speaking out on foreign policy questions with candor and unusual forthrightness. His committee's examination of America's Asian policies in general and Vietnam commitment in particular, and his criticism of President Johnson's response to the Dominican crisis of 1965 are examples of senatorial influence on foreign policy. Most of America's postwar foreign policies might not have been possible without the assistance of another senator, Arthur D. Vandenberg, Republican from Michigan. His influence on such historic policies as the Marshall Plan and the Truman Doctrine cannot be overemphasized.

None of America's foreign policies can be implemented without money. The House of Representatives, therefore, through its participation in the control of appropriations, contributes importantly to the foreign policy-making process. On occasion, the House passes resolutions, as does the Senate, on questions of foreign policy. These express the opinion of the House, or of the Congress, and may be regarded as suggestions to the administration to do something or to avoid doing something. For example, in September, 1965, the House passed by an overwhelming margin a resolution calling for unilateral intervention by the United States anywhere in Latin America in order to meet the threat of Communist subversion. Resolutions aside, the most important facet of the House of Representatives' role in foreign affairs remains the granting of funds for carrying out foreign policy decisions and programs, together with the follow-up on how these funds are spent.

In spite of the substantial formal powers the Senate and House have in foreign policy matters, there was an unmistakable erosion of this power in the 1960s. Partly because of the divisive Vietnam experience, however, and partly because of the opportunity created by a weakened president in the wake of the Watergate scandal, some progress was made in reasserting some degree of Congress' traditional foreign policy prerogatives, as discussed in Chapter 4. Following congressional steps to forbid the continuation of American bombing in Cambodia, congressional leaders and the president agreed that such bombing would cease on August 15, 1973.

The Department of State

Heading the numerous departments and agencies which assist the chief executive in the development and implementation of foreign policy is the Department of State. This department is headed by the Secretary of State, whom the president appoints and the Senate confirms. He is specifically charged with the conduct of American foreign relations. Although the president has other advisers the Secretary of

State has traditionally been considered his senior adviser on foreign policy. Under Richard Nixon, much of the policy input came from special presidential adviser Henry Kissinger. The administrative duties of the Secretary of State remained, however, in the hands of William P. Rodgers until his resignation. The Secretary of State is the chief administrator of the State Department, including its extensive activities overseas. Embassies, consulates, missions, and legations are under the control and direction of this department. The Secretary of State and his immediate subordinates are often called before congressional committees to explain, defend, or rationalize the government's handling of foreign relations.

The Policy Planning Staff

An important unit within the Department of State is the Policy Planning Staff, an elite organization involved in questions of long-range foreign policy planning rather than in the day-to-day functions of the department. The purpose of this group is to anticipate the twists and turns of an adversary's foreign policy and to attempt to develop a policy or series of policies to meet or counteract the thrust of that policy. The Policy Planning Staff has been credited with some successes, the most important being the development of the containment policy in 1947, which calls for the United States to resist the further spread of Communist influence, by force if necessary.

Over the years, this unit has been led by some distinguished personalities. Its first director, who is credited with the policy of containment, was George F. Kennan. More recently W. W. Rostow, a highly regarded economic historian and foreign policy analyst, and Zbigniew K. Brzezinski, a Columbia University professor specializing in Communist affairs, have held important positions in this group. Critics of United States foreign policy argue however, that the nation's policy has been characterized more by reaction than by initiative. In other words, these critics insist that, instead of initiating policies and thus placing the opposition on the defensive, American foreign policy reacts to moves by adversaries.

The Agency for International Development

Also working under the overall direction of the Department of State, this agency administers the economic aid of the United States to friendly nations. The AID mission in a given country coordinates all nonmilitary aspects of United States assistance to that country. Its role has come in for some scrutiny and criticism as a result of United States involvement in Vietnam.

The Treasury, Commerce, and Agriculture Departments

When Thomas Jefferson referred to America's desire for "peace, commerce, and honest friendship with all nations," he recognized the fact that commercial interests would be one of the cornerstones of American foreign policy. He was right. In some instances, especially in the Caribbean and in Central America, the United States has even used force to protect or advance the economic interests of individuals or enterprises. Trade and commerce still remain important goals of foreign policy, and the Treasury, Commerce, and Agriculture Departments carry out these economic objectives of the United States government.

The Department of Defense

In the past 30 years the United States has entered into a number of military alliances and commitments around the globe. For this reason the Department of Defense participates closely and quite actively in the formulation and execution of American foreign policy. It administers the sometimes extensive United States military aid to friendly nations. Military power has always served as a lever in foreign policy. To a great power like the United States, military strength and preparedness is vital to the effective operation of the entire foreign policy process. In this respect, the Secretary of Defense is usually one of the president's top advisers on foreign affairs. Few, for instance, would discount Robert S. McNamara's foreign policy role in the Kennedy and Johnson administrations or Melvin Laird's role under Nixon.

The National Security Council

The nation's most important advisory body on security policy is the National Security Council, which is probably best known today from the role of its director, Henry Kissinger. Established in 1947, it is designed to offer the president coordinated advice on political, economic, and military policies related to national security. By statute, members of this body are the president, the vice president, the Secretaries of State and of Defense, and the director of the Office of Emergency Planning. The director of the Central Intelligence Agency (CIA) and the chairman of the Joint Chiefs of Staff are advisory members. The president, at his discretion, may invite others to take part in the deliberations of the National Security Council. During John F. Kennedy's presidency, for example, Robert F. Kennedy, the president's brother and United States Attorney General, and Adlai Stevenson, the United States ambassador to the United Nations, were included in the meetings of this high-level policy and planning body.

The Central Intelligence Agency

The nation's most important agency for gathering and evaluating information relating to national security is the CIA. The activities of this organization are extensive and, most of the time, secret. In order to gather the necessary information efficiently, the CIA utilizes the most up-to-date techniques and equipment, such as high flying SR-71 reconnaissance aircraft, as well as traditional methods like spying by paid agents who participate in political intrigues, bribery, and even political manipulation. In spite of determined efforts to work in secrecy, CIA activities have not always succeeded in avoiding publicity. In 1960, for instance, a CIA U-2 (predecessor of the SR-71) was brought down over Russia, and Nikita Khrushchev used the incident to sabotage a meeting with President Eisenhower in Paris. In 1961, the CIA's role in the abortive invasion of Cuba at the Bay of Pigs came to light and was criticized in the press and in the halls of Congress. When Khrushchev was suddenly dismissed by his successors in the Kremlin in 1964, the CIA was criticized for not having forecast the turn of events.

In 1966, a group of senators headed by Eugene McCarthy, Democrat of Minnesota, sought to gain closer supervision over CIA activities. Their efforts failed. Questions have been raised about the propriety of such an organization in an open society especially after it was disclosed in 1967 that the CIA had subsidized the activities of the National Students Association (NSA) and many other private groups. These questions are disturbing, to be sure, but in the minds of many people, including key members of Congress, they are overridden by international conditions which require a supersecret agency with virtually unlimited resources—even in a democratic society.

The Joint Chiefs of Staff

Consisting of general officers (usually of four-star rank) who represent the interests of all the armed services, this body offers the president military advice. The chairman is appointed by the president, usually on the basis of his experience. Occasionally, however, the president will give weight to political considerations as well as to experience. For example, in 1961 President Kennedy brought Maxwell Taylor out of retirement to head the Joint Chiefs. This appointment reflected the fact that presidents will often choose someone who agrees with their policies and in whom they have personal confidence.

The United States Information Agency

Since the contemporary conflict between East and West is a contest for the minds of men perhaps more than for territory, raw material, and markets, the USIA was created in 1947 in order to project a good image of the United States overseas. Every nation wishes to be seen in a good light by friend, foe, and potential adversary. The United States is no different in this regard. In a very real sense, the USIA is a propaganda agency; and it has often been criticized within the United States for giving foreigners a distorted, glamorous picture of the nation, its people, and its problems.

Functioning under the overall direction of the Department of State, the USIA operates the Voice of America, a vast radio and television network which broadcasts to most parts of the world, in dozens of languages and dialects, including broadcasts to countries behind the Iron Curtain. It also operates libraries, art, trade, and commercial exhibits, and many other informational activities. USIA libraries and other facilities are easy targets for attack by student mobs and other groups in countries dissatisfied with American foreign policy. Such acts demonstrate that foreigners are well aware that USIA functions are closely related to American foreign policy goals and objectives.

The Peace Corps

A highly successful, and by far the most inexpensive, foreign policy effort of the United States has been the Peace Corps. Created in 1961 as a result of a promise made by John F. Kennedy during the 1960 campaign, the Peace Corps sent volunteers to many of the world's underdeveloped nations. They took with them good will without strings attached, idealism characteristic of America at its best, a willingness for hard work with little pay under poor working conditions, and a sense of mission that has gained the admiration even of those who originally were skeptical regarding the success of the program. Many contemporary observers, both foreign and domestic, regard the accomplishments of the Peace Corps as one of the most striking foreign policy innovations of the Kennedy administration.

Informal Presidential Advisers

Over the years, successive presidents have established the practice of bringing into the administration individuals to advise them on issues of foreign policy. The president may accept or reject the advice, but often the influence of these unofficial advisers is substantial. Woodrow Wilson had his Colonel House, and Franklin D. Roosevelt his Harry Hopkins, while more recently President Eisenhower relied heavily on Sherman Adams, and John F. Kennedy respected the opinion of men like Theodore C. Sorensen, Arthur M. Schlesinger, Richard Goodwin, and McGeorge Bundy. President Johnson's foreign policy attitudes were influenced by Walt Rostow and Bill Moyers who, from all indications, were more than simply the president's speechwriter and press secretary. Under President Nixon, Henry Kissinger played this key role. Many credit Kissinger alone with the striking foreign policy initiatives of the Nixon administration.

THE MAIN ISSUES OF UNITED STATES FOREIGN POLICY

This section will examine briefly what are generally considered the most important challenges to America and its foreign policy. These challenges confront the entire world as well. As a great power, the United States has worldwide interests. In turn, these interests entail obligations and responsibilities. Chief among the responsibilities facing the United States is to prevent thermonuclear holocaust, an awesome challenge. Although there is disagreement as to what the other main challenges to American foreign policy are, the following issues are examined in what the authors consider to be their order of importance.

The Lessons of Vietnam

One of the most perplexing, costly, frustrating, and divisive entanglements of postwar American foreign policy was the Vietnam commitment. It is not the purpose here to examine in detail the recent history of Indochina, part of which is now Vietnam. Before examining United States involvement, it should be pointed out that warfare is nothing new to the Vietnamese. The inhabitants of that unfortunate corner of Southeast Asia have been fighting outsiders—Japanese, French, and Americans—and one another for more than a generation.

When John F. Kennedy assumed the presidency, the United States commitment was in essence of an economic and technical nature, with only a few hundred military personnel in advisory positions. Eight years later, America's involvement was immense by any standard. By 1968, total American military strength in the area exceeded 600,000 men, while the cost to the United States was well over two and one half billion dollars per month. By 1972, over $150 billion had been spent and almost 50,000 Americans killed in the most bitter military experience in recent United States history. United States involvement in Southeast Asia was predicated on the policy of containment, in this case expressed in the much discussed "domino theory." Under the principles of the containment policy, Communist expansion beyond the borders of mainland China had to be resisted—by force if necessary. Following this line of reasoning, those who supported the "domino theory" insisted that unless Communism was checked in Vietnam, it would spread to the rest of Southeast Asia, with its tentacles eventually reaching Australia, New Zealand, Japan, Indonesia, Malaya, the Philippines, and perhaps even Hawaii.

Those who opposed United States commitment in Southeast Asia argued that the "domino theory" still remains a theory—that it is not certain or immutable that if Vietnam fell to the Communists the rest of Asia would meet the same fate. Others opposed America's position in Vietnam on what they considered the historic proposition that the United States, or any other European power for that matter, should never become involved in a war on the land mass of Asia. These same people insisted that the course of American foreign policy in Asia ran the risk of involving us in just such a war.

The point here is that American foreign policy became enmeshed in a predicament in Asia and particularly in Vietnam. The costs of the Vietnamese war have been enormous; and as United States involvement became greater, the costs, in terms of wealth, loss of life, and misery also mounted. Will the people of the United States support such undertakings in the future? We believe not, for one of the main lessons of Vietnam is that a great power like the United States cannot become involved in what is essentially a civil war without suffering a loss of face or prestige. At the same time, such entanglements always run the risk of involving the United States in a direct confrontation with another nuclear power, here with China or the Soviet Union, over an issue of peripheral importance to the national interest. Another lesson is that conventional military tactics, including tactical and strategic bombing, are essentially ineffective against armed guerrilla groups and against a society like North Vietnam's, which is primarily rural and agricultural. A third important lesson is that the United States can no longer act as a world policeman. This is the main assumption underlying the Nixon Doctrine, enunciated by President Nixon in Guam in the spring of 1969. In effect, President Nixon said "no more

Civilian Casualty in Indochina

Editorial cartoon by Paul Conrad; © 1972 The Los Angeles Times, reprinted with permission.

Vietnams." After Vietnam, the president said, the United States would offer aid and assistance to its allies and friends but not foot soldiers.

The United States and Europe

Because alliances are at best marriages of convenience, the "Grand Alliance" of the United States, Great Britain, and the Soviet

Union during World War II began developing cracks in its structure almost immediately after its main objective, the defeat of the Axis powers, was accomplished. With the fall of Berlin and the Japanese surrender, wartime cooperation developed into peacetime suspicion and distrust. Even before the victory celebrations were over, there were signs that promises made during the war were not going to be kept. This was especially true in Eastern Europe, that large portion of the European continent which had been "liberated" by Soviet troops. It also became increasingly evident that a large part of Western Europe and those nations on the periphery, such as Greece, Yugoslavia, and Turkey, were in grave danger of falling into the Soviet camp by the new, efficient, and not very costly method of subversion from within. To meet this challenge, and to contain the further expansion of Soviet influence, the Western powers agreed that a combined effort was necessary. Thus the North Atlantic Treaty Organization (NATO) was created.

In April, 1949, the North Atlantic Treaty was signed by twelve countries: the United States, Great Britain, France, Canada, Denmark, Iceland, Belgium, the Netherlands, Luxemburg, Norway, Portugal, and Italy. With Greek and Turkish membership in 1952, and West German participation in 1955, the number of NATO nations is presently fifteen.

The NATO alliance has served its purpose well. Members do not hesitate to point with considerable pride to the fact that since 1949 not one inch of NATO-protected territory has fallen under Soviet domination. But alliances do not last forever. And while Soviet expansionism has been contained, there has been the development on both sides of the Iron Curtain of what can best be described as "polycentrism." The term polycentrism, first used by Italian Communists to describe the condition of international Communism after Stalin's death, is as relevant to the Western bloc of nations as to the Eastern. It signifies the existence of more than one center of authority and power instead of a monolithic condition. Typically one among the members of an international movement, such as Communism, or an alliance, such as NATO, directs and in a large way controls the affairs of that movement or alliance.

When polycentrism first developed in the mid-1950s, the NATO countries welcomed it. And some East European nations were encouraged to the point of rising against Soviet efforts to maintain their authority intact. One of these revolutions, the Polish revolution, succeeded halfway; but that in Hungary failed under the might of Soviet mechanized units. More recently Rumania and Czechoslovakia (until its independent course was crushed by the Soviet Union in 1968) have manifested a strong attachment to the principles of polycentrism.

The Atlantic alliance is also facing the problems of polycentrism. Although there have been no bloody revolts against the chief protagonist within NATO, the United States, there have developed the cracks and schisms that have characterized alliances for thousands of years. What has plagued NATO is a seeming inability, or perhaps an unwillingness, to conform to new and fast-changing conditions. Most Europeans and many North Americans, for example, recognize the fact that the danger of Soviet expansionism is not as great today as it was a few years ago; conditions have changed and are constantly in a state of flux. Yet because great powers and alliance systems have traditionally preferred the status quo to change, most efforts at redirecting the NATO emphasis from a purely military to a quasi-political coalition have been in vain. Hence the problems exemplified by the late President de Gaulle's stubborn insistence on removing France from NATO's unified command structure should not have come as a surprise.

Since alliances are marriages of convenience, the leading powers of an alliance must constantly strive to keep the rest of the members satisfied. It goes without saying that this task is a very difficult one indeed, and the Atlantic alliance is experiencing the stresses and strains of that condition. As Henry Kissinger has written:

> In the life of societies and international systems, there comes a time when the question arises whether all the possibilities of innovation inherent in a given structure have been exhausted. At this point, symptoms are taken for causes; immediate problems absorb the attention that should be devoted to determining their significance. Events are not shaped by a concept of the future; the present becomes all-inclusive. However impressive such a structure may still appear to outsiders, it has passed its zenith. It will grow rigid and, in time, irrelevant.[4]

Peaceful Coexistence or Nuclear Annihilation

For a quarter century the world has lived precariously with the threat of nuclear destruction. Man's imagination, aided by almost incredible technological advances, has created weapons of such destructive capacity that they can only be termed nightmarish. In the process, man may have given birth to a veritable monster, one that threatens to turn around and destroy its creators. Nothing has concerned civilized man more in the past 25 years than the question of how to deal effectively with the weapons of mass destruction at his disposal. Certainly all the nuclear powers, including the late-comers to the nuclear club, France and Communist China, have shown that they are aware of the dangers inherent in the development and stockpiling of nuclear weapons. The

---

[4] *The Troubled Partnership* (New York: McGraw-Hill, 1965), p. 249.

Robert Bastian in The San Francisco Chronicle

United States and all of mankind is painfully aware of the devastation wrought upon the Japanese cities of Hiroshima and Nagasaki by, in comparison to present-day nuclear weapons, infinitesimally small atomic bombs. We have arrived at a point in the development of nuclear energy that, if used for peaceful purposes, it could bring great benefits to mankind. But if used for purposes of war, it could bring about the end of civilization. John F. Kennedy put it quite succinctly in September, 1963, before the United Nations: "We have the power to make this the best generation of mankind in the history of the world or to make it the last."

The United States was first to develop nuclear weapons. In 1945, Japan was compelled to surrender unconditionally after two of its cities were completely destroyed by atomic bombs. Soon after the Japanese surrender, the wartime coalition between the Soviet Union and the West began to fall apart. Between 1945 and 1949, the Soviet Union was frantically working to develop atomic weapons of its own in order to counteract the arms superiority of the United States. Finally, in 1949, somewhere in remote Siberia, Soviet scientists successfully exploded a nuclear device. Since the early 1950s, therefore, a condition has prevailed that Winston Churchill aptly described as "the balance of terror." Odd as it may seem, the possession of nuclear weapons by more than one power may be a blessing in disguise. Realizing the potential destructiveness of these weapons, both the United States and the Soviet Union have acted responsibly and with commendable restraint. Someone once noted that it might not be too farfetched an idea if the Nobel Peace Prize were awarded to the hydrogen bomb: After all, has it not kept the peace in the world?

The United States government has always realized that unless something was done to control the spread of nuclear weapons disastrous consequences would follow. Since 1946, therefore, a number of plans and proposals have been advanced to accomplish these objectives, at least in part. Of all these proposals, only three seems to have met with any success. First, in the summer of 1963, after lengthy negotiations at Geneva and at the United Nations, the main nuclear powers, the United States, Great Britain, and the Soviet Union, agreed to cease further atmospheric testing of nuclear weapons. This agreement is the Nuclear Test Ban Treaty which has been signed by virtually every nation of the world, with the exceptions of France, China, Cuba, and Albania. Since testing is essential to the development of nuclear weapons, the test-ban agreement was a step in the direction of eventual limitation of all types of armaments.

A second step in the right direction was the nonproliferation agreement signed by the major nuclear powers in the summer of 1968. According to this treaty, the signatories agreed not to supply nuclear weapons or technical and material aid for the production of such weapons to countries that do not already possess a nuclear arsenal. France and China, the other two nuclear powers, did not participate in the negotiations and did not sign the treaty.

The third recent move which had the effect of reducing the threat of thermonuclear war was the conclusion of the first phase of the Strategic Arms Limitation Talks (SALT) in 1972. As a result of those talks, the United States and the Soviet Union agreed to hold constant the number of missiles in their respective arsenals and to confine themselves to two Anti-Ballistic Missile (ABM) sites each. Much more remained to be negotiated, however, including the number of warheads on each missile and the use of space satellites as weapons.

Negotiations toward disarmament continue at Geneva. A number of countries participate in these negotiations, but the protagonists are still the United States and the Soviet Union. The United States Arms Control and Disarmament Agency, created in 1961, coordinates this nation's disarmament efforts. The Soviets are also anxious to talk about further disarmament moves. Often the objectives of the two superpowers in this general area are similar; the means, however, desired to reach these objectives differ. They often disagree on how to make certain that a disarmament agreement is going to be carried out and its provisions observed. In other words, they disagree about what kind of inspection system or procedure is to be utilized.

Is disarmament possible? Most people would like to think that it is. Realistically speaking, though, the probability of complete disarmament is very small indeed. This is not to say that some sort of agreement for the limited use of arms or for the cessation of further production of arms is unlikely. But there is a vast difference between limitation of arms and complete and total disarmament. This issue leads to another question: Is coexistence possible? Before an attempt is made to answer this query, let us see what coexistence means.

Soviet attitudes toward the West changed markedly between 1953 (Stalin's death) and 1956 (Khrushchev's rise to power). At the Communist Party Congress held in the spring of 1956, Nikita Khrushchev, in his capacity as First Secretary of the Party's Central Committee, came out in favor of peaceful coexistence between Communist and non-Communist nations. It would be folly, he said, to think that ideological differences could be solved by force in the age of thermonuclear bombs. In a nuclear conflict between his country and the United States, Khrushchev told Party functionaries, there would be no winners, only losers. He advocated, instead, competition in all fields—ideological, political, economic—so long as it did not lead to a nuclear confrontation. It goes without saying that this was a radical departure from the Stalinist position which viewed war between Communism and capitalism as inevitable. Khrushchev believed, however, and his successors are still convinced, that Communism will ultimately triumph throughout the world, but without recourse to war.

How then is peaceful coexistence possible? In view of the alternatives, not only is it possible, it is imperative. And while the United States' guard must always be up, the search for peace must never cease. Current developments in the Communist world—the independent course of Chinese Communism, and the reduction of controls in Eastern Europe and Russia—suggest that there is room on this planet for all types of ideology and points of view, so long as they do not threaten to blow all mankind into oblivion.

The Challenge of Underdevelopment

According to an eminent British economist, the contemporary world is no longer divided between East and West (between Communism and democracy); rather it is divided into North and South.[5] The North

---

[5] Barbara Ward, *Spaceship Earth* (New York: Columbia University Press, 1966).

is the industrialized and advanced part of the globe: Europe, the Soviet Union, and North America. The South includes much of Asia (some north of the equator), the Middle East, Africa, and Latin America. Mankind, if it is to exist in relative tranquillity, must narrow the immense gap that separates the developed part of the world from the underdeveloped part. The implications for the advanced countries of the world are clear: They must take the initiative and narrow the widening gap between the affluent and the poor of the world.

Another analyst points out that modern developments in transportation and communications have been instrumental in compressing the world into an interdependent whole. The consequences of this development can only be described as revolutionary. But in spite of the apparent closeness of modern man, in a physical sense, his separation, in terms of material well-being, is incredibly wide. Robert Heilbroner's concern about this condition is eloquently expressed in the following passage:

> As a result [of advances in transportation and communications] what was once a gulf which divided two wholly separate worlds is rapidly becoming a rift which divides one self-conscious human community. With each painful step forward, the peoples of the world become more alive to the conditions of humanity in countries other than their own. And of all these conditions the one which stands out is the terrible disparity of living conditions in their own lands compared with the lands of a favored few. The division of the world into the abjectly poor and the grossly rich—a condition of which the poor were always dimly aware, but which appeared as a matter of immutable fate, as an inscrutable destiny—suddenly becomes a dispensation of human history which seems iniquitous, intolerable, and infuriating. Their economic development, their catching up, becomes not just a matter of social policy, but of social justice.[6]

As the world's greatest industrial nation whose economic power is unequalled, the United States faces a challenge without parallel in the history of man. The responsibilities entailed in this challenge are tremendous, but the United States government and people have shown a willingness to respond to the needs and aspirations of the developing world. To its credit, the foreign policy of the United States in the post-war period has shown foresight and imagination in regard to the economic inequities of the world. Numerous programs have been devised to assist the less fortunate members of the community of nations to lift their people from the depths of poverty, disease, and ignorance. In

6 Robert L. Heilbroner, *The Future As History* (New York: Harper and Row, 1960), p. 162.

this respect, foreign policy-makers have been quite realistic. They have recognized the fact that unless the more obvious manifestations of poverty, illiteracy, and disease are steadily reduced or eliminated throughout the world, the United States, along with the rest of mankind, will suffer.

The United States and in recent years the economically prosperous European nations, as well as Japan in the Far East, have been involved in a variety of programs designed to assist needy countries to develop their economies and improve their social conditions. The United States government devotes approximately two to three percent of its annual budget to foreign aid, both military and economic. A greater effort may be necessary if livable conditions are to prevail worldwide. Congress, however, largely because of the costs of the war in Vietnam, reduced the 1969 foreign aid appropriations to the lowest level since the end of World War II. Relatively low levels of spending on foreign aid continued into the 1970s.

Will the United States continue to meet the challenge of underdevelopment? It probably will for two reasons: First, it is in the nation's self-interest to be surrounded by countries that are economically strong and thus able to resist the appeals of revolutionary doctrines such as Communism. Second, the United States as a nation and Americans as individuals have a tradition and a long history of compassion and concern for the condition of people in other parts of the world. A commentator not long ago suggested that the economic ills of the world could be solved, and a possible catastrophe averted, by an economic offensive of massive proportions administered by the United Nations:

> Launched now, a World Marshall Plan just might, and I stress the word might, make life on this planet livable and meaningful by the year 2000. If not, the crises of food and water shortages, pollution, epidemic, famine, overpopulation, illiteracy, and despair are liable to overwhelm the fragile veneer we call civilization.[7]

Such a proposal is worth serious consideration. Furthermore, it would be in keeping with the best traditions of the United States to contribute, from its considerable economic and moral resources, to such an undertaking.

The Challenge of Revolution

In a Senate speech criticizing President Johnson's response to the revolt in the Dominican Republic in April, 1965, J. William Fulbright, more in anguish than in anger, noted that the United States ran the risk

[7] Sherwood Ross, "A World Marshall Plan," *The Progressive* (April, 1966), p. 30.

of appearing to be a counter-revolutionary power, a conservative, contented society that desired to maintain the status quo. Other political figures and commentators have expressed similar sentiments in light of United States behavior vis-à-vis revolutionary developments in many parts of the developing world. What concerns Senator Fulbright and those who share his views is that one of the most revolutionary societies in existence, a society and civilization born through the process of revolution, seems to be losing or abrogating what has been considered its historical role as a leader of social, economic, and political change.

There is little doubt about it. The United States is seriously challenged by the prospect of revolution in Latin America, Asia, and Africa. To a great power like the United States, this challenge is immensely frustrating. However it is met, someone is bound to be displeased and disappointed. No one likes upheavals and violent change; an established great power prefers peaceful, gradual change, or no change at all, to revolutionary transformation. Yet it can be argued that the United States is indirectly as much to blame for these revolutions as is any other country, ideology, or political system. The American experience—that is, the development of a great nation in a relatively short period of time—has had the most revolutionary effects in modern history. The Asian, the African, or the Latin American who sees American films and television programs or listens to broadcasts of the Voice of America must be impressed by the fact that the standard of living in the United States is so much higher than his own. He does not hesitate to follow the leadership of those who promise to bring him closer to that standard, even if it has to be done at the expense of public order and tranquillity. And sad to say, the revolutionary path in some societies appears to be the only avenue to improvement through change.

Has the United States fulfilled its promise as a revolutionary force? In all candor, it must be admitted that it has not. To begin with, the United States has failed to meet the challenge of revolution in its immediate sphere of influence, Latin America. A cursory examination of the political map of the continent south of the Rio Grande indicates that well over two-thirds of the people living in that area are under some form of dictatorial rule. And what is more distressing, dictatorships in Latin America, except Castro's, are treated by the United States government on a par with the few democracies there. Moreover, while the United States has in the past intervened, sometimes by force, in support of the status quo in South America, it has not chosen to intervene when democracy was being threatened and subverted by antidemocratic elements. There are numerous illustrations in this regard, but two will suffice to make the point.

The people of the Dominican Republic, after more than 30 years of dictatorial rule under Trujillo, in 1963 elected by an overwhelming vote Juan Bosch as their president. Seven months after his inauguration, Bosch was ousted by a military junta on the pretext that he was soft on Communists and a poor administrator. After a brief period of protest, the United States resumed military and economic aid to the dictatorial regime of the Dominican Republic. When pro-Bosch elements of the armed forces revolted in April, 1965, the United States intervened militarily because, it was argued, Communists were about to subvert the Dominican Republic. As it turned out, the intervention may have averted a Dominican bloodbath; but that is beside the point. Supporters of the principles of democratic revolution wonder why the United States did not intervene in support of Bosch in 1963.

Another case in point occurred in Argentina. In July, 1966, the popularly elected, but not necessarily effective, government of Arturo Illia was overthrown by the military. It was replaced by a group headed by retired General Juan Ongania who, immediately after gaining control of the government, set about to destroy the vestiges of democratic institutions—political parties, the national and provincial legislatures, and courts—that had been built after the fall of Juan Peron in 1955. After initially condemning the turn of events in Buenos Aires, the United States resumed diplomatic relations and economic assistance programs with the Argentine dictatorship.

An important change in the American attitude toward revolutionary developments in other countries occurred in 1969 with President Nixon's speech on foreign policy now referred to as the Nixon Doctrine. In that speech, the president reaffirmed United States support for governments combating internal revolutionary groups, but announced that this support would not take the form of United States troops. This certainly was a major change from the Johnson Doctrine as applied in Vietnam in the 1960s and the Dominican Republic in 1965. A specific trial for the Nixon Doctrine was the election victory of Marxist Salvador Allende as President of Chile in November 1970. Would the United States send troops to aid those elements in the Chilean military who wished to prevent Allende's taking office? The Nixon administration decided against such a course and maintained a cool detachment from the situation throughout Allende's term in office. This was, perhaps, the clearest illustration of the Nixon Doctrine in practice.

It should not be inferred from this discussion that the United States favors dictatorships over democratic regimes. Indeed it does not. What should be emphasized is that conditions prevailing in much of the world are likely to give rise to revolutions. Many of these revolutions, with all their imperfections and shortcomings, can be guided toward democracy rather than totalitarianism. The United States should become the leader, as it is the example, of democratic revolutions.

The Challenge of Communism

Since 1917, the world has been confronted with a unique and, in many respects, powerful challenge. Revolutionary Marxism (or what today often goes by the name Communism) is one of the greatest challenges of our time. It has gained the attention not only of statesmen, politicians, and academicians, but of the general public as well. In some parts of the world, the Communist challenge could not be countered, and what presently goes by the name Communism has triumphed: Eastern Europe, mainland China, and Cuba.

The world has faced similar challenges in the past. The American War for Independence in 1776 and the French Revolution in 1789, for example, and the ideas emanating from them challenged very seriously the status quo in Europe. In order to meet the challenge, the European powers worked frantically to form alliances and coalitions to protect themselves and their interests against the forces of change. Ultimately they succeeded, in 1815, in defeating Napoleon's armies, but the ideas of the French Revolution proved to be invincible. In this respect the victory against Napoleon at Waterloo was a Pyrrhic one: the war was won, but the battle for the minds of men was lost. The ideas coming out of the American and French revolutions succeeded in fundamentally altering European politics because they promised something which previously was unavailable to the masses: equality of citizenship.

From the middle of the nineteenth century, Marxism, under various forms and interpretations, has been preaching another form of equality. Since Marx and his followers believed that everything rests on economics, they deemphasized such notions as political equality and instead called for drastic, sometimes revolutionary, measures that would bring about economic leveling. Because of the conditions prevailing in Europe during the beginning of the Industrial Revolution, Marxism made an impact on intellectual circles and through them on the masses. The odd thing, however, is that revolutionary Marxism did not succeed, as Marx said it would, in the industrialized countries of Western Europe—France, Great Britain, and Germany. It succeeded instead in the backward, peasant environment of Imperial Russia. Moreover, since 1917, revolutionary Marxism has met with success in China and Eastern Europe, while it has made only minor inroads in the economically advanced nations of the world. What inferences can be drawn from this pattern of successes and failures? Clearly, Communist movements thrive on underdevelopment and backwardness compounded by social and political discontent.

The danger which Communist governments pose for the United States in particular and for democracy in general cannot be dismissed. Communism, however, is only one among the many challenges that the United States must face and meet if it is to survive and if democracy is to prevail. Communism should not be assigned top priority among problems that threaten our society, although some individuals and groups disagree with this appraisal. Democracy must find a way to meet and solve the problems of hunger, disease, ignorance, and prejudice, both at home and abroad. If these are eradicated, the threat and appeal of Communism will be greatly minimized. The fact that Communism has made no important gains in the great democracies of the West—America, Great Britain, Canada—testifies to its lack of appeal in genuinely open societies.

The Communist challenge is threefold: ideological, economic, political. As an ideology, Communism offers simple and apparently straightforward solutions to all of man's needs and aspirations. Essentially, Communism stresses the theory that a particular society's economic system determines the nature of its political, social, and spiritual institutions. To improve conditions, Communists argue, one need only alter the economic structure of society in such a way as to distribute the wealth equally. To be sure, this element of Communist ideology is a powerful one. It is particularly appealing to groups, classes, or individuals who have no stake in their society as it exists. For instance, to the peasant of South America or Asia who has nothing to call his own except misery, Communism offers an escape. For this reason, one of the basic assumptions of such United States programs as the Alliance for Progress called for radical and widespread social and economic reforms.

Does the Communist ideology appeal to the workers of industrialized societies? Although the ideology itself may have some abstract appeal, practically speaking, Communism does not pose a threat in developed countries. What can it offer the average factory worker in the United States? A Cadillac instead of a Ford? More and bigger appliances? A shorter workweek? These he has, thanks to the labor unions and the good sense of businessmen. This discussion leads to one conclusion: Communism as an ideology will find followers and converts in people with empty stomachs and among the world's dispossessed.

The Communist party in the United States has failed to attract large numbers of followers from the disadvantaged minorities. While this fact may seem unexpected, it could be argued that ideology is irrelevant to the plight of racial and ethnic minorities in the United States. The seeming adherence of disadvantaged minority groups to the norms and values of the American system might be attributed either to a lack of opportunity to do anything about their condition or to a basic belief in the system's inherent ability to change over time. In any event, until recent years radical approaches to the solution of minority problems such as those offered by the Communist party, have found a very limited number of followers in the United States.

When Khrushchev was in power, he liked to boast that the Soviet Union would eventually catch up and surpass the capitalist world, especially the United States, in the economic sphere. The fact is, however, that Russia has much to do to catch up to, let alone surpass, the United States. Therefore the economic challenge of Communism poses no grave threat for America and the West European nations. While few will refuse to give the Russians credit for almost spectacular technological successes, exemplified by Sputnik and other achievements in outer space, they have also suffered some rather remarkable economic setbacks. They have had difficulties, for example, with the agricultural sector of their economy, as manifest by their purchases of wheat from the United States and Canada. (Massive quantities of American wheat were imported in the early 1970s.) One explanation of Khrushchev's dismissal is that he failed to deal effectively with Russia's farm problems.

In industry, as in agriculture, the Russians have had difficulties. The quality of their manufactured products leaves much to be desired, and their central planning system has been criticized as inefficient; there have been perennial shortages of some goods and overproduction of others. In recent years, Soviet economists and industrial planners have in essence admitted that certain capitalist principles may have to be utilized in order to develop the Soviet economy to its fullest potential. These might include a greater emphasis on the profit motive and a heavier reliance on the principles of supply and demand to regulate production. The Chinese Communists rarely miss an opportunity to castigate their Russian brethren for behaving more and more like capitalists instead of upholding the true spirit of Marxism-Leninism.

As far as the Soviet economy goes, one thing seems clear: The Russian leaders are discovering, slowly but surely, that a complex economic system cannot be operated along the lines of a rigid ideology. Consequently, they seem inclined to disregard the teachings of orthodox Marxism and willing to make use of what appears to have worked successfully elsewhere. To that degree, they are pragmatic.

Some groups in the West, especially conservatively oriented groups, insist that the political threat posed by Communism is as great today as it was, say 25 years ago. A close examination of this proposition leads to quite a different conclusion. There are three reasons for regarding the Communist threat as less dangerous than it once was. First, it can be argued that as a political system, Communism lacks appeal. While the ideological side of Communism appeals to societies in the process of development, offering them a method for accelerated industrial growth, few are eager to accept Communism as a political system. In fact, wherever Communist regimes exist today—in the Soviet Union, Eastern Europe, China, Cuba—they are sustained by the element of force.[8] In none of these cases have the people, by majority vote, elected to establish a Communist form of government.

Second, it can also be argued that most people prefer freedom to tyranny, democracy to authoritarianism. And if aspirations and needs can be met by a democratic form of political organization, men will support it in preference to Communism or any other form of authoritarian government.

Finally, Communism poses no real threat to "the American way of life" because of the crisis of disintegration in international Communism. Until the early years of the postwar period, the non-Communist world was impressed and concerned with the apparent unity of the Communist bloc. Until Yugoslavia's break with Moscow in 1948, it was generally assumed that international Communism was controlled and directed from a powerful center in Moscow, with Stalin pulling the necessary strings. After Stalin's death, the apparent unity of world Communism began to erode. First the East Germans revolted in 1953 and had to be subdued by Russian troops. Then in 1956 the Poles and the Hungarians violently expressed their disapproval of Soviet overlordship. Even though Russia did not allow Poland and Hungary to leave the Communist camp, concessions were made. West European and Scandinavian Communists have always had a degree of independence from Moscow, but since 1956 they have operated under the proposition of polycentrism. More recently the Rumanians and the North Koreans have expressed nationalistic sentiments. In a much more spectacular way, the reform-minded Communist leaders of Czechoslovakia attempted to follow a more independent course in 1968, but were thwarted in that attempt.

[8] The case of Allende in Chile, discussed above, does not apply here because his regime was Marxist-socialist rather than Communist. Although Chile's Communist party backed Allende's election, they were junior partners in the governing coalition (Union Popular).

The outstanding example of the disintegration of world Communism is the conflict between Russia and China. This is no place to examine the many facets of this supposedly "fraternal disagreement," but it has tremendous implications for the United States and its allies, for the Soviet Union and its supporters, and, ultimately, for the entire world.

GLOSSARY

Alliance for Progress The policy initiated by President Kennedy toward Latin America; the United States was to assist in the economic and social development of Latin American countries.

Cold War The protracted conflict between the United States and the Soviet Union for 25 years after World War II, which never quite reached the level of full-scale military activity.

Domino theory The belief that if one country is taken over by a Communist government its neighbors are likely to be threatened in a similar manner; used as a justification by many for the United States effort in Vietnam.

Executive agreement An understanding between the leaders of nations; in the United States it does not require ratification by the Senate as would a formal treaty.

Grand Alliance The alliance of the United States, the U.S.S.R., and Great Britain during World War II.

Isolationism The basis of early United States foreign policy, which sought to avoid all alliances and all international involvement.

Johnson Doctrine The willingness of United States leaders to inject United States money and troops into Civil War situations where leftist forces may be winning; the phrase refers especially to United States intervention in the Dominican Republic in May, 1965.

Marxism An economic and political philosophy which rests on a commitment to economic equality for all citizens.

Marxism-Leninism A belief that the fight for a better society must be led by revolutionary workers groups.

Monroe Doctrine A policy first announced in 1823 whose primary feature was a warning to European powers not to meddle in the affairs of the Western Hemisphere.

Nixon Doctrine A declaration that United States support for allied governments would not include American troops; support for our allies should be aimed at making them self-sufficient.

Nonalignment A policy followed by many Third World governments, especially during the Cold War period, which meant not being allied with either the United States or the U.S.S.R.

Peaceful coexistence The tacit agreement of American and Russian leaders since 1945 that the two superpowers can compete on many levels without triggering a thermonuclear war.

Satellite A country whose government is totally subservient to another government (as Bulgaria is to the Soviet Union).

Summit diplomacy Direct meetings between heads of state (as between Nixon and Brezhnev in June, 1973).

SUGGESTIONS FOR FURTHER READING

BUCHAN, ALISTAIR. *Power and Equilibrium in the 1970s.* New York: Praeger, 1973.

CARLETON, WILLIAM G. *The Revolution in American Foreign Policy.* New York: Random House, 1964.

CLEVELAND, HARLAN. *The Obligations of Power.* New York: Harper and Row, 1966.

DAHL, ROBERT A. *Congress and Foreign Policy.* New York: Norton, 1964.

FALL, BERNARD. *The Two Viet-Nams.* New York: Praeger, 1964.

GADDIS, JOHN LEWIS. *The United States and the Origins of the Cold War.* New York: Columbia University Press, 1973.

HALLE, LOUIS J. *The Cold War as History.* New York: Harper and Row, 1967.

HALBERSTAM, DAVID. *The Best and the Brightest.* New York: Random House, 1973.

HOROWITZ, DAVID. *The Free World Colossus.* New York: Hill and Wang, 1965.

KENNAN, GEORGE F. *American Diplomacy, 1900-1950.* New York: Mentor, 1958.

KISSINGER, HENRY A. *Nuclear Waepons and Foreign Policy.* New York: Doubleday, 1958.

KISSINGER, HENRY A. *American Foreign Policy.* New York: Norton, 1969.

SAPIN, BURTON M. *The Making of United States Foreign Policy.* New York: Praeger, 1966.

SCHLESINGER, ARTHUR M., JR. *Bitter Heritage.* Boston: Houghton Mifflin, 1968.

SCHULMAN, MARSHALL. *Beyond the Cold War.* New Haven: Yale University Press, 1965.

STILLMAN, EDMUND, and WILLIAM PFAFF. *Power and Impotence: The Failure of America's Foreign Policy.* New York: Random House, 1966.

WALTON, RICHARD J. *Cold War and Counterrevolution: The Foreign Policy of John F. Kennedy.* New York: Viking, 1972.

Chapter 11
Domestic Challenges of the 1970s

The purpose of this brief book on the United States political system has been twofold. First, like all books of its kind, it has been designed to give the student a greater awareness of the political system in which he lives. Second, it has intended to raise as many questions as it answers. The authors have hoped to stimulate an interest in politics so that the student will find it useful and enjoyable to read further into the field. One aim has been to show that, in a democracy, politics as a vocation can be both honorable and rewarding. If this book has even partially accomplished these ends, we have been rewarded for the effort of writing it.

Certainly, the political system of the United States is not perfect; many facets of it could be improved and changed. And changes there will be, because government and politics in a democracy must be constantly reorganized and updated. If a democracy is to remain dynamic, some of its institutions and practices need to be periodically reevaluated, brought up to date, or even cast aside in favor of more appropriate ones. "Conventional wisdom," as John Kenneth Galbraith calls the accepted mode of thought and behavior, has very little applicability to democratic politics or to enlightened economics. What may have been appropriate at some time in the past is not necessarily suitable for the present or the future. If the demands of new situations are to be met, it may be necessary to rely very heavily on "unconventional wisdom," that is, on bold experimentation and innovation. This process has been going on in the American system since 1787, and it is likely to continue.

Chapter 10 examined briefly several of the challenges that the United States is facing internationally. This final chapter will undertake a brief examination of some of the domestic issues that challenge the nation. The viability of our political system may ultimately depend on how these challenges are met. Similar challenges confronting less stable systems and less sophisticated societies have very often proved fatal.

THE CHALLENGE TO CONFIDENCE IN DEMOCRACY

The greatest challenge confronting democratic government today is the person who mocks, ridicules, and questions faith in the democratic process. Some critics of democratic politics ask: "Is democracy possible?" "Is government by the people really possible?" And they answer with an emphatic "No!" by exposing some of the contradictions within democratic politics and concluding that democracy is really a façade for government by an elite of some kind.

This thesis was presented by the distinguished Columbia University sociologist, the late C. Wright Mills.[1] American politics, Mills argued, is not really controlled by those elected to public office but by a small group of corporate executives, military leaders, and influential bureaucrats and administrators. Professor Mills was not an antidemocratic elitist, but he was concerned with what he felt to be the trend in American politics, a trend away from democracy and toward greater power exercised by an elite not responsible to the majority. While Mills insisted that there exists in American politics a "power elite," he failed to demonstrate how and under what conditions such an elite group influenced specific matters of public policy. Moreover, he treated the military-industrial-bureaucratic elite as if it were some form of monolithic conspiracy with well-defined purposes. Yet he was not explicit in describing how this allegedly powerful force is organized and functions. Disregarding the relative merits or shortcomings of the book for the moment, *The Power Elite* did make an impact on the popular mind. Moreover, on retiring from the Presidency in early 1961, Eisenhower advised the American people to beware of the power wielded by the military-industrial Establishment.

[1] *The Power Elite* (New York: Oxford University Press, 1956).

The issue depends on how the term *democracy* is defined in the first place. If by democracy its critics mean that system which briefly existed in Athens 2500 years ago, then they are right; that kind of "direct" democracy is no longer possible in any large and complex society. But men have devised something that approaches the Greek ideal of democracy—indirect or representative government—which was discussed in Chapter 1.

Next, critics of democracy marshal arguments intended to demonstrate that most of the world is governed, to one degree or another, undemocratically. They point to Eastern Europe and the Soviet Union and to most of Asia, Africa, and Latin America as areas where the method of government is not democratic. But does this evidence mean that democracy is impossible or undesirable? Or does it simply substantiate the notion that the economic, social, and political conditions for democracy are not present in those countries? Clearly the answer is the latter. It has been demonstrated, in Western Europe and in North America especially, that democracy is not only possible; it is, indeed, the system preferred by the overwhelming majority of the body politic. In the last analysis, most of those who insist that democracy is not possible fear and distrust the judgment of the average man.

Another argument raised by critics of democracy is that it is an inefficient method of government. Since government is a necessary evil, they argue, why not make it efficient? There is something coldly logical about this proposition, but it is incorrect. It is widely accepted that the most efficient form of political organization is a well-oiled dictatorship. In a stable, well-established dictatorship, there is no opposition to question or criticize the dictator's decisions. When he alone, or with the assistance of a small group of trusted advisers, decides to do something, it is done. Democratic decision making, on the other hand, is a much more complicated and cumbersome business; and sometimes it is frustrating. Nevertheless, it seems that most people do not mind occasional inefficiency as long as they know that they enjoy certain rights and liberties which only democracy, imperfect as it may be, guarantees.

The subject comes up in virtually all conversations about politics. Someone will state categorically that politics is a "dirty" business and that politicians are "scoundrels." Americans in particular have given the term *politician* an unfavorable connotation, implying double-dealing and underhanded deals in smoke-filled rooms and behind closed doors. The career of politician is often viewed with disfavor and distrust. Such statements as "They're all a bunch of crooks" or "What do you expect of a politician? He's only interested in your vote" are heard throughout the country. Yet when every year the Gallup organization publishes the results of their survey of the most admired man, it usually turns out to be the incumbent United States president or a former president, as was the case with Eisenhower.

There are some well-grounded reasons for this popular attitude. First, politicians do make deals—sometimes behind closed doors— because, as was pointed out in Chapter 1, compromise and accommodation are basic ingredients of democratic politics. Moreover, in the

"A victim of Watergate!"

Editorial cartoon by Frank Interlandi; © 1973 The Los Angeles Times, reprinted with permission

mid 1960s, the Johnson administration was afflicted with what was popularly called a "credibility gap." It resulted from widespread public disbelief in government statements and projections about the Vietnam conflict. Accusations of corruption and scandals connected with the Nixon administration, such as alleged irregularities in the settlement of a government antitrust suit against the International Telephone and Telegraph Company, and highlighted by Spiro Agnew's resignation as vice president, further contributed to increasing the public's cynicism about government.

Second, there have been unfortunate cases involving politicians who have abused their position for personal gain. The behavior of the late Representative Adam Clayton Powell of New York is a case in point: Powell was investigated by his colleagues, stripped of his committee chairmanship, and ousted from the House for allegedly taking advantage of his role as chairman of the House Education and Labor Committee for personal purposes. The same year a member of the Senate, Thomas J. Dodd of Connecticut, was censured by his colleagues, upon the recommendation of a special investigating committee, for diverting campaign contributions in excess of $100,000 to his personal use. This severe action by the Senate has been used only seven times in its history. Until now, neither the House nor the Senate has adopted a stringent code of ethics for its members. Despite such instances, the overwhelming majority of those elected to office perform their tasks honestly and without corruption or misfeasance.

Finally, many people seem to believe that politicians are super-human and therefore should behave unlike mortals. The nation was shocked, for example, when the Bobby Baker affair made the headlines a few years ago. It is worth asking what most people would do if they were in Baker's powerful position as secretary of the Senate majority. Politics is not an inherently "dirty" business. In view of the price-fixing scandals involving some of America's largest corporations and tax-evasion convictions of businessmen and labor leaders, it might even be said that politics by comparison does not look so bad.

THE CHALLENGE OF THE CITIES

Many of the most difficult problems facing the United States in the 1970s concern local government. As Chapter 7 brought out, the cities and counties cannot meet these challenges single-handedly; solutions will require cooperation between the states and the national government. With the passage of President Nixon's revenue-sharing program in 1972, which will return in a period of five years about $30 billion of federal tax monies to the states and cities to be used without extensive federal controls, some of the more acute problems of local government may be partially solved. From among a wide range of urban problems that could be mentioned, four of the more vital ones are urban sprawl and decay, air and water pollution, crime and violence, and education. After a brief discussion of the challenges, this chapter will discuss three related issues in the context of violence and "the revolution of rising expectations": demands for equality by blacks and other disadvantaged groups, poverty in the midst of affluence, and political extremism. Although all these problems confront the entire American society, they are particularly acute in the cities. Indeed, the greatest single domestic challenge in the years ahead is often referred to as the "crisis of the cities."

Urban Blight

The most frightening aspect of this multiple crisis is urban decay or urban blight, as it is often called. Because metropolitan areas attract people in ever-growing numbers, local governments have a major difficulty in just keeping up the current level of services to all their inhabitants. The process of urbanization is invariably accompanied by the deterioration of the core city in a pattern commonly referred to as "the cycle of urban decay."

As people continue to move into the city, the property in the central district increases in value; at the same time, taxes increase to keep up the same level of services to an ever-expanding population. As a result middle- and upper-income families move to the suburbs, where property and taxes are less expensive. But many of the major industries also relocate at the fringes of the city. The central city gradually becomes the headquarters for commercial establishments and government offices on the one hand, and crowded, overpriced slum dwellings on the other. Lower socioeconomic groups move into these slums, largely because they belong to minorities and cannot find housing elsewhere. Meanwhile, the margin of profit of the property owner declines as his taxes continue to go up, so that he cannot afford to improve or even maintain the property adequately, and it continues to deteriorate. To complicate the problem, huge freeway complexes are built to carry the white-collar workers, now living in the suburbs, to the central city where many of their jobs are located and to carry the blue-collar workers from the central city to the fringes where much of the heavy industry has relocated. But the freeways gobble up hundreds and thousands of acres of valuable land, thus further reducing the property-tax base.

1984 (OR TOMORROW?)

Peb in The Philadelphia Inquirer

Perhaps most discouraging of all is the fact that although the city may be engaged in a program of urban renewal (that is, removing slums and replacing them with attractive, modern structures), the process of urban renewal almost without exception proceeds more slowly than that of urban decay; new slums develop even before the existing ones can be cleared away.

Air and Water Pollution

Air and water pollution also threaten the quality of life in the cities. Increasing numbers of factories and automobiles, belching forth exhaust and lethal fumes in large quantities, saturate the air with contaminants that kill animals and plants. The internal-combustion engine is responsible for much of this contamination because it is so inefficient that much of the fuel passes through unburned, contaminating the atmosphere with unused hydrocarbons. These unburned gases mix with other elements and, with sunlight acting as a catalyst, produce what is variously called smog, haze, or smaze. Discouragingly, automobile exhaust-control devices which eliminate some 70 percent of these harmful emissions will bring the air-pollution problem back to about the 1960 level, temporarily. As the number of automobiles increases, pollution will again continue to grow worse unless and until some acceptable substitute is found for the gas-burning automobile engine.

If we are not killed off from breathing contaminated air, experts reassure us that we may be done in by polluted water. Water contamination is caused in two ways: by the disposal of industrial wastes into rivers and streams, and by the widespread use agriculturally of insecticides and commercial fertilizers, which make their way into the water supply. Regulating water pollution involves very complex analysis to determine where the contaminants come from, what danger levels are, and what the proper remedy is. Once answers to these questions are found, it will probably develop that pure water is easier to obtain than pure air. For the time being, both seem to be increasingly rare commodities in America's major cities.

Crime and Violence

Crime is another very difficult crisis with which cities must cope. Every major city in the United States has experienced a steady and alarming increase in its crime rate over the past decade. The problem is nationwide, but it is most pronounced in the cities. The attempted explanations for this alarming trend are several, among which are the following:

1. The courts favor the rights of the accused as opposed to those of society and potential victims of crime.
2. Techniques of gathering crime statistics have improved, resulting in more *recorded* instances of crime but not necessarily in more crime per se.
3. The pressures of modern life drive more people to the fringes of distraction and despair, and crime.

The first explanation assumes that would-be criminals rationally evaluate the risks of being caught and convicted and, because of "lenient" court decisions, decide that the risks are not great enough to deter them. This explanation gives criminals credit for rational calculation, which they probably do not undertake. There is no evidence which proves that potential murderers, for example, are less likely to kill if they know they may face a death penalty than if they would not. Crime is very often an irrational act, and sociological studies indicate that the threat of punishment is not an effective deterrent to crime.

Finally, the court decisions blamed, such as *Gideon* v. *Wainwright* (1963), *Escobedo* v. *Illinois* (1964), and *Miranda* v. *Arizona* (1966), do not have the intention of relaxing the penalties for crime, but rather of requiring proper police procedures in the apprehension and conviction of criminals. There is no inevitable conflict between this goal and effective crime prevention, as the experience of the F.B.I. indicates.

Second, it is suggested that the apparent increase in the crime rate is artificial, that it reflects an improvement in crime *detection*, rather than a significant increase in the rate as such. This is a difficult assertion to prove since there are no statistics on the numbers of unrecorded crimes which were committed over the past decade. So this argument at best rests on an unprovable assumption.

The third explanation for the crime-rate increase is the most plausible. It is undeniable that the pressure and tensions of modern living are greater than they were, say, before World War II. The individual is dwarfed by bigness on all sides: big business, big labor, big government, and now the big bomb. He may feel, more than any of his ancestors, that he is the victim or the pawn not only of the forces of nature but also of the equally capricious giant institutions and forces of modern civilization. Modern man, especially if he lives in the big city, is closer to more temptations, both personal and material, than any man in history. If he works, he has more leisure time to brood about his problems, more time to use either for good or evil. And he may be one of the millions of unemployed and unemployable people who despair of satisfying their material needs by socially acceptable behavior; so he turns to crime.

Growing Demand for Education

Part of the solution to the crime problem is education. A person who has at least a high-school education is less prone to crime for two reasons. First, he is able to find productive employment and so is less likely to exist on the fringes of frustration and despair. Second, he is likely to understand the forces at work in society and in himself which threaten his emotional and psychological equilibrium. But education itself is a problem for government because of the growing numbers of children and young adults seeking education and because of the increasing cost per student.

Because education traditionally is paid for by state and local governments, the burden tends to fall on the property owner in most states. The property tax has been the chief source of revenue for schools. But a growing number of Americans do not own property; they rent apartments or homes. Moreover, local property taxes have become so burdensome in many states that property owners are beginning to demand that other sources of revenue be found for schools. In 1965, the Congress enacted the Elementary and Secondary Education Act, extending some aid to local education in partial response to this demand. But massive federal support for education is a brand-new venture in the United States and still meets the opposition of those who prefer the traditional local control and local financing of education. The force of circumstances will probably quiet this opposition over time, and the federal commitment to aid education will undoubtedly be accepted as the only feasible solution to a crisis of enormous magnitude. But whether this aid will be soon enough and substantial enough to meet the challenge remains to be seen.

Concluding Note

In short, the problems of state and local government are many. They will not be solved until there is a new attitude toward government in general and toward local government in particular. In other words, if local governments are to meet the challenges which confront them, the negative attitudes which have long plagued government at this level must be overcome. Local politicians must be willing to innovate. They will have to treat local government as a large enterprise and deal with it in a highly sophisticated way. Unless that is done, and soon, the problems which afflict the states, particularly their cities, may prove insoluble.

VIOLENCE AND THE REVOLUTION OF RISING EXPECTATIONS

In addition to crime in the usual sense,[2] society in the world today—and not least in the United States—is faced with increasing violence in social and political protest. In its extreme form, violent protest manifests itself as looting, sabotage, assassination, and armed rebellion. The political murders of national leaders, including President John F. Kennedy, Dr. Martin Luther King, Jr., and Senator Robert F. Kennedy, led President Johnson in June 1968 to appoint a national commission under the chairmanship of Dr. Milton Eisenhower to study the problem of violence. Meanwhile, Congress has made efforts to tighten gun-control laws.

---

[2] Crime, as it is commonly understood, refers to antisocial acts committed for personal gain or from some private motive such as spite or jealousy.

Various hypotheses have been advanced to explain the epidemic of violence: the tensions of modern life, already noted in connection with crime; the stimulation of mass media, especially television; and the breakdown of public morality (a circular diagnosis that mixes causes with symptoms). One of the most dramatic pictures of the ailment was painted by playwright Arthur Miller in 1968: "From Moscow to Warsaw to Prague to Paris to Rio to Berkeley and New York, there is a deep and boiling rebellion against institutions and institutionalized feeling."

Thus people throughout the world are demanding more from existing institutions, rejecting "institutionalized feeling" (or unfeeling) in response to their demands, and challenging the legitimacy, even their right to exist, of institutions that fail to satisfy popular demands. This phenomenon has been described as "the revolution of rising expectations" by such observers as Hershner Cross, a vice president of the General Electric Company, who analyzed its basic premise as follows:

> . . . the stern philosophy that a man is entitled to the position and the rewards he can carve out for himself is being modified to at least this degree: If he can't get the essentials for himself because of race, age, illness, or an underprivileged early environment, then he will be helped through political action.[3]

When conventional political action fails, the first alternative of the "have-not" is nonviolent civil disobedience as conceived by Thoreau and perfected by Gandhi and Martin Luther King. But if all peaceful avenues seem closed, the modern protester rather quickly turns to violence.

In short, no consideration of violence in the modern world can overlook the social and political context, even if social and political considerations do not explain violence completely. In that context one must consider the three major challenges discussed in the balance of this chapter: blacks and other disadvantaged minorities, poverty in the midst of affluence, and political extremism.

THE CHALLENGE OF THE DISADVANTAGED

One of the great documents of the United States, the *Declaration of Independence,* embodies a principle which is among the most admirable ever put on paper. It states categorically that one of the main assumptions of government in America is the principle of equality: "We hold these

---

[3] "The Executive Environment: 1966," *Harvard Business School Bulletin* (January–February, 1966).

Truths to be self-evident, that all Men are created equal, that they are endowed by their Creator with certain unalienable Rights . . ."

It must be said in all candor that the "self-evident truths" about human equality to which the Declaration of Independence refers were not thought to apply—some insist they still do not apply—to a segment of the United States population whose skin is dark and whose ancestors were originally brought to these shores from Africa as slaves. This segment, the blacks, today constitutes approximately 11 percent of the nation's population.

The problem of race has been with us, in a legal sense, since 1787 although in a human sense it has been with us even longer. (There were persons and groups in the United States before 1787 who opposed slavery on humanitarian grounds.) Chapter 3 noted that one of the compromises reached at the constitutional convention involved the question of representation. It was agreed that those states with large black (slave) populations would be allowed to count a slave as three-fifths of a white person for the purpose of determining the number of representatives allotted to that state in the United States House of Representatives. But this compromise did not affect the slaves themselves in any significant way. For more than fifty years after the creation of the federal union, the position of the slaves and the question of slavery were a central issue in the relations between the northern and southern parts of the union. This issue ultimately contributed to the bloody and divisive war between the states, the effects of which are still being felt more than one hundred years after its conclusion.

At the end of the Civil War, three amendments were added to the Constitution, the Thirteenth, Fourteenth, and Fifteenth. These were to guarantee equality of citizenship regardless of color or previous condition of servitude. Section 1 of the Fourteenth Amendment is singularly important since it makes it illegal for any state to deny a person his rights under the Constitution "without due process of law"; and no one within a state's jurisdiction can be denied "the equal protection of the laws." These two clauses—on due process and equal protection—have been the basis of most court decisions dealing with the matter of civil rights.

The Declaration of Independence, the Constitution, Lincoln's Emancipation Proclamation, the Civil War and the constitutional amendments following it, several civil-rights acts of Congress, and numerous court decisions notwithstanding, the problem of the relations between the majority white population and the large black minority is more acute today than ever before in the history of the republic. In the 1960s, the severity of the problem confronted the body politic in bloody and destructive riots in the Watts section of Los Angeles and in violent clashes and demonstrations in many cities: New York, Chicago, Cleveland, Philadelphia, San Francisco, Omaha, Newark, Detroit. These events point to an inescapable conclusion: There is a wide discrepancy between the declared aims of our society in the realm of human rights and the actual conditions under which the majority of blacks in the United States live. The problems created by these conditions have brought about what is now popularly called the black revolution.

Actually the black effort to attain complete equality of treatment has been multifaceted. It involves efforts for equal opportunities in education, employment, and housing, in addition to the long struggle to attain equality in voting and other political rights in all sections of the United States.

The reversal of the black man's immediate gains after the Civil War has been described by Professor Charles Aikin:

> During the period of Reconstruction after the Civil War, and for a while during the post-Reconstruction years, many former slaves voted. Soon conditons developed in the South and elsewhere that led to a widespread denial of this vote. On the one hand, the judiciary played its part by whittling away some of the Negro's rights and by dulling the edge of congressional statutes adopted to protect him. On the other hand, a growing national lack of interest in the Negro as a voter developed and the nation came to accept him into second-class citizenship.[4]

Restoration of Black voting rights began in 1944 with a Supreme Court decision, in *Smith* v. *Allwright*, outlawing the "white primary" on the ground that a primary election is an integral part of the election process, not a private affair within a clublike political party. In the Civil Rights Acts of 1957, 1960, and 1964, Congress empowered the Department of Justice to sue state election officials to compel registration of citizens disqualified from voting because of race. In 1964 the Twenty-fourth Amendment outlawed a poll-tax requirement for voting in national elections. The Voting Rights Act of 1965, passed after the murder of a civil-rights worker in a freedom march in Alabama, authorized federal action against most remaining voting restrictions, especially the misuse of literacy tests.

While the educational opportunities for blacks have improved markedly in the past fifty years, in certain states the education black children receive—from the elementary to the college level—continues to be inferior to that received by white students. There has been, in this

[4] *The Negro Votes* (New York and London: Chandler Publishing Company, 1962), p. 5.

area, an obvious disregard for some of the most essential aspects of the United States constitutional framework. Many states, especially but not exclusively in the South and border areas, flagrantly disregard the Constitution, common decency, and morality by openly discriminating against blacks in the area of public education.

Until 1954, many states operated their educational systems on the doctrine of "separate but equal" formulated by the Supreme Court in the case of *Plessy* v. *Ferguson* (1896). In that decision, the Court stated that it was acceptable for the states to maintain the separation of the races as long as the facilities provided for each race were equal. This, many states assumed, applied to public education as much as to public transportation and to public accommodations such as train and bus terminals, hotels, restaurants, funeral parlors, and even churches. In May, 1954, the Supreme Court in effect reversed the "separate but equal" principle in the landmark decision of *Brown* v. *Board of Education*. In that case, the Court stated that education received in separate facilities was inherently unequal. It urged the desegregation of public education throughout the United States "with all deliberate speed."

Although he had initial reservations about the *Brown* decision, in 1957 President Eisenhower ordered troops to Little Rock, Arkansas, to enforce the Court's decision to desegregate Central High School. Since then, more and more states in the South have complied with the Court's decisions and related parts of the civil-rights acts of 1957, 1960, 1964, and 1965. But some have complied only under force. Increasingly federal agencies have used the "power of the purse," especially since passage of the Elementary and Secondary Education Act of 1965, by making school desegregation the price of federal aid.

After the Supreme Court banned school desegregation where it was required by law (*de jure*), especially in the South, civil-rights workers turned to school segregation where it existed in fact although not required by law (*de facto*), especially in the North. *De facto* segregation reflects the relation between public school districts and housing patterns. A number of lower-court decisions, before and since *Brown*, have outlawed zoning practices which forced black pupils to leave their neighborhoods to attend segregated schools. Since the *Brown* decision, school districts have faced the question of their obligation to provide integrated education for all children where the segregated schools simply reflect "ghetto" neighborhoods. The methods used to achieve integration include consolidation of school facilities, "benign gerrymandering" of school zones, and voluntary or forced transfers of pupils from ethnically "balanced" to imbalanced zones. School desegregation in the North as well as in the South has become a subject of heated controversy, with protests against "busing," "extravagance," and "social engineering" added to cries protesting "racial mixing." The position of the federal courts has been that elimination of *de facto* segregation is not required by the Constitution but that it is a legitimate objective of state and local school authorities. Again the power of the purse has been used, as both federal and state agencies press local school districts to desegregate not only in law but also in fact. However, busing of schoolchildren for the purposes of racial integration became one of the major political issues of the 1972 presidential campaign. At first Governor Wallace of Alabama raised the issue during the Democratic primaries in the winter and spring of the year. As a result, President Nixon and several of the Democratic contenders like Senators Jackson, Muskie, and Humphrey were forced to take essentially an antibusing position. The 1972 campaign proved that busing was still an emotional and potentially explosive issue in American politics.

School integration progresses steadily but slowly, and national aims, as expressed in judicial decisions, legislative acts, and executive actions, will have been in vain unless equality in education becomes a nationwide standard, in practice as in theory. The Swedish scholar Gunnar Myrdal put it quite bluntly in his monumental and classic study of the condition of the black minority in modern America:

> The American nation will not have peace with its conscience until inequality is stamped out, and the principle of public education is realized universally.[5]

Especially since World War II, organizations such as the National Association for the Advancement of Colored People (NAACP), the Congress of Racial Equality (CORE), and the Urban League—and concerned unorganized white Americans as well—have been making efforts to eliminate inequalities in employment. Their success, however, has been only partial. In spite of state and national legislation, particularly in the Civil Rights Act of 1965, which forbids employers from discriminating on the basis of race, color, religion, sex, or national origin, the unemployment rate for blacks is two or three times higher than that for whites. According to statistics of the United States Department of Labor, in the third quarter of 1972 10 percent of those who lived in so-called urban poverty neighborhoods (for example, black and other nonwhite minorities) were unemployed. The rate of unemployment in predomi-

[5] *An American Dilemma* (rev. ed.; New York: Harper and Row, 1962), p. 907.

nantly white urban neigborhoods during the same period was 6 percent. The national average was 5.5 percent.[6]

Two reasons for the high rate of black unemployment are usually given. First, there is the problem of education. The United States

"... And I say, Gentlemen, it would be simpler to pass a new busing law ... and THEN just let it bog down in technicalities and delays!"

"Grin and Bear It" by George Lichty; © Field Enterprises, Inc. 1973, courtesy of Publishers-Hall Syndicate

economy is highly mechanized and automated. In order to be able to operate the often complicated machinery of modern industry, the worker needs to have a certain amount of education or technical training. Blacks are placed at a disadvantage since their education is very often either inadequate or incomplete. Thus they are technologically un-

[6] United States Department of Labor, Bureau of Labor Statistics, *Employment and Earnings and Monthly Report on the Labor Force.*

employable in good-paying jobs in industry. They either find a menial and low-paying service job or remain unemployed. All authorities agree that it is the unemployed or underemployed black whose frustrations and despair are channeled toward disturbances in urban centers across the United States.

Second, some labor unions are at least partially responsible for the intolerably high rate of black unemployment. While the national government has made it a crime for employers to discriminate in their hiring practices, some have found loopholes. In addition, nothing has been done legally to see that the labor unions follow the same principles. Although some of the industrial unions have fought for the rights of blacks, it is a sad fact that many of the nation's largest craft unions openly discriminate against blacks who are otherwise qualified for membership. At the same time, apprenticeship programs, some financed with government assistance, that ultimately lead toward high-paying jobs in a trade are often closed to black youths. One method some unions have used to keep blacks out of apprenticeship programs is to apply testing procedures that exploit their deficient education.

Decent housing has been inadequately available to blacks throughout their history in the United States. For a number of reasons (most economic, some sociological) blacks have been forced to live in substandard housing, concentrated in dilapidated neighborhoods in the cities, while the rural black, especially in the South, lives under conditions that are even worse than those of poor southern whites.

In order to ameliorate the housing problem of urban blacks, several states and the federal government have passed so-called fair-housing laws. Generally, these forbid property owners to refuse to sell or rent their property to anyone on the basis of his race, color, religion, or national origin. How successful such laws will be in practice it is too early to determine. If the white community's sentiments are reflected in sporadic violent demonstrations against attempts by blacks to move out of the ghetto, then the realization of fairness in the acquisition and disposal of property is still a very long way off. The attainment of the ideal of desegregated housing will encounter two obstacles. First, it is extremely difficult to prosecute and convict anyone who refuses to rent or sell to a person because of his race. Second, there is still a widespread feeling in the United States that property rights take precedence over human rights, those rights which have to do with personal behavior and attitudes.

In the late 1960s, many blacks turned from appeals in the name of constitutional rights, usually made in collaboration with white liberals, to demands made in the name of Black Power. Young blacks particularly, including new leaders of the Student Nonviolent Coordinating

Committee, became impatient while their legal equality was acknowledged but their social equality seemed as elusive as ever. Taking a leaf from the history of immigrant groups—notably Irish- and Italian-Americans and citizens of Eastern European extraction—many blacks sought political power. The ends and means of Black Power remained uncertain in the presidential election years of 1968 and 1972, to friend and foe alike, even (perhaps especially) to its champions. To many, Black Power means no more than bloc voting with the aim of getting the largest possible number of blacks into public office at all levels. To a few, it means separatism, an attempt to build a nation within a nation. To even fewer, it means taking arms in "self-defense" against a rather vaguely defined enemy. To most, it means, chiefly, group pride and self-assertion. Whatever it means, Black Power has struck a chord which echoed in assertions of Brown Power among Mexican- and other Spanish-Americans and of Bronze Power among American Indians.

From this brief examination the implications of the most important aspects of the Black Revolution should be clear. Unless the people of the United States, as a society, make it a national purpose to erase prejudice and to improve considerably the lot of the black man, the Black Revolution is likely to be more violent and destructive, not less. The "long hot summers" of the late 1960s offer ample evidence of this danger. In Detroit alone, more than 30 lives and more than $500 million worth of property were lost in less than a week of rioting in 1967. And when the dreams of betterment of advocates of nonviolence like Martin Luther King are not fulfilled, their nonviolent leadership of the black man's struggle for equality is going to be subverted by those who demand immediate action regardless of the consequences.

THE CHALLENGE OF POVERTY

United States society is frequently described as *affluent*. Even before the publication of John Kenneth Galbraith's *The Affluent Society* in 1958, the United States had the reputation, and the accomplishments, of the most affluent society on the face of the earth. By all standards of measurement—personal income and gross national product, number of automobiles produced and sold annually, the large number of labor-saving devices and appliances available to the average middle-class housewife—Americans in general enjoy a standard of living without parallel in human history.

Yet there are people in the richest nation on earth who do not enjoy the benefits of this apparent affluence but exist in various levels of poverty. This is one of the great contradictions in this modern, highly advanced civilization. In other words, the affluent society has another side, which is neither pleasant nor complimentary—that segment which Michael Harrington aptly calls the "other America." In the early 1960's there were, according to figures supplied by Harrington, between 40 and 50 million people in the United States, or approximately 20–25 percent of the total population, who lived in poverty.[7] Although it is difficult to determine exactly what constitutes poverty, it is estimated that an urban family of four earning less than $5000 per year lives in a state of poverty.

The revelation that perhaps one fourth the total population of the United States lives in substandard conditions may seem unrealistic and even shocking. Where are these poor people? Most Americans—three fourths, according to this estimate—have not been exposed to a great deal of poverty; nor have they personally suffered from its consequences. Therefore, their knowledge of poverty has been at best second-hand. They have read news stories about "pockets of poverty" in the Appalachian region; they have seen television documentaries about the poor in the mining areas of West Virginia or in the slums of Chicago. But their relationship to poverty has been an impersonal one. They just do not see all these poor, and seldom do they have contact with them because the majority of those living in poverty are, as characterized by Harrington, "invisible."

There are always those who argue that people are poor in the land of plenty because they like it that way, they are lazy, or they simply lack the initiative to better their condition. This explanation may have limited validity, although it is difficult to imagine anyone liking poverty. A much more reasonable explanation of poverty is the one offered by Harrington:

> . . . the real explanation of why the poor are where they are is that they made the mistake of being born to the wrong parents, in the wrong section of the country, in the wrong industry, or in the wrong racial or ethnic group.[8]

So, who are these other Americans? They are the many persons over sixty-five years of age who must live on monthly incomes of less than $200—and those under eighteen who cannot provide for themselves. (Together, these two groups constitute one third of the nation's poor.) They are the Puerto Ricans of New York City, the Mexican-Americans of Texas and California, the black and white sharecroppers of the South, the impoverished American Indians, the slum-dwellers of the big cities.

[7] Michael Harrington, *The Other America* (New York: Macmillan, 1963), pp. 180–183.
[8] *The Other America*, pp. 14–15.

They are the "Okies" and "Arkies" who never left the marginal farms of the 1930s; the technologically unemployed miners of Appalachia; the migrant farm workers of the rich valleys of California and of the fertile plains of Texas and other parts of the Southwest.

Most Americans, however, do not see this poverty; it is largely invisible. Harrington gives a poignant answer to the question, where are the poor?

> Poverty is often off the beaten track. It always has been. The ordinary tourist never left the main highway, and today he rides interstate turnpikes. He does not go into the valleys of Pennsylvania where the towns look like movie sets of Wales in the thirties. He does not see the company houses in rows, the rutted roads (the poor always have bad roads whether they live in the city, in towns, or on farms), and everything is black and dirty. And even if he were to pass through such a place by accident, the tourist would not meet the unemployed men in the bar or the women coming home from a runaway sweatshop.[9]

One aspect of President Johnson's Great Society program was designed to deal with some of the most corrosive side effects of poverty. In fact, the great portion of the program was committed to a "war against poverty." Many of the president's efforts, however, met congressional opposition. A few—the rat-extermination bill, for example—were initially met by congressional laughter and ridicule. It took a major riot in Newark in the summer of 1967 to make some Congressmen reconsider their stand on this issue.

Yet, while the war against poverty has been going on for some time, the issue of poverty still remains a very troublesome thorn in the side of an unquestionably affluent society. There is no question that some gains in the struggle against poverty have been made. By 1972, the percentage of the poor had decreased from 20–25 percent of the population to about 10–15 percent. The passage of the medicare program in 1965, for example, alleviated some of the problems faced by senior citizens. But such gains, in relation to the total problem, are infinitesimal. Even the first director of the antipoverty program, Sargent Shriver, often stated publicly that the program, while certainly not a total failure, left much to be desired. In 1966, Shriver was asked if he ever envisioned an absolute end to poverty. He answered emphatically in the affirmative and pointed out that it would take $10 billion a year for ten years to defeat poverty totally by the year 1976—the two-hundredth anniversary of the Declaration of Independence. To many people, of course, the figure of $10 billion per year for ten years is a fantastic one. But it it really, when

[9] *The Other America*, p. 3.

the national budget for fiscal 1972–1973 was approximately $220 billion and the gross national product was over $1 trillion? Is $10 billion such an unrealistic figure when expenditures for defense in fiscal 1972–1973 will probably exceed $90 billion?

What all this implies is that as a people Americans must reevaluate priorities. They must look at themselves realistically and make the sacrifices and commitments necessary to make the United States a truly great and affluent society. It is part of what Galbraith calls the "conventional wisdom" to think that the nation can appropriate vast sums of wealth for weapons of destruction while expenditures for winning the war against poverty, certainly a constructive and worthwhile undertaking, are declared "nonessential."

As a society the United States must do much more to see that poverty is no longer self-perpetuating, that generations of poor do not follow generations of poor. And to do this, the nation must first improve the educational and health services of poor communities or of poor sections within relatively affluent communities. Galbraith puts it this way:

> To eliminate poverty efficiently we should invest more than proportionately in the children of the poor community. It is there that high-quality schools, strong health services, special provision for nutrition and recreation are most needed to compensate for the very low investment which families are able to make in their own offspring.[10]

To cite a hypothetical example: If the son of a farmworker in Fresno, California, is able to enjoy the above-mentioned benefits and acquire a decent elementary and high-school education, without being taken out of school at age 13 to augment the family's income, he could then go on to Fresno State University and at the end of four years would be able to get a good job. The investment society would have made in such a youngster would be repaid many times over. At the same time, he would not perpetuate his parents' poverty. Instead, he would become a useful, productive, and taxpaying member of the affluent society.

The "negative income tax" is one of the ways proposed to end poverty in America. Oddly enough, this idea has supporters from both conservative economists like Milton Friedman of the University of Chicago and liberals like Galbraith of Harvard. But, for many, it seems such a radical departure from "common sense" that detractors see in it only a "giveaway" to the lazy and shiftless. What the plan proposes is really very simple. If it is estimated that an urban family of four needs $5000 per year to live decently, but the family's sources of income supply

---

[10] *The Affluent Society* (Boston: Houghton Mifflin, 1958), pp. 330–331.

only $3000, the government would supplement that family's income with a grant of $2000. Radical, revolutionary, socialistic? Perhaps. But it does seem to be one of the most sensible proposals made thus far.

There are those who argue that all the efforts to eliminate poverty smack of socialism. The government is attempting, some conservatives insist, to create a society of equals, a society in which the spirit of enterprise and risk taking is eliminated and is instead replaced by the spirit of economic leveling. These same people, incidentally, are also critical of the graduated income tax because, they insist, it hinders initiative. Under close scrutiny, such arguments are misleading. Economists agree that poverty is economically costly, in addition to being a blemish on our society. Michael Harrington, who made a reputation as an expert on the causes and effects of poverty, estimated that the American economy is losing as much as $50 billion per year because the poor are not contributing to the nation's economic growth.

In the end, it simply makes good economic, moral, and political sense to make sure that no one, in a society as developed and as affluent as the United States, lives below a minimum standard of living. It is in the nation's power to eliminate poverty from the face of the country once and for all. It requires only political imagination and courage on the part of leaders to open the way. In the last analysis, public opinion will follow such leadership because compassion for the underprivileged anywhere has been a characteristic quality of the American people.

THE CHALLENGE OF POLITICAL EXTREMISM

In an article written just before his death in 1965, Arthur M. Schlesinger, Sr., examined the issue of extremism in perspective and defined its relationship to the American political scene, past and present.[11] The essence of the article is that extremist political activity is nothing new to the United States. It has existed, in one form or another, virtually since the beginning of the republic. Few will argue with this assertion, although the extremist activity of the present period seems to be more dangerous than ever before in the nation's history for reasons which will be examined later in this section. First, an attempt to define *extremism* and *extremist politics* will be made.

An extremist is one who finds the present political, social, or economic order so objectionable that he wants to see it destroyed or radi-

[11] "Extremism in American Politics," *Saturday Review* (November 27, 1965), pp. 21–25.

cally altered. Thus, extremists find themselves at odds with some of the basic principles and practices of democratic government and politics. In simpler terms, extremists find themselves unable or incapable of conforming to the broad requirements of the politics of consensus. An extremist, in other words, is unwilling to work within the established institutional order to attain the ends he desires. Instead, he either undermines or circumvents those institutions. Thus, it would not be accurate to label Barry Goldwater, the Republican presidential candidate in 1964, and George McGovern, the Democratic standard bearer in 1972, extremists. Although some of the views they held during their campaigns were mildly radical so that they were branded extremist, they still wanted to implement their preferences through the established and popularly accepted constitutional framework.

All extremists, whether of the left or of the right, characteristically view consensus politics as a vast and evil conspiracy intended to destroy or undermine something they deem unique or desirable, or both. Leftist extremists insist, for example, that the working masses are constantly threatened by a conspiracy of businessmen and government functionaries. On the other hand, extremists of the right argue that the governmental-political conspiracy has strayed so far away from the intentions of the Founding Fathers that the purity of the American system has been contaminated. On issues of foreign policy, as on domestic questions, extremists apply the conspiratorial theory of history and politics. To take China as a particular example: Since 1949, right-wing extremists have maintained that Chiang Kai-shek's China was "sold out" in the late 1940s by a group of Communist agents or sympathizers working conspiratorially in the nation's press, in universities, and within the Department of State. Conversely, left-wing extremists have argued that the United States government did not recognize the regime of mainland China because of an anti-Communist, status-quo-oriented conspiracy among persons of power and authority.

Extremist political activity has existed in the United States since the colonial period. In the eyes of the British, for instance, those who signed the Declaration of Independence were dangerous and irresponsible extremists. But never before in the history of the United States has extremism been as great a threat to the viability of the American system as it is now. And while the threat from the radical left should never be underestimated, the dangers from the radical right pose a much more immediate challenge to our way of life. This appraisal is substantiated by the fact that the most radical and potentially dangerous groups on the left—the Communist party of the United States together with its pro-Peking faction and the Progressive Labor party—

are very small in size. (Estimated nationwide membership in both is set at about 10,000.) Moreover, these groups have been plagued by constant feuds and factionalism; their financial difficulties have been notorious. Also, over the years the F.B.I. has been able to infiltrate these groups to such an extent that their activities are always known to the appropriate authorities. It has been said, perhaps in jest, but perhaps not, that about half of those who belong to the Communist party and similar organizations of the left are F.B.I. informers.

Finally, Congress has passed laws prohibiting or severely restricting the activities of such organizations. Three such acts in particular stand out: the Smith Act of 1940, the Internal Security Act of 1950, and the Communist Control Act of 1954. The last declared the Communist party of the United States to be "an instrumentality of a conspiracy to overthrow the Government of the United States." In effect, this act outlawed the Communist party although several Supreme Court decisions have significantly altered provisions of all three acts.

The other extreme of the political spectrum, the right, presents an entirely different picture. The groups are well organized, rich, and at least some of them have been clothed with the mantle of respectability since they appeal to a very basic human emotion—patriotism. Among the groups belonging to the extreme right are the John Birch Society, the Minutemen, the American Nazi party, and the Ku Klux Klan.

Robert Welch, leader of the John Birch Society, views the past 30 years of United States history as a monumental conspiracy to turn the United States over to the Bolsheviks. He has accused all recent American presidents of having been dupes of Communism, either knowingly or unwittingly. He has written that former President Eisenhower and Secretary of State John Foster Dulles aided the Communist cause. The credentials of both, needless to say, were impeccably anti-Communist. Why, then, did Welch make such a preposterous allegation? The answer is that one of the ways extreme political movements attain publicity is through outlandish distortions of the truth. It must be agreed that a statement implicating a national figure such as Eisenhower in an un-American activity has a certain amount of shock value; it is intended to get the public's attention and it succeeds in doing so. Robert Welch had set as one of the aims of his society the impeachment of Chief Justice Earl Warren because, in Welch's opinion, the Supreme Court had been making decisions favoring the enemies of the United States and because it was trying "to make our republic a democracy." While the Birch Society's membership lists are secret, it is estimated that approximately 100,000 persons are dues-paying members. Many have shown a commitment to the cause nearing fanaticism. Birch Society publications, such as its monthly periodical *American Opinion*, are distributed throughout the country, and the Society's annual budget, coming principally from contributions, exceeds $4 million. In 1972, two Birch Society members, John Schmitz and Thomas Anderson, were nominated by the right-wing American [Independent] Party (originally organized in 1968 by George Wallace) for president and vice president.

One of the most dangerous groups on the extreme right is an organization known as the Minutemen. The Minutemen see an imminent take-over of the United States by Communist forces and are training in order to conduct guerrilla operations once the country is in the hands of the Communist enemy. On several occasions over the past several years, veritable arsenals of all types of weapons have been seized by government authorities in different parts of the country. In January, 1967, the national leader of the Minutemen, Robert B. DePugh, and one of his West Coast associates were convicted in federal court for illegal possession of arms. At the same time, the Minutemen central organization reportedly has files on persons whom they consider dangerous or not patriotic enough. The implication is that these persons will be dealt with severely once guerrilla war breaks out.

Other groups on the extreme right include the small but noisy American Nazi party whose espousal of causes brings back memories of Hitler's Germany. Its principal aims are to put the Jews and the blacks, both considered inferior races by the Nazis, in their rightful place and to root out Communists and their sympathizers. It may seem ironic but these people, brandishing swastikas and khaki uniforms, as well as a "Fuhrer" (the late George Lincoln Rockwell), claim to be protectors and defenders of American ideals.

The Ku Klux Klan is another group preaching hate, prejudice, and violence. After almost a generation of relative obscurity, the Ku Klux Klan has been making a comeback, generally in response to the Black Revolution. Its main avowed purpose is to maintain the separation of the races, by force and violence if necessary. Further, the Klan wants the United States to be a "white, Christian nation," a goal which illustrates that the organization is also anti-Semitic. It may seem a contradiction, but the Klan claims to be based on Christian principles.

There are many more groups and countless individuals in all parts of the United States who have undertaken a crusade, either singly or in combination, to defend the rest of us unsuspecting souls from all sorts of conspiracies and plots to subvert and overthrow our constitutional govenment. Radio and television stations across the United States daily inundate the air with messages of fear, gloom, and impending disaster.

Earlier in this section it was stated that the danger from the right

seems more acute than from the left. The extreme left is divided, disor-
ganized, discredited, disreputable, and poor. Conversely, the right,
although speaking in many voices, has uniform objectives, is well organized, has few financial problems, and is, in some quarters at least,
"respectable." The extreme right is dangerous because it abuses continuously an otherwise honest and laudable human feeling, patriotism.
It is dangerous because it creates fears, anxiety, frustration, and despair.
This is a period of great challenges and also of great opportunities. These
challenges and opportunities cannot be met unless actions are guided by
reason rather than by emotion and fear. Survival may depend on how
well man utilizes his power of reason to solve the immense and often
nightmarish problems that confront him. The extreme right is dangerous,
further, because it creates suspicion and distrust. Suspicion and distrust
of the nation's political system, its leaders, clergymen, teachers, newspapers, magazines—suspicion, in short, of the ability of society to deal
with its enemies or potential enemies sternly and decisively if the need
arises.

All right-wing extremists, according to two men who investigated
the movements closely, concentrate on the same theme:

> The enemy is within. We are the victims of subversives at home. The
> real threat to America is not from Russia but from secret agents of
> the communist conspiracy here—your garden-supply dealer, the high
> school principal, the superintendent of the town waterworks, your
> congressman.[12]

As Edith Cavel, a British nurse, said when tried as a spy by the
Germans in World War I: "Patriotism is not enough." Extremists of
the far left and of the far right are easily as patriotic as the average
American, but they are patriotic only in terms of the goals they seek
for the United States. When confronted with institutions or programs
which are widely accepted as desirable and necessary elements in the
United States political system, the extremists are likely to reject them
and call for radical changes. They say they want to make these changes
in the interest of all Americans—they know best what is good for the
United States. And they often advocate extreme measures to achieve
their goals, believing that the end justifies the means. But this is the
point at which their pseudo-patriotism shows its true colors, for if the
American experiment means anything, it means a profound commitment to the principle of majority rule. Only the majority is qualified to
say what is best for America. The majority may not necessarily be right

---

[12] Donald Janson and Bernard Eismann, *The Far Right* (New York: Mc-
Graw-Hill, 1963), p. 5.

in every case. But there is firm faith in the contention that the majority will more often be right than wrong, and that no minority, no elite group, is ever qualified to impose its views on the society as a whole.

So this introduction to United States government and politics concludes with an affirmation of, and a rededication to, the basic principles which underlie the political system of the United States. As a people, Americans face a number of critical problems in the decades ahead, problems unequaled in human history. Some individuals and radical groups will offer miracle cures, panaceas outside the context of the democratic approach. We are of the opinion, however, that the American political system, rooted in democracy, is uniquely equipped to meet these challenges.

GLOSSARY

Affluent society A term coined by John K. Galbraith to describe American wealth and waste.

Black Power At a minimum this term refers to electoral strategies aimed at getting the largest possible number of Blacks into public office.

Black Revolution All of the various movements and processes in recent years which have the effect of erasing discrimination against blacks and giving blacks jobs, incomes, educational opportunities, which are on a par with those available to whites.

Busing Transporting school children to distant schools by bus for the purpose of achieving racial balance.

Civil disobedience Intentional violation of laws thought to be unjust in order to bring about public pressure to change those laws.

Credibility gap Widespread public disbelief in the veracity or sincerity of national leaders' public pronouncements.

Crime An act committed in violation of a law.

De facto segregation Segregation that exists in fact despite official acts or laws.

De jure segregation Segregation that results from official acts or laws.

Disadvantaged Persons who, because of race, age, illness or an underprivileged early environment do not have an equal chance to enjoy "the good life."

Fair housing laws Laws which forbid property owners to refuse to sell or rent their property to anyone on the basis of his race, color, religion, or national origin.

Ghetto An Area of a city occupied by a particular racial group.

John Birch Society A right-wing extremist political action organization.

Minutemen A right-wing extremist vigilante organization often involved in the illegal purchase, sale, and storage of weapons.

Negative income tax   A proposal that would have the federal government bring the income of every family up to certain minimum level through grants.

The other America   A term coined by Michael Harrington to describe the millions of Americans who do not share in the luxuries and conveniences enjoyed by the majority of citizens.

Political extremism   A belief that the present political (and by extension social or economic) order is unacceptable and should be destroyed or radically altered.

Power elite   A term coined by C. Wright Mills to describe the corporate executives, military leaders, and influential administrators who control United States society.

Revolution of rising expectations   The demands of masses of people who have hear about or seen the good things of life to have a share of that good life for themselves.

Smog   The product of the chemical reaction of sunlight on oxides of nitrogen, carbon monoxide, and unburned hydrocarbons (all waste products of automobile engines and power plants).

Urban blight   Deterioration of the core city by which existing housing units become slums.

Urban renewal   Removing slum dwellings and replacing them with modern structures.

SUGGESTIONS FOR FURTHER READING

BEICHMAN, ARNOLD. *Nine Lies About America.* New York: Library Press, 1972.

CAHN, EDMOND. *The Predicament of Democratic Man.* New York: Delta, 1961.

CORNUELLE, RICHARD C. *Reclaiming the American Dream.* New York: Random House, 1965.

ELEY, LYNN W. and THOMAS CASSTEVENS. *The Politics of Fair-Housing Legislation.* New York and London: Chandler, 1968.

FRANKEL, CHARLES. *The Case for Modern Man.* New York: Harper and Row, 1956.

GALBRAITH, JOHN K. *The Affluent Society.* Boston: Houghton Mifflin, 1958.

GORDON, MARGARET S. *Poverty in America.* New York and London: Chandler, 1965.

GURR, TED R. *Why Men Rebel.* Princeton, N.J.: Princeton University Press, 1970.

HACKER, ANDREW. *The End of the American Era.* New York: Atheneum, 1971.

HADDEN, JEFFREY K. et al. *Metropolic in Crisis: Social and Political Perspectives.* Itasca, Ill.: E. E. Peacock, 1967.

HARRINGTON, MICHAEL. *The Other America.* New York: Macmillan, 1963.

HARTZ, LOUIS. *The Liberal Tradition in America.* New York: Harcourt Brace Jovanovich, 1955.

MYRDAL, GUNNAR. *An American Dilemma.* Rev. ed.; New York: Harper and Row, 1962.

PADOVER, SAUL K. *The Meaning of Democracy: An Appraisal of the American Experience.* New York: Praeger, 1963.

REVEL, JEAN-FRANCOIS. *Without Marx or Jesus: The American Revolution Has Begun.* New York: Delta, 1972.

TINDER, GLENN. *The Crisis of Political Imagination.* New York: Scribner's, 1964.

YOUNG, JAMES P. *The Politics of Affluence.* New York and London: Chandler, 1968.

Appendix A
The Constraining of the President*

BY RICHARD E. NEUSTADT, HARVARD UNIVERSITY

The White House was once—and will be again—a great place for a young man to work. I did it myself and have never been sorry. Fate was kind and my age was right: It was Harry Truman's White House, and I worked for Charlie Murphy—Charles S. Murphy, to give him his due. He was the President's Special Counsel, successor to Clark Clifford in that post and one of Truman's senior aides. Working for Murphy and with him for the President was a fine experience, as unlike Egil Krogh's or Gordon Strachan's as day from night. A story illustrates what made it so, and the story is a starting point for looking at the Presidency now, by light of Watergate.

In December, 1950, at the wrenching turn of the Korean war, amidst Chinese attack, American retreat, renewed inflation, fears of

* © 1973 by The New York Times Company. Reprinted by permission.

World War III, Truman met at the White House with the Congressional leaders of both parties. Their meeting in the Cabinet room was largely symbolic, underlining events; it was an occasion for briefings, not actions. Soon after it broke up, a White House usher came to Murphy's office with a memorandum found under the Cabinet table. This was a document of several pages addressed by the staff of the Senate Minority Policy Committee to Senators Robert A. Taft and Kenneth S. Wherry, the Republican leaders. Some of his assistants were with Murphy at the time, and we fell upon it with whoops of joy. As I recall, one of us read it aloud. It dealt with the contingency (which had not arisen) that the President might use that meeting to seek pledges of bipartisan support for the Administration's future conduct of the war. This, the memorandum argued, ought to be resisted at all costs. By Easter recess the war could have taken such a turn that Republicans might wish to accuse Truman of treason, and they should be free to do so. The term "treason" fired in me and my associates an outrage we wanted the world to share. With the loyalty of subalterns, more royalist than the king, we cried, "Get it copied . . . show it to the President . . . leak it to the press!" Murphy smiled at us, took the memorandum from us, sealed it in an envelope, summoned a messenger and sent it by hand to Senator Taft. End of story.

Murphy's conduct showed propriety—indeed, for me defines it— so that much recent White House staff behavior simply shocks me. His conduct also showed prudence. He worked in a White House where seniors had constant incentive to contain themselves and restrain the young.

The Presidency as we know it now took shape in Franklin Roosevelt's time, the product of Depression, war, the radio and Presidential personality. Truman inherited and consolidated. In terms of personnel, both military and civilian, the Federal Government during his later years was roughly the same size as it is now. (The great growth of civilian public service since has been at state and local levels.) In constitutional and statutory terms, the Presidency's formal powers then were much what they are now. Like President Nixon, Truman fought undeclared war, imposed price controls, presided over a great turn in foreign policy, sought changes in domestic policy and championed "executive privilege." But if, in these respects and others, Presidential powers are substantially unchanged, what has changed is a set of inhibitions on their use.

Formal powers stay about the same, but their conversion into actual power—into making something happen—takes place with less restraint than formerly. If the Nixon regime felt itself under siege in 1971, so did Truman's in 1951. Yet there were no do-it-yourself White House horrors. Had propriety not barred them, prudence would have done so.

Almost surely, Watergate's effect upon the Presidency will be to prop up old incentives for restraint, restoring White House prudence to something like its former state. Such a prop is artificial and cannot last forever, but it should hold good for years to come. Score one for Watergate! In that perspective it is not a tragedy—far from it.

So the modern Presidency's past and prospects are bound up with the questions: What was prudence made of? What became of those ingredients? And on what terms does Watergate restore them?

A generation ago, our system's formal checks and balances were strongly reinforced by an array of informal constraints on White House conduct. Some were external, imposed on the White House, equally affecting President and staff. Others were internal, products of his operating style, affecting the staff more than him. External constraints reflected his dependence upon men whom he could not control for work he wanted done. Such men were found in many places, but let me single out three: the Congress, the party and the Cabinet. As for internal constraints I shall single out another three: his schedule, press conferences, and the staff system.

The Congress

Those men on whom the President depended were his "colleagues" in the quite specific sense that while he needed them, their power did not stem wholly from his. To need is to heed, or at least to listen. Truman had one such set of colleagues on Capital Hill: the Speaker of the House, the House and Senate floor leaders and the committee chairmen. As the modern Presidency emerged before and during World War II, it was assumed that those posts would go to men of the same party as the President. So it had been for all but four years since the turn of the century. So it remained in Truman's time for six years out of eight. Under F.D.R. and Truman this assumption was built into Governmental practice, not least at the White House where it moderated tones of voice, promoted consultation and preserved respect, at least for working purposes. Speaker Sam Rayburn and the floor leaders met Truman every week. They were colleagues together: At Rayburn's wish they met alone, no staff—and no recordings.

While all the posts of power on the Hill were manned by men who shared the President's party label, Truman could not do what he did in 1948 and in effect run against Congress, lambasting it for a "do-nothing" record he himself had forced on it by seeking bills he lacked the votes to pass. But that was the 80th Congress, elected two years earlier with Republican majorities in both Houses. Truman could not turn as sharply on an institution led by Rayburn. Nor would he have wanted to. Nor could his staff. Family quarrels were of a different quality than conflict with the rival clan.

And even as he rose to the attack in 1948, Truman carefully walled off from party battle what he took to be the cardinal field of foreign relations, including European policy, and especially the Marshall Plan. Under the aegis of Senator Arthur H. Vandenberg, the Congressional Republicans did likewise. For limited purposes, the Truman-Vandenberg connection linked the White House to Republican leaders as closely as ever to Democrats.

In 1954, Truman's successor General Eisenhower faced the reverse situation when the Democrats regained control of both houses of Congress. He then faced it continuously for six years. Eisenhower was a national hero, consciously so, and only lately become a Republican. He joined Rayburn and the latter's protégé, the new Senate Leader Lyndon Johnson, in a loose but comfortable connection. Over a wide range of issues this served much as Truman's with Vandenberg.

What Truman had for two years and Eisenhower for six, Nixon now has had for more than four, with no prospect of change: Congress organized by the other party. But Nixon, despite intermittent caution in his first term, seems not to have wanted special connections of the sort his predecessors threw across the party breach between themselves and Congress. And after his triumphant re-election, he immediately tried a reverse twist on Truman's warfare with the 80th Congress. Truman had made demands that Congress would not meet, and cried "do-nothing"; now Nixon made budget cuts that Congress would oppose, and readied taunts of "fiscal irresponsibility." In such a game the negative makes for even less restraint than the affirmative. Truman wanted the program he requested but lacked votes and did not get it. Nixon no doubt wants to keep the cuts he made, and wields the veto. Until scandal overtook him I think he was winning hands down—and he is not defeated yet. In all events, little remains of a once-strong constraint.

The Party

Twenty years ago, both parties were what they had been since Andrew Jackson's time: confederal associations of state parties grouped together for the sake of Presidential nominations and campaigns. The state parties, in turn, consisted of some relatively standard parts: city machines, court-house gangs, interest-group leaders, elective office-holders, big contributors. Stitching them all together nationally every fourth year was a task for party regulars assembled in convention. Barons strongly based in interest groups or regions or machines collectively had power to decide, or at least veto, and their number at a given time was never very large. Perhaps 50 or 100 men—buttressed, of course, by aides and friends and clients—were crucial to each party's nomination and campaign, crucial in convention and in canvassing and funding. And they were a known circle, shifting over time but usually quite easy to identify at any moment.

As with Congress, Truman was linked in stable fashion to the party leaders by a common interest: the Presidential succession. Such a relationship constrains one politician's staff in dealing with another politician, and even more so when, as was usually the case with Truman, he needed more help than he could give. Gallup Poll approval of his conduct fell to 32 per cent in 1946 and then as low as 23 per cent in 1951, eight points below Nixon's low last August. Not coincidentally, in 1946 Truman was requested by the Democratic National Committee *not* to campaign for Congress. In 1948 the railroads withdrew credit and his famous whistle-stop tour almost stopped for lack of funds. In 1952 Gov. Adlai Stevenson of Illinois persistently evaded his embrace, insisted on a draft, refused a White House build-up. The party barons out in states and cities may have liked the President and felt some kinship for him, but few if any were prepared to die for him, and none, so far as I know, were content to work through staff in lieu of him. Like Rayburn, they preferred to deal, and to be known to deal, and to be known to deal directly. In Truman's situation their preferences mattered a lot.

As organizations our two national parties have never been twins. But insofar as both shared features of the sort I have described, both are now changed almost beyond recognition. TV and jet aircraft, primaries and ticket-splitting join with education, affluence and population shifts to outmode old customs and weaken old fiefdoms. We have left the age of barons and entered the age of candidates. Its hallmarks are management by private firms, exposure through the tube, funding by direct-mail drives as well as fat-cats and canvassing by zealous volunteers.

For the Republican party nationally, 1964 exposed the passing of the old regime; for Democrats the year was 1972. Nixon in a sense is our first President to deal with party ties wholly in terms of the new conditions. Watergate sheds light on how his White House dealt. What it shows is an inordinate concern for raising money, coupled with a campaign organization run by White House aides. The Committee for the Re-election of the President was wholly independent of the Republican National Committee; it remained in existence after the campaign. Perhaps coincidentially, the White House planned that after the election those aides and others should fan out all over town, taking up sub-Cabinet posts or civil service supergrades in every major agency. Much of this actually happened last winter; it was the most determined such effort by any Administration in memory.

Why grab so much money? Why carry on C.R.P.? Why scatter subalterns all over the place? Likelier than not the answer lies in sheer momentum, in doing what comes naturally (and to excess, as was typical of the Nixon staff). But possibly they are related. It is conceivable these three developments were part of a scheme for dominating not only the Administration, but also the Republican succession. In an age of candidates, could White-House controlled bank accounts combined with White-House controlled agencies provide a substitute for defunct party baronies? As hopefuls crowded the primaries in 1976, could these assets have given the power of decision or veto to the White House staff? In any event, the setting does not make for much constraint!

The Cabinet

Truman's Cabinet officers were his appointees, for the most part, but rarely his creatures. Some of them (not many) had party standing of their own, linked to a faction of those old-style barons. Some bureau chiefs (a lot) had the equivalent in links to leading Congressmen and vital interest-groups. Everyone, regardless of his standing, owed a duty to the statutory programs he administered, and so to the Congressional committees that controlled their life blood: laws and funds. Since the "Compromise of 1789"—when Congress took the power to create departments, leaving the Presidents the discretion to dismiss department heads—it had been recognized in practice, if not always in words, that "executive" agencies of all sorts were subordinate at once to President *and* Congress, a triangular relationship that left them with two masters who could frequently be played off against each other. J. Edgar Hoover's practice of this art in 1971 seems newsworthy today but would have seemed the norm for any self-respecting bureau chief in 1951 or earlier, the period when Hoover perfected his technique.

So it was in Truman's time, and so with variations it appears to have remained. But the variations are important. They suggest that Nixon's White House up to now has rarely felt the full constraint shared mastership used to impose. That Nixon's aides thought otherwise—as their extraordinary memoranda show—hits at either ignorance or paranoia.

Viewed from a distance, two changes stand out. As of, say, 1970 compared with 1950, most Cabinet officers seem less important to the President, while bureau chiefs appear less certain of Congressional support against the President, or anyway less likely to invoke it. The latter change reflects what may have been a passing phase—much of Washington heeds the dictum "never hit a man unless he's down," and Nixon, like Truman before him, has become vulnerable. Or maybe it reflects a downward shift of levels for Congressional support deep into program management, and well below the bureau chiefs, almost out of sight. And possibly the change is greater than it would be if party ties helped connect committees to agencies. But if this change is hard to pin down, the Cabinet change is not.

The low estate of most contemporary Cabinet posts reflects reduced White House dependence on departments as well as increased dependence of departments on each other. Twenty years ago the President relied on Cabinet members for a great deal of the staff work now performed inside the White House. President Eisenhower was the first to pull into the White House the detailed work of lobbying with Congress for Administration bills; Truman had mostly kept it out. And the hiring and firing of agency officials below Cabinet rank is now centralized as never before. Whatever is purpose—partisan or managerial or both—the fanning out of Nixon aides last winter into agencies reflects unprecedented White House planning and initiative in lower level appointments. Initiative once rested mostly with department heads; they usually won their contests with the White House staff. (It has been only a dozen years since Kennedy's Defense Secretary rejected out of hand a White House proposal for Secretary of the Navy, none other than Franklin Delano Roosevelt Jr.)

In Truman's years, moreover, a department head could look down at his bureaus, out to their clients and up to subcommittees on the Hill without having to think hourly about other departments. A bailiwick was still a bailiwick. For many department heads this is no longer true. I once worked closely with the head of the housing agency that preceded HUD. I do not recall that he gave a thought to the Federal Security Agency, the forerunner of H. E. W. But there was then no Model Cities Program.

Since President Johnson got his chance to put through Congress a whole generation's worth of Democratic programs—many stemming from Truman proposals stalled since the nineteen-forties—new endeavors have entangled departmental jurisdictions in such a web of overlapping statutes, funding, staffs and clientele that no one moves without involving others, often painfully. I gather it is even hard to stand still on one's own. In dealing with the consequences, bureaus are important, and so are Presidential staffs; the bureaus can operate, albeit on a narrow front, while the staffs can coordinate, at least in terms of budgets. Department heads are often poorly placed to do either. Their positions often are at once too lofty and too low.

Johnson once wanted supermanagers to rationalize his programs as they built them up. Nixon called for supermanagers to rationalize those programs down, and build up revenue-sharing. From either standpoint, Cabinet posts seemed cramped in White House eyes. In addition, the incumbents were cramped for time. New programs conferred on most departments new relationships with more Congressional committees than before. These Cabinet members still were in position to testify. So they did, over and over. It took a lot of time. But it added little to their weight at the White House. And Ehrlichman condescended.

Down the drain went still another set of Presidential colleagues—and constraints.

The Schedule

As for internal constraints on Truman's Presidency, the first derived from his operating style. He was accessible beyond contemporary belief. Following Roosevelt's peace-time practice and a long Presidential tradition, H.S.T. stood ready to see any member of Congress, granting 15 minute interviews to anyone who asked, if possible within 24 hours of the asking. The same rule held for Cabinet and sub-Cabinet officers, heads of lesser agencies and governors of states—these among others. His days were chopped up into 15-minute segments, morning and afternoon. He managed to include not only those who wanted to see him but also those he wished to see. He was available to staff early and late. And he met weekly, in addition, with the legislative leaders, the Cabinet, the National Security Council and the press—all this on top of ceremonies and aside from reading, late into the night.

Those 15-minute interviews, on the callers' business, at their option, took a large amount of time—no mean constraint—and also follow-up, which constrained his staff all the more, as Truman, like Roosevelt before him, usually met his callers alone. Inefficiencies resulted, and waste motion. But at the same time, this President was personally exposed, day in and out, to what a lot of people wanted from him; he learned what they cared about, believed, hoped and feared. And constraining or not, I think Truman liked the flow. He found in it large compensations.

Eisenhower, by contrast, chafed under it, found it intolerable, channeled off all he could to his aides. Until his heart attack in 1955, members of Congress complained, and so did Cabinet members and others. Afterwards, acceptance set in. Before President Kennedy took office he was warned (to his discomfort) that he would be pressed to resume Truman's custom. But this did not occur. Washington had accepted the Eisenhower custom. Kennedy and Johnson were as free as has been Nixon to receive or put off whom they chose. Their choices were very different from his. But their freedom to make them eased his choice of relative isolation.

The Press

Twenty years ago, another internal constraint derived from White House press relations, above all from the press conference as a regular weekly undertaking. These were no longer the intimate affairs of Roosevelt's time, with reporters crowded compatibly into the Oval Office; by Truman's second term they had become big-scale affairs in larger quarters, less educative for the correspondents, less fun for the President. But they still served many other functions, communications functions *within* Government, connecting our peculiarly separated branches, as well as informing the public. Regular press conferences gave the White House staff a chance to put the President on record unmistakably with Congressmen or bureaucrats or interest groups or partisans who could not be convinced at second-hand. They gave those others chances to check up on the assertions of the staff. They gave the President himself a chance to reinforce or override the claims made in his name by staff and everybody else. They gave him, finally, opportunities to puncture myths and gossip.

Truman did not always turn these chances to his own account. Sometimes he backed into unintended promises, disclosures or embarrassments. Thus press conferences constrained him. But I think they constrained others more, not the least his staff. At any rate, whatever pain they caused, those regular press conferences offered all concerned, the President included, compensations not obtainable from any other source. This was found out after Johnson impaired them by irregularity, still more after Nixon virtually shut them down. By Johnson's time, of course, press conferences had come to be live television shows. He reacted against the risks to his own image and his programs inherent in exposure through an entertainment medium, where many things besides words are conveyed to many publics viewing as a passive audience. Endowed with different style and temperament, Kennedy had faced those risks with relish. Not Johnson, and not Nixon. Seeking to safeguard their public relations, these Presidents backed out of regular press conferences; in the process—inadvertently perhaps—they impaired their internal communications.

The Staff

The last constraint I want to mention arose from Truman's staff system, which as its central feature made him his own chief of staff. He chaired the morning staff meeting; he parceled out assignments; he watched the White House budget; he approved new staff positions. He dealt directly, one by one, with all but junior aides; he allowed few of these, kept an eye on them and made sure that in meetings they saw a lot of him. He was immersed in detail, and it all took time. Thereby he was constrained. His aides, though, were also constrained—by him.

In this and other respects Truman followed rather closely, although not very consciously, the pattern F.D.R. had brought to Presidential staffing in his second term. Roosevelt's pattern had four features; he clung to them consistently, and so did Truman. First, the President, and only the President, was the chief of staff. Second, there was a sharp distinction between "personal" and "institutional" staff. The latter worked in such places as the Budget Bureau, with a mandate to think always of the Presidential office apart from personal politics. The former, the White House staff per se, would think about the President's personal interests, while he could weigh both views and choose between them. Third, personal staff meant only those who helped the President to do what was required of him day by day, manning his schedule, drafting his speeches, guarding his signature, nursing the press corps or, during the war, dealing with Stalin and Churchill. "This is the White House calling" was to mean the President himself or someone reliably in touch with him. Roosevelt cared devoutly for the symbolism of that house. All other aides were "institutional," to be kept out of there and off that phone. He overlapped staff duties, reached out to departments, pored over newspapers, probed his visitors and quizzed his wife. Not only was he chief of his own staff, he also was his own director of intelligence on happenings in his Administration. Except when they embarrassed him, he looked upon press leaks as adding to his sources.

The Rooseveltian pattern has had a curious history over the years. It evolved under Truman and then was abandoned by Eisenhower. The General could not abide it and thought it wrong in principle. Rather than immersion he sought freedom from detail and built a bigger staff than Truman's to relieve him of it. He made someone else his chief of staff, and created a swirl of secretariats to serve committees of Cabinet members. In reaction, Kennedy scrapped most of that and consciously restored the Rooseveltian arrangement, adapting as he went but following all its features. Johnson adapted further, but with less care as he grew more and more immersed in his war. Nixon evolved a different pattern that somewhat resembled Eisenhower's, but with a marked change in its means for tackling policy. Committee secretariats became substantive staffs, with initiative and discretion independent of Cabinet members. A much larger White House staff resulted. Seeking freedom for himself, Nixon left its management to others.

Thus in the more than 30 years since the White House staff became a major feature of our Government, we have alternated between two contrasting patterns for its composition and control. Numbers tell part of the story. In 1952, civilian aides with some substantive part in public business numbered 20. In 1962 the number was the same. In 1972 it seems to have been somewhere between 50 and 75 (depending on how one counts the third-level assistants). Moreover, the alternation follows party lines; the contrasting patterns have almost become matters of party philosophy. At least they are matters of party experience, handed down through the political generations from old cadres to the young. When a Haldeman eloquently testifies on the philosophy of Nixon's system, Democrats scoff. Republicans did likewise at the lack of system in Roosevelt's arrangements, to say nothing of Kennedy's. It naturally is harder now for Democrats than for Republicans to think Nixon could genuinely, if wishfully, not know—and then be cramped in finding out about—the cover-up of Watergate. Students of the Eisenhower Presidency are less skeptical.

A staff system that liberates the President to think frees staff men from his watchful eye. The price he pays for liberty comes in the coin of power. So we have seen with Nixon since last March. This always worried Roosevelt.

It is a matter of coincidence, I think, that even as the old constraints of prudence slackened, the White House staff fell under the control of senior aides so lacking in propriety as those we saw this summer on our television screens. Men like these are the opposite of Truman's Counsel, Murphy. Not everyone who ever served in the White House met his standard. But few if any ever fell so far below it as those Nixon aides. Men of their extraordinary impropriety have not been found there before, at least not in such numbers. Their like might not have been there under Nixon, or not so many of them, had he won the Presidency eight years earlier, succeeding Eisenhower. Even in 1969 they did not have the place all to themselves, but had to share it for a while with seniors of a different sort, men who were old hands at governing, experienced downtown and tempered by long contact with the Hill.

Murphy's sensitivities owed much to the flavor of Congress—especially the Senate (where he himself had been a legislative counsel) and most especially the Senate of the old Southern ascendancy, exemplified by Senator Richard Russell. (In 1951, Russell's masterful performance in the chair of the MacArthur hearings caused the General to fade away, no harm to the Republic, and set a high standard for Senator Ervin.) But in Nixon's White House those most respectful of the Hill's old flavor did not long survive a contest with the masters of new-style campaigning. Zealous for their chief, the winners packed the place with second and third-level men of their own mind, magnified his wishes by their own means and wound up blighting the bright prospect of his second term.

Excess now has bred its own corrective. Watergate puts new life into old constraints, or more precisely, it assures a set of temporary substitutes. If the White House is forced into continuous give-and-take, this is after all what the Constitution intended. If the give-and-take sometimes degenerates into sheer nastiness, that will reflect the way it all began, in White House zealousness. Near-term results are predictable. If he wants, Nixon can have a limited connection with the Congressional leaders, though at a higher price than formerly. Where he does not, stand-offs will ensue, with each side using assured powers to harass the other. Budget cuts and vetoes will be countered by withheld appropriations or rejected confirmations. Bargains will be struck, *ad hoc*, on relatively even terms, a process hardly conceivable six months ago. At the same time there will be fresh support by subcommittees for pet programs, and vice versa, no matter what the White House says or wants. Caught in between, department heads will drift toward their subordinates regardless of the White House or subsist increasingly in lame-duck isolation. Some Cabinet officers will probably emerge as major figures in their own right. And while the President himself cannot now be expected to change operating styles, the senior aides now near him, and particularly those inflicted on him, should be quite able to do so in the direction of caution. Their accessibility compensates a little for his isolation.

If these predictions are borne out, the three-and-one-half years remaining for this President—assuming, as I do, that he fills out his terms—will be neither easy nor tidy; in domestic terms they will produce more noise and less redirection than he wanted, and in foreign terms they will produce less movement than he hoped. But he would have faced some shortfall even if Watergate had not happened. The failure of Phase Three to keep down prices, and the failure of bombing in Cambodia to bring "peace," assured that opposition would revive on the Hill and in the press.

The modern Presidency is a sturdy vehicle. Hardship and untidiness are frequently its lot. But at worst a President retains his formal powers. These put him at the center of the legislative process, the administrative process, national politics, foreign relations; combined they make him central to the news. Accordingly, so long as he has time ahead, there will be men in every part of Washington who are mindful of his wishes because they in their own jobs have need of him in his. Until his last appointment, his last budget, his last veto, his last summit, he cannot sink to insignificance in Government; his office will uphold him. As for changes in the office of the sort now being argued both in Congress and the courts—limiting impoundment, or his use of force abroad, or claims to executive privilege—each dents the Presidency at an outer edge, narrowing discretion, reducing flexibility, but strikes no vital spot. What is vital to the office is that combination: processes, politics, peace and the news. Within our Government the combination is unique, and so confers unique advantages. These remain.

(The Nixon proposal for a single six-year Presidential term is in a different category. It would change the Presidency's central core, to my mind, for the worse. We now have, in effect, an eight-year term subject at midpoint to an opposition audit reviewed by the electorate and then a vote of confidence without which he retires. The required re-election at midterm is one of the most democratic features of the office and adds to its legitimacy in a system of popular sovereignty. Removal of this feature to protect us from its possible corruption is a frivolous proposal for a President to make, especially when his regime has been the most corrupt. Nixon, I hope, was not serious.)

The Supreme Court last interfered with Presidential powers in 1952 when Truman was denied authority to seize the nation's steel mills. But the Court managed not to say it never could be done again in any circumstances. On the contrary, the artful spread of concurring opinions left the future relatively open. The Presidency is limited only a little. This is the likeliest outcome again when current issues reach the highest Court. The net result may be to make some future Presidents work harder, under more restrictions, conciliating more, and forcing issues less than Nixon chose to do in his first term—or Truman at the time of the steel seizures. The Presidency won't be flattened by that!

To write of Truman is to recall the trouble and the pain associated with his Presidency: the pain of the Korean war and those interminable truce talks; the pain of domestic reforms deferred, of foreign developments blighted; the pain of MacArthur, and McCarthy; the China charges; the corruption charges; the list goes on and on. But where is that pain now? The young know nothing of it; the old have long since put it out of mind. A few of us would gladly show our scars, but we have no viewers except for historians, and not even many of them. Truman never captivated the campuses. And so I predict it will be with our current trouble. At the same time, though, short-term results have a way of shedding light on problems for the more distant future.

If the value of Watergate is great as a temporary renewer of old constraints, it is not unqualified. We now are in a period of antipolitical politics, with journalists and politicians playing to their own sense of successive, cumulative, public disillusionments. Watergate feeds the mood. When such a period descended on us in the early fifties we got Eisenhower for President, the hero-above-politics. Since we lack heroes nowadays, the next time could be worse. Moreover, the renewed constraints on Nixon cannot last forever. Watergate's effects will wear off over time, perhaps by his successor's second term (taking us no farther than 1984). As this occurs the weakened state of old constraints will be exposed once more: the parties gone beyond recall, the Congress mortgaged to ticket-splitting, the Cabinet frayed by overlapping jurisdictions, the dependence of all the rest on the President's own style.

But separated powers still define our system, so new colleagues, bringing new constraints, may replace the old, and some of the old may revive. What happens in our parties is especially important. We may face perpetual disarray, a dire prospect. But renewal is by no means inconeivable. For instance, big-state governors, linked to professional managers and money, may revive party baronies in the guise of perpetual candidacies. Reagan and Rockefeller may be precursors. As part of the same vision, or perhaps quite separately, cadres of volunteers funded by direct-mail drives may come into existence state by state to man elective party posts and staff campaigns, substituting, in relatively stable fashion, for old-style machines. "Favorite sons" may come to have renewed significance. The national convention may again become the place for interstate negotiations (especially if the TV networks cut back live coverage). A President, like others, then negotiates again.

If national parties revive, this makes it the more likely that Congress and the White House will some day be run again by men with the same party label. A President then will welcome back old colleagues. As for executive operations, residual price and wage controls—an incomes policy with some sort of club in the closet—may well join revenue sharing and resource regulation as likely long-term features of the Federal scene. White House attention may be focused on them in the future, along with defense and diplomacy. If so, no matter what becomes of traditional Cabinet posts, the President will gain new executive colleagues; corporation officials, union leaders, governors, mayors.

Even the traditional executive positions may again turn more collegial from a President's standpoint than most of them were six months ago. Much depends upon the evolution of relationships with Congress. Senator Walter F. Mondale recently has urged, as one of several new checks on the White House, a televised Senate question-period for Cabinet officers. This is an old proposal, but with the new addition of television, no small matter. Such appearances would distance Cabinet members from the President and so make them more important to him, in the very act of making them perform independently. But television is not without risk. While distancing them, it might also diminish them—and the Senate along with them—especially if viewers were to compare Senate sessions with, say, the press conferences of a J.F.K. The tube is a two-edged sword; thus, so is Mondale's scheme. But it suggests how readily the future may be open to some changes in the status of traditional Cabinet posts.

In short, I think it possible that 20 years from now constraints upon a President will be at least as strong as 20 years ago. While we wait for the emergence of new colleagues or a welcome-back to old, we have little to depend on by way of these informal checks and balances, except constraints of the other sort, those of operating style. Then the man's methods alone define the sense of prudence he may call to the support of his own sense of propriety. All is subjective, turning on him, much as it was until lately with Nixon.

But for a while Watergate supervenes. Nixon's successor, I predict, will not be tarred by it. Indeed he probably will be its beneficiary, winning as a "Mr. Clean." Almost surely he will pledge to make himself accessible and to rein in his staff. So did Nixon five years ago, but the next President will have more need to be serious about it, and more reason, and he may well possess a temperament more suited to the task. Voters, I suspect, will shun secretive types. God willing, they will welcome humor. At worst we should get prudence with a pretense of propriety. At best we will get the genuine article.

Appendix B
Supreme Court Decisions Cited in the Text

*Baker v. Carr, 369 U.S. 186 (1962), 52, 88, 89, 140, 162
Bolling v. Sharpe 347 U.S. 497 (1954)
*Brown v. Board of Education, 347 U.S. 483 (1954), 136, 139, 231, 232, 233, 299
*Civil Rights Cases, 109 U.S. 3 (1883), 227
Communist Party v. Subversive Activities Control Board, 367 U.S. 1 (1961), 217
*Dennis v. United States, 341 U.S. 494 (1951), 214, 215, 217
Dred Scott v. Sandford, 60 U.S. 393 (1857), 55, 139, 226
*Engel v. Vitale, 370 U.S. 421 (1962), 223
*Escobedo v. Illinois, 378 U.S. 478 (1964), 141, 288
*Everson v. Board of Education, 330 U.S. 1 (1947), 222
*Gideon v. Wainwright, 372 U.S. 335 (1963), 141, 288
*Gitlow v. New York, 268 U.S. 652 (1925), 211, 213, 214
Hamilton v. Regents of University of California, 293 U.S. 245 (1934), 221
*McCollum v. Board of Education, 333 U.S. 203 (1948), 222, 224

* Decisions in cases marked with an asterisk are published by Chandler Publishing Company as individually bound reprints in the series Leading Decisions of the United States Supreme Court.

Appendix C
The Constitution of the United States of America

We the People of the United States, in Order to form a more perfect Union, establish Justice, insure domestic Tranquillity, provide for the
common defence, promote the general Welfare, and secure the Blessings
of Liberty to ourselves and our Posterity, do ordain and establish this
Constitution for the United States of America.

Article. I.

SECTION. 1. All legislative Powers herein granted shall be vested
in a Congress of the United States, which shall consist of a Senate and
House of Representatives.

SECTION. 2. The House of Representatives shall be composed of
Members chosen every second Year by the People of the several States,
and the Electors in each State shall have the Qualifications requisite for
Electors of the most numerous Branch of the State Legislature.

No Person shall be a Representative who shall not have attained
to the age of twenty five Years, and been seven Years a Citizen of the
United States, and who shall not, when elected, be an Inhabitant of that
State in which he shall be chosen.

Representatives and direct Taxes shall be apportioned among the several States which may be included within this Union, according to their respective Numbers, which shall be determined by adding to the whole Number of free Persons, including those bound to Service for a Term of Years, and excluding Indians not taxed, three fifths of all other Persons. The actual Enumeration shall be made within three Years after the first Meeting of the Congress of the United States, and within every subsequent Term of ten Years, in such Manner as they shall by Law direct. The Number of Representatives shall not exceed one for every thirty Thousand, but each State shall have at Least one Representative; and until such enumeration shall be made, the State of New Hampshire shall be entitled to chuse three, Massachusetts eight, Rhode-Island and Providence Plantations one, Connecticut five, New-York six, New Jersey four, Pennsylvania eight, Delaware one, Maryland six, Virginia ten, North Carolina five, South Carolina five, and Georgia three.

When vacancies happen in the Representation from any State, the Executive Authority thereof shall issue Writs of Election to fill such Vacancies.

The House of Representatives shall chuse their Speaker and other Officers; and shall have the sole Power of Impeachment.

SECTION. 3. The Senate of the United States shall be composed of two Senators from each State, chosen by the Legislature thereof, for six Years; and each Senator shall have one Vote.

Immediately after they shall be assembled in Consequence of the first Election, they shall be divided as equally as may be into three Classes. The Seats of the Senators of the first Class shall be vacated at the Expiration of the second Year, of the second Class at the Expiration of the fourth Year, and of the third Class at the Expiration of the sixth Year, so that one third may be chosen every second Year; and if Vacancies happen by Resignation, or otherwise, during the Recess of the Legislature of any State, the Executive thereof may make temporary Appointments until the next Meeting of the Legislature, which shall then fill such Vacancies.

No Person shall be a Senator who shall not have attained to the Age of thirty Years, and been nine Years a Citizen of the United States, and who shall not, when elected, be an Inhabitant of that State for which he shall be chosen.

The Vice President of the United States shall be President of the Senate, but shall have no Vote, unless they be equally divided.

The Senate shall chuse their other Officers, and also a President pro tempore, in the Absence of the Vice President, or when he shall exercise the Office of President of the United States.

The Senate shall have the sole Power to try all Impeachments.

When sitting for that Purpose, they shall be on Oath or Affirmation. When the President of the United States is tried the Chief Justice shall preside: And no Person shall be convicted without the Concurrence of two thirds of the Members present.

Judgment in Cases of Impeachment shall not extend further than to removal from Office, and disqualification to hold and enjoy any Office of honor, Trust or Profit under the United States: but the Party convicted shall nevertheless be liable and subject to Indictment, Trial, Judgment and Punishment, according to Law.

SECTION. 4. The Times, Places and Manner of holding Elections for Senators and Representatives, shall be prescribed in each State by the Legislature thereof; but the Congress may at any time by Law make or alter such Regulations, except as to the Places of chusing Senators.

The Congress shall assemble at least once in every Year, and such Meeting shall be on the first Monday in December, unless they shall by Law appoint a different Day.

SECTION. 5. Each House shall be the Judge of the Elections, Returns and Qualifications of its own Members, and a Majority of each shall constitute a Quorum to do Business; but a smaller Number may adjourn from day to day, and may be authorized to compel the Attendance of absent Members, in such Manner, and under such Penalties as each House may provide.

Each House may determine the Rules of its Proceedings, punish its Members for disorderly Behaviour, and, with the Concurrence of two thirds, expel a Member.

Each House shall keep a Journal of its Proceedings, and from time to time publish the same, expecting such Parts as may in their Judgment require Secrecy; and the Yeas and Nays of the Members of either House on any question shall, at the Desire of one fifth of those Present, be entered on the Journal.

Neither House, during the Session of Congress, shall, without the Consent of the other, adjourn for more than three days, nor to any other Place than that in which the two Houses shall be sitting.

SECTION. 6. The Senators and Representatives shall receive a Compensation for their Services, to be ascertained by Law, and paid out of the Treasury of the United States. They shall in all Cases, except Treason, Felony and Breach of the Peace, be privileged from Arrest during their Attendance at the Session of their respective Houses, and in going to and returning from the same; and for any Speech or Debate in either House, they shall not be questioned in any other Place.

No Senator or Representative shall, during the Time for which he was elected, be appointed to any civil Office under the Authority of the United States, which shall have been created, or the Emoluments whereof shall have been encreased during such time; and no Person holding any Office under the United States, shall be a Member of either House during his Continuance in Office.

SECTION. 7. All Bills for raising Revenue shall originate in the House of Representatives; but the Senate may propose or concur with amendments as on other Bills.

Every Bill which shall have passed the House of Representatives and the Senate, shall, before it becomes a Law, be presented to the President of the United States; If he approve he shall sign it, but if not he shall return it, with his Objections to that House in which it shall have originated, who shall enter the Objections at large on their Journal, and proceed to reconsider it. If after such Reconsideration two thirds of that House shall agree to pass the Bill, it shall be sent, together with the Objectons, to the other House, by which it shall likewise be reconsidered, and if approved by two thirds of that House, it shall become a Law. But in all such Cases the Votes of both Houses shall be determined by yeas and Nays, and the Names of the Persons voting for and against the Bill shall be entered on the Journal of each House respectively. If any Bill shall not be returned by the President within ten Days Sunday excepted) after it shall have been presented to him, the Same shall be a Law, in like Manner as if he had signed it, unless the Congress by their Adjournment prevent its Return, in which Case it shall not be a Law.

Every Order, Resolution, or Vote to which the Concurrence of the Senate and House of Representatives may be necessary (except on a question of Adjournment) shall be presented to the President of the United States; and before the Same shall take Effect, shall be approved by him, or being disapproved by him, shall be repassed by two thirds of the Senate and House of Representatives, according to the Rules and Limitations prescribed in the Case of a Bill.

SECTION. 8. The Congress shall have Power To lay and collect Taxes, Duties, Imposts and Excises, to pay the Debts and provide for the common Defence and general Welfare of the United States; but all Duties, Imposts and Excises shall be uniform throughout the United States;

To borrow Money on the credit of the United States;

To regulate Commerce with foreign Nations, and among the several States, and with the Indian Tribes;

To establish an uniform Rule of Naturalization, and uniform Laws on the subject of Bankruptcies throughout the United States;

To coin Money, regulate the Value thereof, and of foreign Coin, and fix the Standard of Weights and Measures;

To provide for the Punishment of counterfeiting the Securities and current Coin of the United States;

To establish Post Offices and post Roads;

To promote the Progress of Science and useful Arts, by securing for limited Times to Authors and Inventors the exclusive Right to their respective Writings and Discoveries;

To constitute Tribunals inferior to the supreme Court;

To define and punish Piracies and Felonies committed on the high Seas, and Offences against the Law of Nations;

To declare War, grant Letters of Marque and Reprisal, and make Rules concerning Captures on Land and Water;

To raise and support Armies, but no Appropriation of Money to that Use shall be for a longer Term than two Years;

To provide and maintain a Navy;

To make Rules for the Government and Regulation of the land and naval Forces;

To provide for calling forth the Militia to execute the Laws of the Union, suppress Insurrections and repel Invasions;

To provide for organizing, arming, and disciplining, the Militia, and for governing such Part of them as may be employed in the Service of the United States, reserving to the States respectively, the Appointment of the Officers, and the Authority of training the Militia according to the discipline prescribed by Congress;

To exercise exclusive Legislation in all Cases whatsoever, over such District (not exceeding ten Miles square) as may, by Cession of Particular States, and the Acceptance of Congress, become the Seat of the Government of the United States, and to exercise like Authority over all Places purchased by the Consent of the Legislature of the State in which the Same shall be for the Erection of Forts, Magazines, Arsenals, dock-Yards, and other needful Buildings;—And

To make all Laws which shall be necessary and proper for carrying into Execution the foregoing Powers, and all other Powers vested by this Constitution in the Government of the United States, or in any Department or Officer thereof.

SECTION. 9. The Migration or Importation of such Persons as any of the States now existing shall think proper to admit, shall not be prohibited by the Congress prior to the Year one thousand eight hundred and eight, but a Tax or duty may be imposed on such Importation, not exceeding ten dollars for each Person.

The Privilege of the Writ of Habeas Corpus shall not be suspended, unless when in Cases of Rebellion or Invasion the public Safety may require it.

No Bill of Attainder or ex post facto Law shall be passed.

No Capitation, or other direct, Tax shall be laid, unless in Proportion to the Census of Enumeration herein before directed to be taken.

No Tax or Duty shall be laid on Articles exported from any State.

No Preference shall be given by any Regulation of Commerce or Revenue to the Ports of one State over those of another; nor shall Vessels bound to, or from, one State, be obliged to enter, clear or pay Duties in another.

No Money shall be drawn from the Treasury, but in Consequence of Appropriations made by Law; and a regular Statement and Account of the Receipts and Expenditures of all public Money shall be published from time to time.

No Title of Nobility shall be granted by the United States: And no Person holding any Office of Profit or Trust under them, shall, without the Consent of the Congress, accept of any present, Emolument, Office, or Title, of any kind whatever, from any King, Prince or foreign State.

SECTION. 10. No State shall enter into any Treaty, Alliance, or Confederation; grant Letters of Marque and Reprisal; coin Money; emit Bills of Credit; make any Thing but gold and silver Coin a Tender in Payment of Debts; pass any Bill of Attainder, ex post facto Law, or Law impairing the Obligation of Contracts, or grant and Title of Nobility.

No State shall, without the Consent of the Congress, lay any Imposts or Duties on Imports or Exports, except what may be absolutely necessary for executing it's inspection Laws: and the net Produce of all Duties and Imposts, laid by any State on Imports or Exports, shall be for the Use of the Treasury of the United States; and all such Laws shall be subject to the Revision and Controul of the Congress.

No State shall, without the Consent of Congress, lay any Duty of Tonnage, keep Troops, or Ships of War in time of Peace, enter into any Agreement or Compact with another State, or with a foreign Power, or engage in War, unless actually invaded, or in such imminent Danger as will not admit of delay.

Article. II.

SECTION. 1. The executive Power shall be vested in a President of the United States of America. He shall hold his Office during the Term of four Years, and, together with the Vice President, chosen for the same Term, be elected, as follows

Each State shall appoint, in such Manner as the Legislature thereof may direct, a Number of Electors, equal to the whole Number of Senators and Representatives to which the State may be entitled in the Congress: but no Senator or Representative, or Person holding an Office of Trust or Profit under the United States, shall be appointed an Elector.

The Electors shall meet in their respective States, and vote by Ballot for two Persons, of whom one at least shall not be an Inhabitant of the same State with themselves. And they shall make a List of all the Persons voted for, and of the Number of Votes for each; which List they shall sign and certify, and transmit sealed to the Seat of the Government of the United States, directed to the President of the Senate. The President of the Senate shall, in the Presence of the Senate and House of Representatives, open all the Certificates, and the Votes shall then be counted. The Person having the greatest Number of Votes shall be the President, if such Number be a Majority of the whole Number of Electors appointed; and if there be more than one who have such Majority, and have an equal Number of Votes, then the House of Representatives shall immediately chuse by Ballot one of them for President; and if no Person have a Majority, then from the five highest on the List the said House shall in like Manner chuse the President. But in chusing the President, the Votes shall be taken by States, the Representation from each State having one Vote; a quorum for this Purpose shall consist of a Member or Members from two thirds of the States, and a Majority of all the States shall be necessary to a Choice. In every Case, after the Choice of the President, the Person having the greatest Number of Votes of the Electors shall be the Vice President. But if there should remain two or more who have equal Votes, the Senate shall chose from them by Ballot the Vice President.

The Congress may determine the Time of chusing the Electors, and the Day on which they shall give their votes; which Day shall be the same throughout the United States.

No Person except a natural born Citizen, or a Citizen of the United States, at the time of the Adoption of this Constitution, shall be eligible to the Office of President; neither shall any person be eligible to that Office who shall not have attained to the Age of thirty five Years, and been fourteen Years a Resident within the United States.

In Case of the Removal of the President from Office, or of his Death, Resignation, or Inability to discharge the Powers and Duties of the said Office, the Same shall devolve on the Vice President, and the Congress may by Law provide for the Case of Removal, Death, Resignation or Inability, both of the President and Vice President, declaring what Officer shall then act as President, and such Officer shall act accordingly, until the Disability be removed, or a President shall be elected.

The President shall, at stated Times, receive for his Services, a Compensation, which shall neither be encreased nor diminished during the Period for which he shall have been elected, and he shall not receive within that Period any other Emolument from the United States, or any of them.

Before he enter on the Execution of his Office, he shall take the following Oath or Affirmation:—"I do solemnly swear (or affirm) that I will faithfully execute the Office of President of the United States, and will to the best of my Ability, preserve, protect and defend the Constitution of the United States."

SECTION. 2. The President shall be Commander in Chief of the Army and Navy of the United States, and of the Militia of the several States, when called into the actual Service of the United States; he may require the Opinion, in writing, of the principal Officer in each of the executive Departments, upon any Subject relating to the Duties of their respective Offices, and he shall have Power to grant Reprieves and Pardons for Offenses against the United States, except in Cases of Impeachment.

He shall have Power, by and with the Advice and Consent of the Senate, to make Treaties, provided two thirds of the Senators present concur; and he shall nominate, and by and with the Advice and Consent of the Senate, shall appoint Ambassadors, other public Ministers and Consuls, Judges of the Supreme Court, and all other Officers of the United States, whose Appointments are not herein otherwise provided for, and which shall be established by Law; but the Congress may by Law vest the Appointment of such inferior Officers, as they think proper, in the President alone, in the Courts of Law, or in the Heads of Departments.

The President shall have Power to fill up all Vacancies that may happen during the Recess of the Senate, by granting Commissions which shall expire at the End of their next Session.

SECTION. 3. He shall from time to time give to the Congress Information of the State of the Union, and recommend to their Consideration such Measures as he shall judge necessary and expedient; he may, on extraordinary Occasions, convene both Houses, or either of them, and in Case of Disagreement between them, with Respect to the Time of Adjournment, he may adjourn them to such Time as he shall think proper; he shall receive Ambassadors and other public Ministers; he shall take Care that the Laws be faithfully executed, and shall Commission all the Officers of the United States.

SECTION. 4. The President, Vice President and all Civil Officers of the United States, shall be removed from Office on Impeachment for, and Conviction of, Treason, Bribery, or other high Crimes and Misdemeanors.

Article. III.

SECTION. 1. The judicial Power of the United States, shall be vested in one supreme Court, and in such inferior Courts as the Congress may from time to time ordain and establish. The Judges, both of the supreme and inferior Courts, shall hold their Offices during good Behaviour, and shall, at stated Times, receive for their Services, a Compensation, which shall not be diminished during their Continuance in Office.

SECTION. 2. The judicial Power shall extend to all Cases, in Law and Equity, arising under this Constitution, the Laws of the United States, and Treaties made, or which shall be made, under their Authority;—to all Cases affecting Ambassadors, other public Ministers and Consuls;—to all Cases of admiralty and maritime Jurisdiction;—to Controversies to which the United States shall be a Party;—to Controversies between two or more States;—between a State and Citizens of another State;—between Citizens of different States;—between Citizens of the same State claiming Lands under Grants of different States, and between a State, or the Citizens thereof, and foreign States, Citizens or Subjects.

In all Cases affecting Ambassadors, other public Ministers and Consuls, and those in which a State shall be Party, the supreme Court shall have original Jurisdiction. In all the other Cases before mentioned, the supreme Court shall have appellate Jurisdiction, both as to Law and Fact, with such Exceptions, and under such Regulations as the Congress shall make.

The Trial of all Crimes, except in Cases of Impeachment, shall be by Jury; and such Trial shall be held in the State where the said Crimes shall have been committed; but when not committed within any State, the Trial shall be at such Place or Places as the Congress may by Law have directed.

SECTION. 3. Treason against the United States, shall consist only in levying War against them, or in adhering to their Enemies, giving them Aid and Comfort. No Person shall be convicted of Treason unless on the Testimony of two Witnesses to the same overt Act, or on Confession in open Court.

The Congress shall have Power to declare the Punishment of Treason, but no Attainder of Treason shall work Corruption of Blood, or Forfeiture except during the Life on the Person attainted.

Article. IV.

SECTION. 1. Full Faith and Credit shall be given in each State to the public Acts, Records, and judicial Proceedings of every other State. And the Congress may by general Laws prescribe the Manner in which such Acts, Records and Proceedings shall be proved, and the Effect thereof.

SECTION. 2. The Citizens of each State shall be entitled to all Privileges and Immunities of Citizens in the several States.

A Person charged in any State with Treason, Felony, or other Crime, who shall flee from Justice, and be found in another State, shall on Demand of the executive Authority of the State from which he fled, be delivered up, to be removed to the State having Jurisdiction of the Crime.

No Person held to Service or Labour in one State, under the Laws thereof, escaping into another, shall, in Consequence of any Law or Regulation therein, be discharged from such Service or Labour, but shall be delivered up on Claim of the Party to whom such Service or Labour may be due.

SECTION. 3. New States may be admitted by the Congress into this Union; but no new State shall be formed or erected within the Jurisdiction of any other State; nor any State be formed by the Junction of two or more States, or Parts of States, without the Consent of the Legislatures of the States concerned as well as of the Congress.

The Congress shall have Power to dispose of and make all needful Rules and Regulations respecting the Territory or other Property belonging to the United States; and nothing in this Constitution shall be so construed as to Prejudice any Claims of the United States, or of any particular State.

SECTION. 4. The United States shall guarantee to every State in this Union a Republican Form of Government, and shall protect each of them against Invasion; and on Application of the Legislature, or of the Executive (when the Legislature cannot be convened) against domestic Violence.

Article. V.

The Congress, whenever two thirds of both Houses shall deem it necessary, shall propose Amendments to this Constitution, or, on the Application of the Legislatures of two thirds of the several States, shall call a Convention for proposing Amendments, which, in either Case, shall be valid to all Intents and Purposes, as Part of this Constitution, when ratified by the Legislatures of three fourths of the several States, or by Conventions in three fourths thereof, as the one or the other Mode of Ratification may be proposed by the Congress; Provided that no Amendment which may be made prior to the Year One thousand eight hundred and eight shall in any Manner affect the first and fourth Clauses in the Ninth Section of the first Article; and that no State, without its Consent, shall be deprived of it's equal Suffrage in the Senate.

Article. VI.

All Debts contracted and Engagements entered into, before the Adoption of this Constitution, shall be as valid against the United States under this Constitution, as under the Confederation.

This Constitution, and the Laws of the United States which shall be made in Pursuance thereof; and all Treaties made, or which shall be made, under the Authority of the United States, shall be the supreme Law of the Land; and the Judges in every State shall be bound thereby, any Thing in the Constitution or Laws of any State to the Contrary notwithstanding.

The Senators and Representatives before mentioned, and the Members of the several State Legislatures, and all executive and judicial Officers, both of the United States and of the several States, shall be bound by Oath or Affirmation, to support this Constitution; but no religious Test shall ever be required as a Qualification to any Office or public Trust under the United States.

Article. VII.

The Ratification of the Conventions of nine States, shall be sufficient for the Establishment of this Constitution between the States so ratifying the Same.

done in Convention by the Unanimous Consent of the States present the Seventeenth Day of September in the Year of our Lord one thousand seven hundred and Eighty seven and of the

Independence of the United States of America the Twelfth In witness whereof We have hereunto subscribed our Names,

Go. WASHINGTON—Presidt.

and deputy from Virginia

AMENDMENTS TO THE CONSTITUTION

Amendment [I.] *

Congress shall make no law respecting an establishment of religion, or prohibiting the free exercise thereof; or abridging the freedom of speech, or of the press; or the right of the people peaceably to assemble, and to petition the Government for a redress of grievances.

Amendment [II.]

A well regulated Militia, being necessary to the security of a free State, the right of the people to keep and bear Arms, shall not be infringed.

Amendment [III.]

No Soldier shall, in time of peace be quartered in any house, without the consent of the Owner, nor in time of war, but in a manner to be prescribed by law.

Amendment [IV.]

The right of the people to be secure in their persons, houses, papers, effects, against unreasonable searches and seizures, shall not be violated, and no Warrants shall issue, but upon probable cause, supported by Oath or affirmation, and particularly describing the place to be searched, and the persons or things to be seized.

Amendment [V.]

No person shall be held to answer for a capital, or otherwise infamous crime, unless on a presentment or indictment of a Grand Jury, except in cases arising in the land or naval forces, or in the Militia, when in actual service in time of War or public danger; nor shall any person be subject for the same offence to be twice put in jeopardy of life or

---

* Brackets enclosing an amendment number indicate that the number was not specifically assigned in the resolution proposing the amendment.

limb; nor shall be compelled in any criminal case to be a witness against himself, nor be deprived of life, liberty, or property, without due process of law; nor shall private property be taken for public use, without just compensation.

Amendment [VI.]

In all criminal prosecutions, the accused shall enjoy the right to a speedy and public trial, by an impartial jury of the State and district wherein the crime shall have been committed, which district shall have been previously ascertained by law, and to be informed of the nature and cause of the accusation; to be confronted with the witnesses against him; to have compulsory process for obtaining witnesses in his favor, and to have the Assistance of Counsel for his defence.

Amendment [VII.]

In Suits at common law, where the value in controversy shall exceed twenty dollars, the right of trial by jury shall be preserved, and no fact tried by a jury, shall be otherwise re-examined in any Court of the United States, than according to the rules of the common law.

Amendment [VIII.]

Excessive bail shall not be required, nor excessive fines imposed, nor cruel and unusual punishments inflicted.

Amendment [IX.]

The enumeration in the Constitution, of certain rights, shall not be construed to deny or disparage others retained by the people.

Amendment [X.]

The powers not delegated to the United States by the Constitution, nor prohibited by it to the States, are reserved to the States respectively, or to the people.

Amendment [XI.]

The Judicial power of the United States shall not be construed to extend to any suit in law or equity, commenced or prosecuted against one of the United States by Citizens of another State, or by Citizens or Subjects of any Foreign State.

Amendment [*XII.*]

The Electors shall meet in their respective states and vote by ballot for President and Vice-President, one of whom, at least, shall not be an inhabitant of the same state with themselves; they shall name in their ballots the person voted for as President, and in distinct ballots the person voted for as Vice-President, and they shall make distinct lists of all persons voted for as President, and of all persons voted for as Vice-President, and of the number of votes for each, which lists they shall sign and certify, and transmit sealed to the seat of the government of the United States, directed to the President of the Senate;—The President of the Senate shall, in the presence of the Senate and House of Representatives, open all the certificates and the votes shall then be counted;—The person having the greatest number of votes for President, shall be the President, if such number be a majority of the whole number of Electors appointed; and if no person have such majority, then from the persons having the highest numbers not exceeding three on the list of those voted for as President, the House of Representatives shall choose immediately, by ballot, the President. But in choosing the President, the votes shall be taken by states, the representation from each state having one vote; a quorum for this purpose shall consist of a member or members from two-thirds of the states, and a majority of all the states shall be necessary to a choice. And if the House of Representatives shall not choose a President whenever the right of choice shall devolve upon them, before the fourth day of March next following, then the Vice-President shall act as President, as in the case of the death or other constitutional disability of the President—The person having the greatest number of votes as Vice-President, shall be the Vice-President, if such number be a majority of the whole number of Electors appointed, and if no person have a majority, then from the two highest numbers on the list, the Senate shall choose the Vice-President; a quorum for the purpose shall consist of two-thirds of the whole number of Senators, and a majority of the whole number shall be necessary to a choice. But no person constitutionally ineligible to the office of President shall be eligible to that of Vice-President of the United States.

Amendment XIII.

SECTION 1. Neither slavery nor involuntary servitude, except as a punishment for crime whereof the party shall have been duly convicted, shall exist within the United States, or any place subject to their jurisdiction.

SECTION 2. Congress shall have power to enforce this article by appropriate legislation.

Amendment XIV.

SECTION 1. All persons born or naturalized in the United States and subject to the jurisdiction thereof, are citizens of the United States and of the State wherein they reside. No State shall make or enforce any law which shall abridge the privileges or immunities of citizens of the United States; or shall any State deprive any person of life, liberty, or property, without due process of law; nor deny to any person within its jurisdiction the equal protection of the laws.

SECTION 2. Representatives shall be apportioned among the several States according to their respective numbers, counting the whole number of persons in each State, excluding Indians not taxed. But when the right to vote at any election for the choice of electors for President and Vice President of the United States, Representatives in Congress, the Executive and Judicial officers of a State, or the members of the Legislature thereof, is denied to any of the male inhabitants of such State, being twenty-one years of age, and citizens of the United States, or in any way abridged, except for participation in rebellion, or other crime, the basis of representation therein shall be reduced in the proportion which the number of such male citizens shall bear to the whole number of male citizens twenty-one years of age in such State.

SECTION 3. No person shall be a Senator or Representative in Congress, or elector of President and Vice President, or hold any office, civil or military, under the United States, or under any State, who, having previously taken an oath, as a member of Congress, or as an officer of the United States, or as a member of any State legislature, or as an executive or judicial officer of any State, to support the Constitution of the United States, shall have engaged in insurrection or rebellion against the same, or given aid or comfort to the enemies thereof. But Congress may by a vote of two-thirds of each House, remove such disability.

SECTION 4. The validity of the public debt of the United States, authorized by law, including debts incurred for payment of pensions and bounties for services in suppressing insurrection or rebellion, shall not be questioned. But neither the United States nor any State shall assume or pay any debt or obligation incurred in aid of insurrection or rebellion against the United States, or any claim for the loss or emancipation of any slave; but all such debts, obligations and claims shall be held illegal and void.

SECTION 5. The Congress shall have power to enforce, by appropriate legislation, the provisions of this article.

Amendment XV.

SECTION 1. The right of citizens of the United States to vote shall not be denied or abridged by the United States or by any State on account of race, color, or previous condition of servitude.

SECTION 2. The Congress shall have power to enforce this article by appropriate legislation.

Amendment XVI.

The Congress shall have power to lay and collect taxes on incomes, from whatever source derived, without apportionment among the several States, and without regard to any census or enumeration.

Amendment [XVII.]

The Senate of the United States shall be composed of two Senators from each State, elected by the people thereof, for six years; and each Senator shall have one vote. The electors in each State shall have the qualifications requisite for electors of the most numerous branch of the State legislatures.

When vacancies happen in the representation of any State in the Senate, the executive authority of such State shall issue writs of election to fill such vacancies: *Provided,* That the legislature of any State may empower the executive thereof to make temporary appointments until the people fill the vacancies by election as the legislature may direct.

This amendment shall not be so construed as to affect the election or term of any Senator chosen before it becomes valid as part of the Constitution.

Amendment [XVIII.]

SECTION 1. After one year from the ratification of this article the manufacture, sale, or transportation of intoxicating liquors within, the importation thereof into, or the exportation thereof from the United States and all territory subject to the jurisdiction thereof for beverage purposes is hereby prohibited.

SEC. 2. The Congress and the several States shall have concurrent power to enforce this article by appropriate legislation.

SEC. 3. This article shall be inoperative unless it shall have been ratified as an amendment to the Constitution by the legislatures of the several States, as provided in the Constitution, within seven years from the date of the submission hereof to the States by the Congress.

Amendment [XIX.]

The right of citizens of the United States to vote shall not be denied or abridged by the United States or by any State on account of sex.

Congress shall have power to enforce this article by appropriate legislation.

Amendment [XX.]

SECTION 1. The terms of the President and Vice President shall end at noon on the 20th day of January, and the terms of Senators and Representatives at noon on the 3d day of January, of the years in which such terms would have ended if this article had not been ratified; and the terms of their successors shall then begin.

SEC. 2. The Congress shall assemble at least once in every year, and such meeting shall begin at noon on the 3d day of January, unless they shall by law appoint a different day.

SEC. 3. If, at the time fixed for the beginning of the term of the President, the President elect shall have died, the Vice President elect shall become President. If a President shall not have been chosen before the time fixed for the beginning of his term, or if the President elect shall have failed to qualify, then the Vice President elect shall act as President until a President shall have qualified; and the Congress may by law provide for the case wherein neither a President elect nor a Vice President elect shall have qualified, declaring who shall then act as President, or the manner in which one who is to act shall be selected, and such person shall act accordingly until a President or Vice President shall have qualified.

SEC. 4. The Congress may by law provide for the case of the death of any of the persons from whom the House of Representatives may choose a President whenever the right of choice shall have devolved upon them, and for the case of the death of any of the persons from whom the Senate may choose a Vice President whenever the right of choice shall have devolved upon them.

SEC. 5. Sections 1 and 2 shall take effect on the 15th day of October folowing the ratification of this article.

SEC. 6. This article shall be inoperative unless it shall have been ratified as an amendment to the Constitution by the legislatures of three-fourths of the several States within seven years from the date of its submission.

Amendment [XXI.]

SECTION 1. The eighteenth article of amendment to the Constitution of the United States is hereby repealed.

SEC. 2. The transportation or importation into any State, Territory or possession of the United States for delivery or use therein of intoxicating liquors, in violation of the laws thereof, is hereby prohibited.

SEC. 3. This article shall be inoperative unless it shall have been ratified as an amendment to the Constitution by conventions in the several states, as provided in the Constitution, within seven years from the date of the submission thereof to the States by the Congress.

Amendment [XXII.]

SECTION 1. No person shall be elected to the office of the President more than twice, and no person who has held the office of President, or acted as President, for more than two years of a term to which some other person was elected President shall be elected to the office of the President more than once. But this Article shall not apply to any person holding the office of President when this Article was proposed by the Congress, and shall not prevent any person who may be holding the office of President, or acting as President, during the term within which this Article becomes operative from holding the office of President or acting as President during the remainder of such term.

SEC. 2. This Article shall be inoperative unless it shall have been ratified as an amendment to the Constitution by the legislatures of three-fourths of the several States within seven years from the date of its submission to the States by the Congress.

Amendment [XXIII.]

SECTION 1. The District constituting the seat of Government of the United States shall appoint in such manner as the Congress may direct:

A number of electors of President and Vice President equal to the whole number of Senators and Representatives in Congress to which the District would be entitled if it were a State, but in no event more than the least populous State; they shall be in addition to those appointed by the States, but they shall be considered, for the purposes of the election of President and Vice President, to be electors appointed by a State; and they shall meet in the District and perform such duties as provided by the twelfth article of amendment.

SEC. 2. The Congress shall have power to enforce this article by appropriate legislation.

Amendment [XXIV.]

SECTION 1. The right of citizens of the United States to vote in any primary or other election for President or Vice President, for electors for President or Vice President, or for Senator or Representative in Congress, shall not be denied or abridged by the United States or any State by reason of failure to pay any poll tax or other tax.

SECTION 2. The Congress shall have power to enforce this article by appropriate legislation.

Amendment [XXV.]

SECTION 1. In case of the removal of the President from office or his death or resignation, the Vice President shall become President.

SEC. 2. Whenever there is a vacancy in the office of the Vice President, the President shall nominate a Vice President who shall take the office upon confirmation by a majority vote of both houses of Congress.

SEC. 3. Whenever the President transmits to the President pro tempore of the Senate and the Speaker of the House of Representatives his written declaration that he is unable to discharge the powers and duties of his office, and until he transmits to them a written declaration to the contrary, such powers and duties shall be discharged by the Vice President as Acting President.

SEC. 4. Whenever the Vice President and a majority of either the principal officers of the executive department or of such other body as Congress may by law provide, transmit to the President pro tempore of the Senate and the Speaker of the House of Representatives their written declaration that the President is unable to discharge the powers and duties of his office, the Vice President shall immediately assume the powers and duties of the office as Acting President.

Thereafter, when the President transmits to the President pro tempore of the Senate and the Speaker of the House of Representatives his written declaration that no inability exists, he shall resume the powers and duties of his office unless the Vice President and a majority of either the principal officers of the executive department or of such other body as Congress may by law provide, transmit within four days to the President pro tempore of the Senate and the Speaker of the House of Representatives their written declaration that the President is unable to discharge the powers and duties of his office. Thereupon Congress shall decide the issue, assembling within 48 hours for that purpose if not in session. If the Congress, within 21 days after receipt of the latter written declaration, or, if Congress is not in session, within 21 days after Congress is required to assemble, determines by two-thirds vote of both houses that the President is unable to discharge the powers and duties of his office, the Vice President shall continue to discharge the same as Acting President; otherwise, the President shall resume the powers and duties of his office.

Amendment [XXVI.]

The right of citizens of the United States, who are 18 years of age or older, to vote shall not be denied or abridged by the United States or by any state on account of age.

Index

Printer and Binder: Vail-Ballou Press, Inc.
78 79 80 81 8 7 6 5 4 3 2

065 1